SMART OFFICE

11 Steps to a User-Friendly Office

SMART OFFICE

11 STEPS TO A USER-FRIENDLY OFFICE

**JUDITH VERITY AND
IAN ELLIOTT SHIRCORE**

BLOOMSBURY

All rights reserved: no part of this publication may be reproduced, stored in a retrieval system, or transmitted in any form or by any means, electronic, mechanical, photocopying or otherwise, without the prior written permission of the publisher.

The information in this book was correct to the best of the editor's and publisher's belief at the time of going to press. While no responsibility can be accepted for errors and omissions, the editor and publisher would welcome corrections and suggestions for material to include in subsequent editions of this book.

This edition first published in 1996 by
Bloomsbury Publishing plc
2 Soho Square
London, W1V 6HB

Copyright © 1996 by Judith Verity and Ian Elliott Shircore

The moral right of the authors has been asserted

A copy of the CIP entry for this book is available from the British Library

ISBN 0 7475 2479 3

10 9 8 7 6 5 4 3 2 1

Designed by AB3
Typeset by Hewer Text Composition Services, Edinburgh
Printed and bound in Great Britain by Butler and Tanner, Frome and London

CONTENTS

Foreword		vii
Step 1	**THE OFFICE COMES SECOND!**	1
	Good people plus good systems = smart offices	
Step 2	**WHO NEEDS AN OFFICE ANYWAY?**	21
	How to set up and run the smarter office	
Step 3	**LOOK AFTER THE POUNDS AND THE PENNIES DON'T MATTER**	37
	Taking control of the office	
Step 4	**MAKING IT HAPPEN**	61
	The impact of computers on office management	
Step 5	**TOWARDS THE UFO**	77
	Matching the workplace to the people	
Step 6	**HEALTH AND SAFETY FIRST FOR PRODUCTIVITY THAT LASTS**	99
	Looking after your major assets	
Step 7	**TIME TO PUT ECO BEFORE EGO**	119
	Growing greener gracefully	
Step 8	**TRUST TEAMS TO WORK**	133
	Positive team building	
Step 9	**LEARNING TO LEAD AND LIGHT**	155
	Will you take on the role?	
Step 10	**FROM NETWORKING TO INTERNETWORKING**	171
Step 11	**LASTING IMPRESSIONS**	191
	Smart presentations work	
Appendices		
	Doing it Right: Back to Basics	215
	Doing it Right: Paper Trails and Finding Systems	221
	Doing it Right: In Time, Every Time	229

Doing it Right: Money Matters	239
Doing it Right: People Practices	245
Doing it Right: Travel with Confidence	253
References	267
Index	271

FOREWORD

UFOS MAKE SENSE!

In the past, it was offices first, people last.
Now it's people first, offices second.

The Office Revolution is happening now. There is a tremendous power shift taking place, from the traditional focus on hard cost control of routine operations to workplaces focused on enhancing the performance of knowledgeable people tackling non-standard tasks.

The Smart Office describes the 11 steps to the UFO, the user-friendly office, which represents the ultimate in office efficiency. The idea behind this annual handbook is to create a dynamic, regularly updated Everyman's Guide to the turbulent times that lie ahead as the office adapts from the old procedure-dominated workplace to the flexible, project-driven environment of the future.

At its best, today's office is the crucible in which the skills of the people and the capabilities of the new technologies come together to create a fusion with tremendous productive potential.

Goodbye to the pyramid

The offices of the sixties and seventies were dominated by hard, numerically-based control systems. The environment was spartan, as a matter of principle, and the accountants called the tune in most matters of policy and procedure. Offices were built on a model taken directly from the Victorian factory, with massed ranks of typists and input clerks lined up to carry out mass processing tasks that were seen in crude production line terms. Computers were used only for control and management information purposes. The master/servant relationship between bosses and workers lived on, with a rigid hierarchy of directors, senior management, middle management, supervisors and foremen forming a perfect and symmetrical pyramid.

Information trickled down the organisation in a slow, haphazard way and feedback coming up from frontline staff stood little chance of reaching anyone who mattered. Personnel policies were built on job descriptions, evaluation procedures, minutely graded car entitlements and doorstop-thick manuals full of lists of don'ts. Bureaucracy reigned. Regimentation and discipline stifled initiative and creative thinking. The top companies in every sector of industry thought they had a divine right to be there for ever and acted accordingly, perpetuating conservative policies and seeing the office and its people as necessary evils – overhead costs that had to be strictly controlled.

Diamonds are trumps now

Information technology has changed all that. Knowledge itself is power, as Francis Bacon said 400 years ago. And never more so than in the last few years, since PCs and communications networks have made almost limitless specialist knowledge available to almost everybody.

Dog-in-the-manger hardliners are having to adapt to the nimble, flexible, personal project-driven future, whether they want to or not. Intelligent people demand careers, not jobs. They are task-driven and target-oriented, keen on working in multi-functional teams, inspired by accountability and leadership and resentful of traditional supervision. Today's people are *taxi drivers*, not bus drivers. They know where they are going and they're getting there by their own routes.

The organisations that are taking shape around the new workers and the new technologies are no longer pyramids. They are more like a diamond, reflecting the shape of a rapidly changing workforce with more women, more older people and many more highly educated workers.

There is no longer the neatly tapering triangle with the broad clerical base supporting fewer professionals, topped by even fewer managers. Instead, the realisation that the professionals or knowledge workers are the key to success is leading to the new orthodoxy of the magic diamond.

While the inhabitants of the professional layer are keen to work to their own goals in their own ways, they are generally fairly self-reliant and responsible. They need some clerical support, but most have basic keyboard skills and do not expect to be mollycoddled by an army of secretarial staff. In the same way, as long as they feel they are getting suitable inspiration and guidance from senior management, they do not want or need supervisors standing over them.

But the shift from pyramid to diamond is not the whole story. The other factor that is dissolving the old office culture is mobility. *Today's office is wherever you are.*

Ergonomics means profits

With PC power available everywhere and laptops offering most of the same facilities, the workforce is becoming vastly more mobile. In a single week, a busy consultant might easily spend two days working on clients' premises, two days working from home and another day or more in his or her own office. The changes in working habits have been quick and radical and the office has to be able to change, too, to accommodate the changing work patterns new technologies make possible.

There is no doubt that the focus has rightly swung back onto the people. "Our people are our greatest asset," has become an almost mandatory sentence in every Chairman's Report. But words are cheap and it's worth asking just how many companies can show action to match the rhetoric.

Everyone knows that British firms have invested millions of pounds in information technology to improve financial performance through cost control and productivity schemes. But the overall productivity gains have been dispiritingly modest. Independent research shows one possible reason for this. Large companies have piled their IT investment into short-term performance improvement measures, buying computers, printers and faxes for use in parts of the business where the money spent can easily and visibly be justified by cutting back on staff costs.

But the problem is that very little has been invested in the ergonomic refinements which are a necessary part of making users more comfortable and productive in the new electronic office environment. Better ergonomics doesn't give the same instant payoff of being able to turn round, swing the axe and chop another two or three junior office staff off the payroll.

What it does do is help to ensure that the more important, specialised and highly-paid people are able to give full value for money. Losing a junior clerk might cut payroll costs by, say, £10,000 in a full year. Enhancing the ability of a couple of £30,000-a-year specialists to do their jobs well could have a far greater impact on the business.

Let's suppose that having exactly the right comfortable and stimulating environment, the ideal tools for the job and the right sort of leadership and motivation meant that these two big hitters could each get through 20 per cent more work. That is a modest enough target to aim for. But that would immediately be worth £12,000 a year to the company – already rather more than the saving from getting rid of the office junior. It would very probably mean that more business was being brought in through the office, thus helping to spread all the fixed costs over a larger revenue base. And the quality of the work that was being done would almost certainly be better and more consistent.

The point is that the boundaries of what can be done with new technologies, especially computing and communications equipment, are almost always set by the limits of human capabilities. By balancing the needs and preferences of real people with the requirements of the technologies involved, sound ergonomic design and planning has become one of the primary means of improving productivity.

It is this interface between people and technology – the user-friendliness at the heart of the UFO concept – that forms the focus of this book.

How different is the UFO?

Progressive companies that have cottoned on to the potential that lies hidden in this area have already started to make substantial gains. Among the well-known names from both sides of the Atlantic, some of the best examples have come from people like Federal Express, Hyatt Hotels, Hewlett Packard and Arthur Andersen. Each of them is proving conclusively that UFOs can and do make very down-to-earth sense.

User-friendly offices are the safest, the cleanest and the most comfortable workplaces. They are also, by no coincidence at all, the most productive.

This is partly because they work well as machines for getting things done, but also because they are attractive, motivating places in which to work. Morale and productivity tend to go hand in hand in all offices. In the UFO, they can be mutually reinforcing to an extraordinary degree.

The revolution in the office that puts people first and offices second epitomises a major shift away from the old school of organisational thinking in recent years. In parallel with this, there are a number of other important shifts that are happening now and which will need to be taken into account in planning and designing the UFOs of the future. You could probably nominate many more of your own, but here are some very obvious examples that strike me as significant:

From rules to guidelines
From bigness to smallness
From boss focus to customer focus (internal and external)
From fear of failure to admiration for initiative
From centralised to decentralised operations
From impersonal, inflexible to personal, flexible relationships
From departmentally minded to project organised
From vertically structured to horizontally networked
From authoritarian to collegiate thinking
From alienated to involved workers
From numbers to knowledge
From processing simple tasks to solving complex problems
From traditional to transactional environments
From don'ts to dos

From DOS to Windows
From overheads to opportunities
From fear to fulfilment
From mechanical, inhuman places of work to human, flexible workplaces
From dumb jobs to smart careers.

The Smart Office takes you from the rigidities of the past, through the present, to a better future that is within our grasp. It offers hundreds of positive, practical suggestions to help the facilities manager or office manager. For some FMs in progressive companies, backed by open chequebooks and wholehearted boardroom commitment, progress will be swift and straightforward. For the majority, it is more likely to be a question of inching the company in the right direction – unobtrusively and within the bounds of existing budgets.

Whichever way you approach it, though, we are talking about a necessary revolution that cannot be put on hold. This book shows how office managers, even in the most traditional firms, can begin to introduce and influence positive changes. Above all, it underlines the unstoppable nature of the shift from oppressive cost control environments, with their unjustified aura of logical infallibility, to the new concept of maximising people's potential and performance through the creation of the smarter office, the UFO or user-friendly office.

Smart offices and the vortex of virtue

It is the harmonisation of good people with good office systems in a physically comfortable and mentally stimulating environment that makes the smart office come to life. Get it right and the momentum builds up quickly into a virtuous circle of awesome power.

More comfortable environments bring better morale. Better morale means higher motivation. Higher motivation leads to increased productivity. Increased productivity lowers unit costs. Lower costs mean higher profitability. And higher profits bring even better morale. And so on and so on, in a self-reinforcing cycle, a vortex of virtue, that benefits employees and management, shareholders and pensioners, suppliers and customers – indeed everyone who has any contact with the firm. It's not just like win/win solutions in a two-way negotiation. It's win, win, win, for everyone involved, with no inherent reason why it should ever come to a halt. I believe this book can show you how to do it. Good luck – and enjoy the trip from bureaucracy to buccaneering. I promise it'll be a memorable journey, whatever point you're starting from.

Peter Frost
February 1996

Can't you make up your mind?

One serious problem that has troubled us in the writing of this book – and caused great anguish among our friends, the editors and proof readers at Bloomsbury Publishing – is the question of consistency.

Inevitably, this book touches on many different fields of human endeavour, some of them thoroughly metric in the measurements they use, others defiantly (or Americanly) imperial in their chosen units.

As a result, there has been much discussion about whether we should plump for one unified system, in order to avoid confusion.

However, if there's one thing we have consistently tried to do in this book, it's stay in touch with the real world, rather than some tidied-up theoretical model. And that means accepting that, for now, it is pointless to talk about computer screens as being 35.5cm, 38cm or 43cm models, when everyone in the business, from top to bottom, knows the standard sizes as 14, 15 or 17 inches.

Diskettes are mostly 3½ inches now. Desks are measured in millimetres. Standard drawing pins are 11mm, while the big paper clips are still two-inchers. Envelopes may well be DL or C6 size (ultimately defined in metric terms). But your 70gsm envelope will be quoted as being 3½ inches by 6 inches, with a window panel of, say, 39 × 93mm.

It gets worse, too. The most popular size of continuous listing paper used in British offices is 241mm wide. It is universally known, and ordered, as 11 × 241 – eleven inches by 241 millimetres.

That way madness lies. So, in the interests of sanity and practical relevance to the job in hand, we have adopted a firm policy of judicious inconsistency, dealing with each case entirely on the basis of normal usage in real offices.

Conundrums like the 11 × 241 listing paper are beyond us to unravel, so we'll just take comfort in the words of one of America's greatest poets, Ralph Waldo Emerson, whose prophetic warning was penned in the 1840s:

A foolish consistency is the hobgoblin of little minds.

STEP 1
THE OFFICE COMES SECOND!

Step 1 | **The Office Comes Second!**

GOOD PEOPLE PLUS GOOD SYSTEMS = SMART OFFICES

It's probably a symptom of what's wrong with the nineties that there are an awful lot more people rushing round reinventing the corporation these days than reinventing the office.

The management gurus have had their fun up at the super-strategic level. Pursuing excellence has led on to getting to wow. The giants have learned to dance and delayering has cut the distance between the factory floor and the penthouse suite. Desktop computing and networks have totally changed the nature and scope of what can be done by office workers in companies large and small.

Yet how much has the office actually changed?

Not half as much as it's going to over the next few years. Because if it doesn't change and change again, keeping pace with new technologies and some radically new ways of working, it is going to become a dead weight and a liability, rather than a vital part of every forward-looking company.

The vision that is beginning to emerge is one in which the office becomes both more comfortable and more productive.

From the management point of view, it develops into a tool for raising productivity and drawing the best out of the workforce. From the individual employee's point of view, it becomes a lot more personally tuned to his or her needs – much more of a home from home. With abundant computer power wherever it's needed, thoughtfully planned equipment and furnishing and a controlled, pleasant environment, the office will be a much more encouraging place to work in.

It's about fun, as well as productivity

The perfect office is probably too much to hope for. But the smart office, otherwise known as the UFO or user-friendly office, is well worth striving towards.

Even where budgets or other constraints limit what can be done, there are very significant gains that can be made by modifying approaches and working methods, paying more attention to the dynamics of team working and helping people to get more fun and satisfaction into their working days. Happy offices are productive offices – which is one reason why the smart office approach is making its presence felt at a very appropriate time.

In a period when many people have felt pressured and insecure in their jobs, it is important to shake off the feeling that going to work has to be a grim struggle. It doesn't. And if that's what it feels like to the employee, it usually means that he or she is being let down by the management – or, at least, not getting the support and encouragement that is one of the main planks of the smart office approach.

OFFICE MANAGER OR UFO MANAGER?

There aren't many jobs that have changed as much as the office manager's over the past few years. The new status, sometimes reflected in subtle changes of title (office manager to facilities manager, perhaps), is mainly the result of the revolution in computing and communications. This has made it abundantly clear to everyone that there are technical factors and complexities in the job that demand specialist knowledge.

The other half of the job, of course, is all about people management, just as it always has been. This is actually far more complex and demanding, but lacks the jargon, the glamour and the expensive hardware, so noone is quite so awed by it. There's always been a tendency for office management skills to be taken for granted, as if the job only demanded practical common sense and an ability to count. But the fact that today's facilities manager is likely to be at the nerve centre of the company's communications network has helped in the reassessment and revaluation of the role. As the business potential of the user-friendly office becomes more generally accepted, this upgrading process will continue.

Talking about the facilities

Office managers in the bad old days tended to do their job by decree. There was plenty of communication, but the office manager wasn't usually involved. It was everybody else, from the MD to the messenger, who muttered in corners and grumbled (but only to each other) about delays in the post room, lack of Tipp-Ex or the wrong biscuits. The up side of this negative situation was its democratic, levelling effect. Like the blitz, it brought people together in adversity and gave them something to talk about. You could blame a lot of problems on the wrong size of envelopes or running out of coffee and nobody had to take the responsibility for doing anything about it.

Nowadays facilities managers still deal in nuts and bolts. But they're not ruling by decree any more. They are still keeping an eye on the detail, but the nuts and bolts are used for building visions, not cages. The only problem is that they have to make sure that the visions

Step 1 | The Office Comes Second!

they're building are the same ones everybody else is dreaming of. A cage is a cage, but dreams can be dangerous.

That's why today's FM has to be more than a meticulous bean counter, a computer and communications expert and a manager of his own time and everyone else's. On top of all this, it's his business to know what everyone wants, what everyone needs and what the difference is.

New to the job? TIP 1: Do nothing

When you first arrive in a new office, taking over from someone who has left the firm or moved across to a different role, you are not likely to be short of advice from those around you.

The first thing to remember is that what you find awaiting you – whether it strikes you as a mess or a model of ordered efficiency – is what everyone else is used to. Until you start to make changes and impose your own mistakes, you have a good deal of licence to blame anything that goes wrong on the previous incumbent. Take advantage of it.

It takes a lot longer to upset people by being slow to reform an established, inefficient system than it does to rub them up the wrong way by bringing in wholesale changes – whether they turn out to be right or wrong.

So listen to everyone's grumbles without commenting too freely. Note what seems like good sense and clear the rest out of your mind as quickly as possible, while you build up your own picture of what needs to be done.

Then think, plan and act. But remember, once your systems are in place, the problems are down to you too.

Try asking

Finding out what people want and need is not as easy as it looks. If you just ask people what they want, they're likely to tell you what they think they'll get or what they think you want to hear. It takes a little bit longer to get at the real requirements – but it's worth the time and effort.

Smart Office | 11 Steps to a User-Friendly Office

Try again

How you do it depends on the organisation or lack of it.

In some companies a rather formal approach works well. If you call a meeting and ask people to go away and consider what changes or improvements they would like to make, and maybe even what their vision of an ideal working environment would be, they will know you're taking them seriously. In this kind of set-up you might even want to consider using questionnaires and setting up planning groups.

But there are some offices full of sceptics where that kind of approach would be seen as an empty paper exercise, with zero credibility. If your company's like that, you'd do a lot better to approach people in small, natural groups and talk to them in the canteen, in the pub or after a project meeting.

Whatever approach you take, though, you must take it seriously and give it time. Making any useful progress towards the user-friendly office always depends on knowing your company and knowing your people. And there are no short cuts to getting that right.

New to the job? TIP 2: Explore your environment

There are always aspects of your new office that you need to find out about and that are not going to be spelt out in any job description or official documentation.

What sort of moral atmosphere is there among your new workmates? How ambitious are those around you – both for themselves and for the company? These things matter. They'll make a big difference to the way you feel when you come in to work each morning and to the way you organise things.

If the atmosphere is rational, cost-conscious and harshly competitive, you may be able to make big changes surprisingly fast, as long as you can wheel in the facts and figures to support your arguments. In a softer, more compromising environment, you may find that even the most harmless improvements can be seen as stepping on people's toes.

In fact, the most warmly informal offices are often the trickiest minefields. Personal affections and obligations can make apparently logical solutions quite out of the question.

Step 1 | **The Office Comes Second!**

> Until you know what's going on at this level, you will waste a lot of time and energy. So make a point of chatting to people individually. Pay attention to everything they are telling you, including the asides, the body language and the tone of voice, as well as the formal content.
>
> Your researches will stand you in good stead in working out what is possible, what can be done with people's willing consent and what could only be driven through in the teeth of real opposition.

UFOs can be scary

Converting a company to UFOs may take a while. For some people, it will be such a radical challenge to the way they've always thought about their workplace that it might have quite a destabilising effect. There's certainty and comfort in feeling free to grumble about the way things are run if nothing that goes wrong is your fault. There's also a get-out clause if you can't work as effectively as you should because it's too cold or too hot and there's no toner for the copier.

So don't expect your consultation initiative to be unconditionally welcomed at first. People instinctively know that the down side of getting involved in decision making is having to take responsibility if things don't work. You have to convince them that the benefits outweigh the disadvantages.

The most powerful argument in your favour here is that it's all going to happen anyway. There aren't so many people sitting in rows from nine to five any more, processing the work that they're given and rushing for the door in mid-calculation as soon as the clock sets them free. Computers do that kind of processing now and they don't stick to 40-hour weeks. Now that people are in direct competition with computers for available work, they can only win by doing things computers can't – and the field is narrowing fast.

To stay ahead of the computer in the workplace, people have to abandon routine and repetitive tasks and start thinking creatively, being answerable for their own work and organising the tools they need for themselves. The survivors in the business world will be entrepreneurial individuals who are ready and willing to take responsibility for the projects they are given to run and for their environment as well.

Business wants adaptable, independent employees who are constantly upgrading their skills in response to the needs of the market place and who have a self-employed attitude to their careers. People like this are not going to waste time worrying about paper clips. If they don't have the tools they need to do the job, they'll get them or make sure somebody else does. They will be too focused on the project in hand to worry about the cosmetic details of the working environment, but they are likely to be pretty demanding when it comes to what's really necessary. For people like this to work effectively, they need fast response

Smart Office | 11 Steps to a User-Friendly Office

facilities management that gives them the support they need when – or, ideally, just before – they need it.

It's what you do, not the way that you do it

"If it wasn't for me, this place wouldn't keep going," the office manager used to say. And keeping the place going used to be seen as pretty central to his role. Suddenly, though, the place doesn't seem to matter so much. People have realised that it's the revenue that pays the rent and not the rent paying that creates the revenue.

People are working in self-managed teams, being their own project managers and taking responsibility for what they do.

They are working towards goals rather than working to rule. And the rules by which the old office managers lived have largely gone. Instead of lists of rules, the job is now about fulfilling a collection of different roles – real, demanding roles which put the office manager or FM at the focal point of change and growth, instead of patrolling the perimeter fences of the organisation in the old-fashioned way.

Whether it's user-friendly, smart or just about average, the office still needs systems and procedures, of course. But these days they have to be tailored to the real needs of the people and projects they support.

"You'll soon fit in," recruits used to be told by their new colleagues. But people shouldn't have to fit the facilities any more, to shoehorn themselves into uncomfortable ways of working, inflexible routines and regimented procedures. That is not how anyone delivers the best he or she can give. People have jobs to do and it's the job of the facilities manager to support them and give them what they need to be productive. If that means constantly updating and adapting the facilities and the equipment that is provided, that only goes to prove how vital the FM's contribution has become. Nowadays, in fact, facilitators might be a better name for facilities managers (and probably for office managers as well).

New to the job? TIP 3: Think like a millionaire

Noone says you have to spend like a millionaire. Indeed, if you chose that as a short-term strategy, it would virtually guarantee your firm didn't need to worry about a long-term strategy at all.

But learning to think like a millionaire adds another technique to the repertoire of the office manager, or anyone else in a practical problem-solving role.

Step 1 | The Office Comes Second!

> Thinking like a millionaire provides a useful lever to help you see situations from a different angle.
>
> It works because things look different when your perspective changes. And seeing them differently offers you new choices about how to tackle problems.
>
> How would you solve this one if money did not matter? Who would you get to design/advertise/present/negotiate that for you, if you could afford a star name?
>
> What would you do next if you had unlimited working capital? How many niggling complexities could be ironed out if you could afford to delegate the details to a team of specialists?
>
> Millionaires simplify, clarify, prioritise, focus and take decisions, while the rest of us are still wondering where to start.
>
> Because they ruthlessly ignore trivial costs, they get into the habit of carrying out instant, intuitive benefit analysis on every decision, from whether to walk or take a cab to whether or not to launch a takeover bid. But it will be pure benefit analysis first – cost only comes in as a factor if the benefits look promising.
>
> Step into a millionaire's shoes and the world will look easier to manage. Step back and you may bring with you some workable ideas and insights that would never normally have occurred to you.

A high-powered patent lawyer in the City tells the story of her "job from hell".

A few years after qualifying, she was headhunted by one of the most prestigious patent law firms in London. She was flattered and delighted and accepted the job, knowing that she would be the only woman in the company (apart, of course, from secretaries and support staff, who didn't really count). Anxious to prove her worth, she worked longer and harder than anyone else and, one Friday afternoon, a couple of months into the job, she found she had filled up all her audio tapes with dictation. Dropping the full tapes on her secretary's desk, she called in on the administrator and requested another box.

"How many have you used?" said the administrator.

"Eight," said the lawyer. "I need some more."

Smart Office | 11 Steps to a User-Friendly Office

"Noone has more than eight. That's the standard allocation. I've only got one box spare and if I give you that everyone's going to want extra."

"So what do you expect me to do for the rest of the afternoon? I've got another two hours of dictation to tie up the work for the week. I'm in meetings all day on Monday and my secretary will run out of work by lunchtime."

"Why don't you just write it out for her?" said the administrator. "Several of the partners prefer that to dictation."

"Have you any idea what we do for a living here?" gasped the lawyer. "Our clients are in the forefront of technology, inventing things that help other people work faster. What do you think their reaction would be if they knew I was writing reports in longhand before handing them over to be typed on an electric typewriter? I still can't believe we haven't even got computers yet!"

"Yes we have," said the administrator, huffily. "We've got some in Accounts."

"If you don't get this organisation into the 20th century, you won't have any accounts to worry about," said the lawyer and stormed out in the direction of the nearest office supplies shop to buy her own tapes.

On the way down Chancery Lane she met a former fellow-student and told her story. One month later she handed in her notice and joined a rival firm, having been promised, in advance, that she could have as many tapes as she wanted and a workstation of her own. She still has lunch with her ex-secretary, who tells her that she wasn't really missed, especially by the administrator, but that the senior partners are worried about the number of long-standing clients who seem to be taking their business to a rival firm.

How do you set up a supportive, reliable working environment, with predictable systems that ensure invoices don't get lost and enough paper gets ordered while, at the same time, keeping it flexible, responsive and people-friendly?

It's a tall order, but one way to tackle it might be by redefining yourself as a project manager, rather than an office manager or an organiser of lighting, phones and laser cartridges. This immediately entitles you to borrow some of the fashionable (and effective) performance management ideas on your own UFO-building project. If nothing else, it will give you some insight into what everybody else is doing. It's surprising how many of the current theories about inspiration, creativity and motivation can be applied just as easily to the nuts and bolts of running a business as they can to hammering out its strategic mission statement.

Get the picture right before you hang the wall on it

There's a very popular management training technique around at the moment called visualisation. Like a lot of good ideas, it started on the sports field. It has been used by tennis

Step 1 The Office Comes Second!

players such as John McEnroe, athletes like Linford Christie and many rugby players, including Rob Andrew and Will Carling, with the aim of reaching peak performance by training the mind when the muscles can't take any more.

It's particularly useful in the business world because, while it can help people improve their performances as individuals and team players, it can also be used for doing dry runs on big decisions like office moves or business diversification. People who are in the habit of trying their big decisions out for size, as well as checking the numbers on the page, have a better chance of getting what they really want.

There's more to visualisation than making mental To Do lists and it may take a bit of practice before it becomes really easy. Some people have no difficulty in running full colour stereo movies in their heads, or, better still, virtual reality scenarios with full sensory input. It's easy for them to get a feel for things (including office set-ups) in advance. But a lot of us are still sitting at the back of the cinema, with only a partial view of a badly worn black and white silent film. You may not want to play rugby for England, but you can save a lot of time, money and stress with realistic mental run-throughs, so it is a skill that's well worth acquiring.

Trying this technique out on your office set-up is a good way to test it. After all, planning for an ideal working environment shouldn't just be a second-rate paper exercise. It should be a visual – and a visionary – one as well.

You may be planning to move into a new office or you may only be able to afford a coat of paint for the old one. It doesn't matter. Before you wear yourself out with phone calls and brochures, use some mental energy to fix what you want firmly in your mind. Ask yourself what sort of office you really want. Does the answer you give yourself sound right? Do you have a clear view of what that office would look like? Do you have a feel for what kind of structure and setting your business needs?

What would you like your business to look, feel and sound like? It's not such a strange question. Unless you know what you really want, you have little chance of achieving an environment that is functional and feels good.

Let's be specific. What would your ideal office be like to walk into? Start at reception and give yourself a guided tour. Notice the lighting, the colours, the sounds and the atmosphere. As you walk through, help yourself to a coffee, take a look at the equipment that is being used and try out a chair and a desk for size. And, before you leave, you may want to visit the bathroom.

If your organisation is already up and running, compare your ideal with the reality. If it's even close, you are one of the fortunate few. If there's a lot to be desired, you can at least start to identify what changes are needed, whatever the constraints. From there you can sort out what changes can actually be made and begin to shape your action plan.

If you aren't in business yet, you have the advantage of starting with a clean slate. Unfortunately clean slates often come with small budgets. But you have to set up something, somewhere. So why not start moving in the direction you really want to go?

Smart Office | 11 Steps to a User-Friendly Office

Turning fantasies into facilities

Once the inspiration is firmly in place, you can work on the reality. But don't lose the vision. For every business that goes bankrupt through ignoring its budget, there's another one that loses its way in detail and ends up with more structures to support than services to sell.

Everybody knows that writing things down makes them more likely to happen. It's also a well known fact that people who make lists and organise things are compulsive, uninspired individuals – just the job description, perhaps, for an old-school facilities manager? In the past, when the paper clips had to be counted and so did the people, that might have been true. But the successful facilities manager on the flight deck of the potential UFO needs goals, as well as the means to get to them. How about setting some smart targets for getting it to fly?

Four little words: "Leave it to me."

The facts of life for facilities managers and office managers include spending a great deal of time chasing round picking up other people's litter and saving their bacon.

You're going to end up doing this anyway, so make the most of it. Smile. The franking machine is misbehaving and there's not a 25p stamp in the place. Smile.

You're having to spend two days this week interviewing, because one of your people has been moved on to higher things. Smile – the interviews may bring in someone really valuable to the company.

You've been lumbered with organising the MD's whistle-stop tour of Europe, with a press conference for the trade journals when he gets back. Smile. You said you wanted the job to be more than just routine and you know it will all be good experience once you get stuck into it. Practise your line: "Leave it to me."

There's no better way of building job security, making contacts, winning contracts and getting what you want out of your working life. Sure, you'll need a lot of advice and factual back-up for some of these tasks. But don't worry. That's all here in the rest of this book. Leave it to us.

Step 1 | **The Office Comes Second!**

The SMART approach to facilities management

The first thing to do, whether you're taking on new office premises or reorganising your old office space, is to be very clear about who is responsible for managing the facilities. Exactly what is involved? After all, office management and facilities management can cover almost everything, from controlling the credit facilities at the bank to cleaning the necessary facilities in the office itself. A lot depends on the size of the business, of course – if you happen to be a one-man band, then it's usually fairly obvious who does what. But once you get two or more gathered in the same place for working purposes, there's room for negotiation, co-operation or inefficiency.

Responsibility for managing the facilities might well be shared out among quite a number of people, but it only works if somebody, somewhere, has overall control. As you are reading this book, let's assume *it could be you*.

Take the vision and break it down into what's needed. Set some targets for getting each detail right – starting from the building (if there is one) and going right through to the last teacup.

Run the SMART reality check on every decision and acquisition. To be smart, it needs to be:

Specific	*What exactly do you need?*
Measurable	*How will you know when you've got it right?*
Affordable	*Boring, but undeniably important.*
Realistic	*Is it really possible?*
Time-related	*It doesn't have to happen immediately, but restrict your planning to the next financial year at this stage.*

Take a few moments to try this out now. Pick something that's a real and current issue for your organisation. It might be an office move – or it might be closing down the office and turning everyone into teleworkers. It might be a new computer system. Or it could just be a question of getting a new copier. Run the SMART test and see if anything turns up that you didn't know before. It usually does.

Begin, with or without a building

Let's assume you've made a start. You're either reviewing your current situation and figuring out how to make it work better or you're planning something a bit more ambitious: a new start, a new office, or even no office. The office space may be less important than the mission statement now, but it's still important to get it right. How do you make sure you have the kind of office your organisation needs?

You know UFOs make sense. The idea that the office can be reshaped and rethought to make it usable, comfortable and genuinely stimulating, with a direct knock-on effect on

Smart Office | **11 Steps to a User-Friendly Office**

productivity and profit, is not difficult to grasp. And if the details of how the new technologies can be used to implement the UFO concept are still a little hazy, there's a lot more information to come throughout this book – both in the main 11 Steps and in the Doing It Right sections at the back.

The smart office is not just an abstract idea. And it is something you can move towards, starting from the here and now. But how do you take the first steps?

Start by thinking about your people. Then take some time to think about your company mission or, to put it another way, what you're selling and how much of it you plan to sell. Bring these two elements together and move on to the next stage, which is to ask yourself: What do these people need to make it easy for them to manage this mission successfully?

What surroundings and support would be appropriate to enable them to tackle their projects energetically and creatively, with the resources they need to hand and just the right balance of stimulation and security that will impel them forward to contact the customers and make the sales?

Whether you are opening your first office or revamping one for somebody else, don't underestimate the critical importance of the working environment in terms of:

- Motivation
- Creativity
- Staff health, attendance and retention
- Satisfaction and commitment
- Productivity
- Morale

The company that looks good usually feels good too. It has nothing to do with size or glitz, but it's got a lot to do with comfort and support. With a bit of planning, you can create a working environment that runs smoothly for your organisation, as opposed to running it.

The mistake many people make when they start up a business is assuming that, because they can't afford the city-centre multi-storey landmark they really want, there is no point in bothering about the details of the working environment at all. They typically move into the first place they can afford and acquire the cheapest equipment from the first salesman who comes past and smells blood. They assume they haven't got time to worry about that sort of thing until they've sold enough of their new widgets to make them a household name. Over the years, this assumption has been the first step on the road to failure for many promising small companies.

How big is a UFO, anyway?

Of course, a lot of companies, large and small, have also been brought down by the excessive scale and grandeur of their marble halls. It's not just about size. It's about the right size – and the right style and the right feel and the right look as well.

Step 1 | The Office Comes Second!

Once you have matched the needs, the budgets and the practicalities and have moved into (or out of) an office, it's time to spend some time on getting it all to work. Get back to the traditional manager's list of what needs taking care of on a regular basis. Set up some systems and work on them until they work for you. And when the system doesn't seem to work any more, change it! Don't try to fit the work back into the system.

You've got to do whatever works

American envelope manufacturer, unconventional business guru and author Harvey Mackay specialises in shocking his readers out of their usual habits of thought. He knows all about the importance of tidy, orderly offices. After all, this is a man who has spent his adult life running an office supplies business. And what policy does he adopt to make sure things he keeps putting off finally get done?

He throws them on the floor.

He jots down an outline of what needs doing on a piece of yellow legal notepaper and chucks it on the carpet near his desk. Then he tries to forget about it.

But, of course, every time he goes back to his desk he has to walk round it, or step over it or tread on it, until eventually he cracks. At the point where the nuisance value of this scrap of paper outweighs the gain from putting the job off, it gets done.

People have strongly polarised feelings about Harvey Mackay, but there are a lot of unexpected ideas in his original bestseller, *Swim with the Sharks without Being Eaten Alive*. And it does have some of the shortest chapters ever seen in a management book, which has to be some form of recommendation.

Choosing the right anthill

Good working environments promote good work, satisfied staff and contented customers. Give the decisions about the environment, large or small, the attention they deserve. Take into account as many factors as you can. Don't assume that big budgets and prestigious addresses count for everything. But don't assume that cheapest is best either. You may not be looking at it from all the possible angles.

Smart Office | 11 Steps to a User-Friendly Office

> *One businessman in Putney, in southwest London, made the move recently from cheap, practical, downmarket offices to a smart modern office block a stone's throw away on the sunny side of the street. For years, he had bragged about how much he was saving on overheads by working out of rundown premises above a Chinese restaurant. After the move, it turned out that he was actually in pocket, despite the higher rent. Suddenly he could invite his oil company clients to visit him, instead of having to go up to central London every time a meeting was needed. He saved two hours of his own time per meeting (costed at £100 per hour) plus train and taxi fares. And when lunch was involved and his firm was paying, he soon found that restaurants in SW15 were heartwarmingly cheaper than those in SW1.*

It's not just the people *in* the office who matter — the people *around* the office make a difference too. Offices shouldn't be ivory towers and it's worth taking into account neighbourhoods, external support systems and other individuals who also contribute, if only indirectly, to your success.

What happens when the people are the system?

Organising people is one of the most difficult and undervalued skills of the office manager or facilities manager. Objects are much easier. It's far more straightforward to plan the ergonomic seating and set up a new computer system than it is to synchronise the people you need to support your sales and production teams.

Organisations don't work in isolation. Everybody knows you need customers and suppliers, but there's always a local ecosystem of some kind that can make all the difference to the atmosphere and culture of a business, as well as its efficiency. Smaller offices often lean quite heavily on surrounding businesses, while business parks and business centres create artificial communities which can provide useful support for new ventures. But even the multi-storey, one-company office blocks can be seen, on close inspection, to be swarming with people who aren't actually employees.

Dealing with contractors, suppliers, cleaners and tradesmen

They may not be on the payroll, but these are the backstage people who support the performers. These outsiders who supply the paper or repair the roof when it leaks are often just as important as the physical bricks and mortar of the office premises. After all, it's better for morale to use the local sandwich shop than the office kitchen when it hasn't been cleaned — and if it's going to be kept clean, somebody has to do it.

Step 1 | **The Office Comes Second!**

Getting the wrong people to give your organisation the support it needs can be almost as disastrous as getting your recruitment wrong on the inside. Obviously a dishonest cleaner or an incompetent plumber may not be able to wreak havoc on the same scale as a corrupt financial controller, but it's still worth spending some time and effort to find the right suppliers and tradesmen.

- Check what and who the other businesses around you are using. Don't just ask the people next door – compare a few. Even so, it does make sense to use the same cleaners as other people in the building, provided they are efficient. You cut down on the potential security risks and you become more important to the cleaning firm, because you are collectively bigger customers. The same argument often applies to anyone who delivers anything. Stationery supplies are more likely to arrive promptly and regularly if the company delivers to other people in the same area.
- Check more than one costing for regular services and supplies. Once you have made up your mind, run a comparison with the competition every year or so to make sure you are still getting a good deal for your money. Squeeze the maximum value from the exercise by letting the people you use know from the start that their services will be re-costed regularly like this.

Creature comforts

Assuming that you've got the people on the outside working for the common good, the next consideration is the comfort and productivity of the ones on the inside.

The facilities you provide will naturally depend on how many people you have to provide for and the budget and image you are working on. If there are only two of you, a kettle and a couple of mugs, plus use of the loo and washbasin on the next floor, will probably do. Very small firms are generally too busy surviving to fret about their surroundings.

If you are slightly bigger, however, it's worth remembering that the better you treat people, generally, the better they perform. Unlike the nineteenth-century workplace, where staff were only allowed to answer calls of nature once a day and eating and drinking were forbidden, some modern offices are almost surrogate homes. Other remain vilely Victorian, with the bleakest and most unhygienic of facilities. They are clearly intended to give the message that satisfying bodily needs is to be allocated the minimum amount of attention during the working day.

All this may seem trivial, compared with selecting copiers and purchasing software. But you will save your business a lot of money and improve staff morale immeasurably if you make well informed and carefully costed decisions about the basic issues.

- What equipment are you going to install?
- Who will clean and service it?

- What rules will you have for its use?
- What are staff expected to provide for themselves?

Don't make the cloakrooms an excuse

There is one school of thought which believes that comfortable, separate, male and female lavatories encourage lingering, chatting and smoking during working hours. Unheated unisex loos, on the other hand, supposedly discourage people from taking over-long comfort breaks. The down side is that they also tend to be less well treated, less hygienic and bad for morale.

Well-appointed washrooms are not only good for your staff; they will also be noticed by your visitors. If employees are spending too much time in them, it won't be because they like the decor. It's much more likely to be because they don't like the work. And that's another problem altogether.

You need to be quite a large operation before it is worth paying an outside contractor to visit you weekly to sanitise loos and empty bins in the ladies. A firm of fewer than 20 people can probably manage with washrooms that are cleaned by the regular cleaning staff. Think about whether you go for hot-air dryers or paper towels and liquid soap dispensers rather than the real thing. Hot-air dryers used to be considered more hygienic. Recent surveys, however, have shown that most people don't like them because they take so long and tend to break down a lot. As a result, people often come out grumbling, with wet hands, or else use toilet paper as a makeshift towel, which is expensive and messy, as well as being inefficient.

Keep the kitchen simple

Everyone has a prejudice or two about what sort of kitchen ought to be provided at work. But which works best in practice? Does a nicely fitted little kitchen with a microwave and a toaster lower productivity by encouraging staff to spend hours preparing gourmet lunches and mid-afternoon snacks?

Or does it simply mean that they are more likely to make a toasted sandwich and take it back to their desks, so that they can continue working through the lunch break? Then again, do you want soup in your keyboards and greasy patches on the correspondence? Wouldn't it be better to encourage people to pop out for half an hour and take a proper break, clear their minds, make crumbs in the sandwich bar and not in the office, and come back refreshed and ready to concentrate?

It's a good idea to provide basic facilities, including a fridge. But do resist the temptation to install a complicated range of equipment that needs a lot of cleaning and maintenance. Doing this can cause more problems than it solves and can trigger all kinds of tensions and unrest.

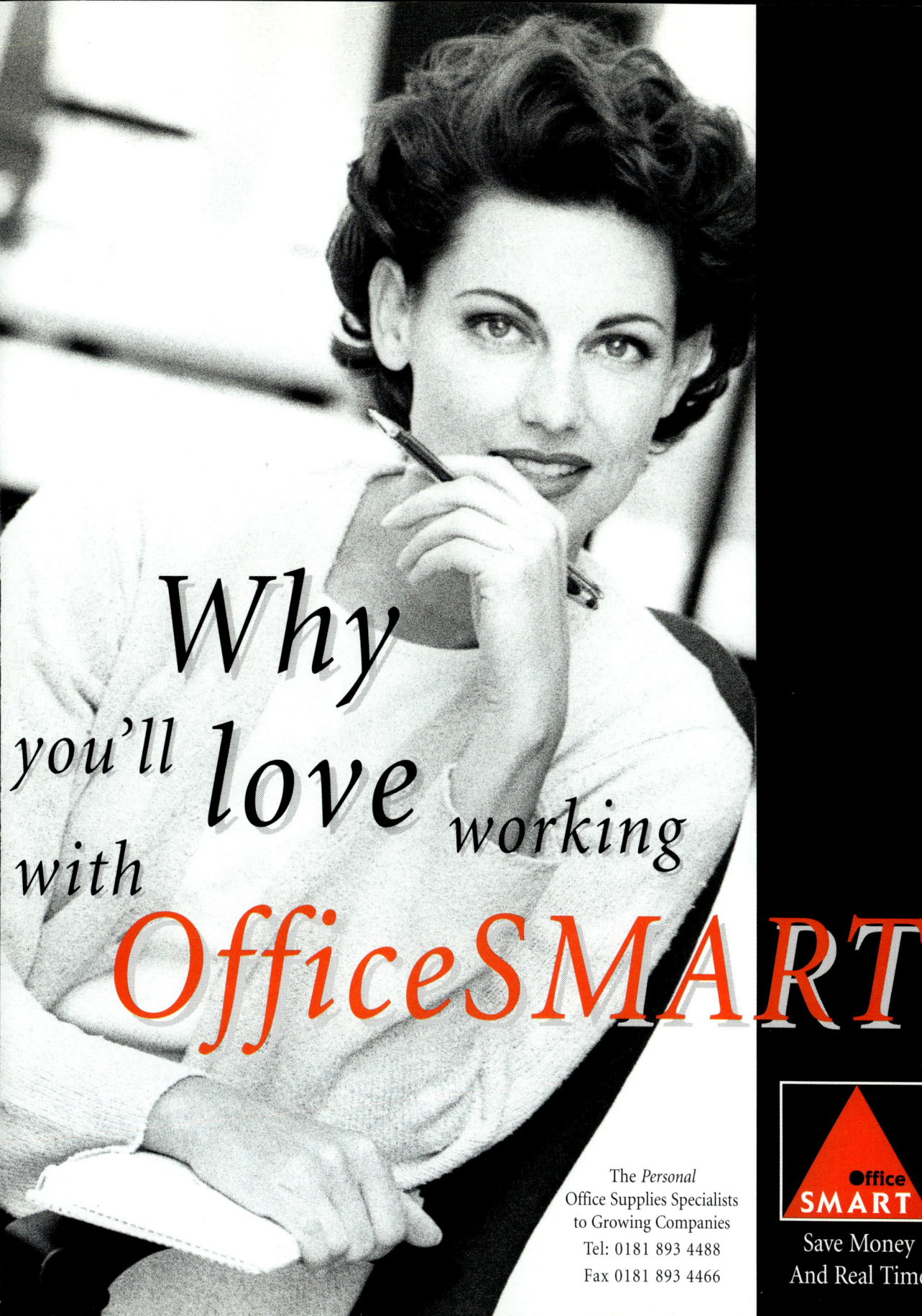

Step 1 | The Office Comes Second!

There's always someone who eats someone else's peanut butter and expects the coffee mugs to wash themselves. But there's always someone who is sufficiently fussy about coffee to brew a fresh pot every morning, too. So if you provide a large insulated jug, there's just a chance this person will make enough for everyone else as well.

Can coffee breed co-operation?

The big decision for companies of a certain size is always whether or not to have a drinks machine. If you decide to go for this option, investigate several and cost your commitment carefully. Some machines really are better than others and some are more expensive than you think. Allow for the cost of the maintenance and supplies, in addition to the monthly rental. If you do install an automatic, at least provide a back-up kettle as well. Some people really can't drink the almost-tea that comes out of machines and need their raspberry and camomile to keep them going, to say nothing of the demand for Lemsip during the winter months.

The days of the tea trolley are gone, and many people still miss it. It was a beacon of hope – something to look forward to in the middle of a long morning or afternoon and an excuse to break concentration and grapple with a sticky bun. But whatever kitchen space and equipment you provide for your staff, experience shows that it's better to stick to a minimum of actual supplies. Tea, coffee, milk and sugar are all that is needed, plus, of course, the washing-up liquid, the dish scrubber and several tea towels (it's quite remarkable how many otherwise well-equipped offices can only rise to one).

Building self-managing teams in the kitchen

This minimalist approach has nothing to do with cost cutting, though. It's simply that the more you provide, the more discontent there will be. The biscuits will never please everyone. If there is Earl Grey, someone is bound to want Lapsang Souchong. But if you leave it to the staff, it's often quite a neat way of building up a bit of camaraderie and co-operation. People will share their pepper and salt and sweeteners and Ryvita and will find ways of regulating for themselves who uses what, rather than expecting the management to do everything for them. It's actually quite a positive frame of mind to encourage.

This may sound a bit like the seaside landlady syndrome. But if you don't make it clear what you expect of people in terms of washing-up duties, they will invent their own rules and there will be as many versions of these as there are members of staff. Whoever imposes the rules is bound to be the butt of people's grumbles occasionally – it's less disruptive if it's a disembodied managerial "them" than if one person has to take on the role of special constable.

Smart Office | 11 Steps to a User-Friendly Office

You can take off on a wing and a prayer

Whatever the physical shape and size of your premises and however lavish or spartan the facilities, the important thing to remember about the smart office principle is that there is always something positive you can do to make things better.

In the later chapters of this book, there is plenty of very concrete, specific advice about improving the physical aspects of the office environment, managing your responsibilities under health and safety legislation and exploiting the new possibilities offered by computers, databases and the Internet. But it is the people who set the tone in any office and create the most important influence on the atmosphere. However much thought and investment goes into sorting out the decor, the architecture or the equipment, it is the warmware that counts.

That means, of course, that there is scope for the ambitious facilities manager to begin making a real difference at any time, even in the middle of a total budget freeze. Anything you can do to start wheeling people round towards the positive, collaborative attitudes and ways of working outlined in this book will represent valuable progress, which should be quite tangible and measurable within a matter of weeks. If you're out to create a true UFO, you are going to need some budget behind you at some stage. But it's surprising how far you can go just by helping people make minor, detailed changes in the way they work and the way they approach other people. High-tech ergonomic chairs may be expensive, but talk's cheap. And if you can show results before there is any money in the kitty, it will certainly put you in a strong position to make the business case for later investment.

STEP 2
WHO NEEDS AN OFFICE, ANYWAY?

Step 2 | Who Needs an Office, Anyway?

HOW TO SET UP AND RUN THE SMARTER OFFICE

WHAT'S THE OFFICE THERE FOR?

One essential part of the smart office approach is changing the way you think about the office. Why have one at all, for example? What do you get through having an office that could not be achieved by piecing together some carefully planned system of subcontracting and teleworking?

If you take a long, cool look at these questions, the answers may startle you.

In the past, the social model implicit in most commercial firms was an almost feudal master/servant relationship. The office environment was all about control. The main reason for setting up offices and office systems was to allow the necessary work to be done without the need to hire high quality workers. A handful of well-drilled and authoritarian managers and supervisors could guide, bully and cajole the most unpromising squad of staff into doing what needed to be done. Historical factors played a part in this, too, as those who had experienced life in the forces during the war or on National Service applied a quasi-military approach to motivation and discipline. Initiative was not required and a chronological pecking order usually emerged, with the longest-serving staff holding the whiphand.

This kind of set-up is chillingly depicted in any number of 1950s movies, where the vast, regimented insurance office or typing pool is part of a world of tyrannical bosses, meek company wives and harassed, insecure and incompetent workers.

In today's offices, there is less dumb routine work, less shouting and more talking. No one is sent off to paint the coal white. Newcomers receive training, which is now rather more than just watching and copying someone else. But the biggest change is that people are expected to understand what they are doing, take responsibility for it and be flexible enough to modify their approach as circumstances change. That takes initiative. But it also demands the kind of co-operation that lets one person benefit from another's ideas, knowledge and experience – in a word, teamwork.

It's the teamwork that adds the value. Teamwork is such a cynically overused term these days that it's worth pausing for a moment to think about what its real significance is. Often, talk about teamwork is just so much hot air and window-dressing. But if it means anything at all, it surely means a bunch of individuals, working closely together and clicking in a way that delivers remarkable results – results that add up to more than you could reasonably expect from their individual efforts and talents. If the whole is not more than the sum of the parts, teamwork is not happening, despite the gloss that managers or PR departments may be trying to put on the situation.

Teamwork, however, cannot develop in the abstract. It needs to be located in time and place. And that's where the office makes a vital, and often unacknowledged, contribution. The office is not an unproductive overhead. It adds value simply by being the crucible in which the reactions take place that make teamwork a reality.

OFFICE MANAGER OR FACILITIES MANAGER?

Whatever label you apply to it, the job of running and managing the office, balancing responsibilities for people, systems and the environment, is a much more subtle and complex role than it ever used to be. The title of "office manager" doesn't really do it justice any more, which is probably why so many of the more forward-thinking people doing this sort of job have opted for the alternative title of "facilities manager".

In practice, these days, the two titles are probably more or less interchangeable, though the old guard will probably gravitate towards OM, while the Young Turks naturally like the sound of FM.

The important thing is that today's facilities manager or office manager sees the big picture and acts accordingly. He or she understands the organisation and its people and takes on board the goals of the managing director, the senior strategy-makers and the business as a whole.

In a small firm where you may be MD, chief accountant, facilities manager and several other people rolled into one, maintaining this big picture perspective demands no special effort. It can be quite different if you are responsible for a branch office in Inverness and the corporate HQ is located in Crawley. Under those circumstances, it will often take a real, conscious effort to ensure that you are kept plugged in and properly informed about the shifts and nuances of strategy that should be part of your thinking.

Making a fuss or making a difference?

It may be tactless to mention it, but not all traditional office managers have always been assets to their companies. A lot of pensioned-off sergeant majors and petty officers arrived

Step 2 | **Who Needs an Office, Anyway?**

in Civvy Street in the fifties and sixties and found themselves cosy niches as petty tyrants. The classic ex-Navy PT is almost an endangered species now, though you will still occasionally find a fine one-off specimen, blithely ignorant about how the company makes its living but fanatically correct about enforcing rules and insisting on the forms needed for paper clip supplies or the issue of a new fax roll.

Oddly enough, though, alongside these walking caricatures, the modern facilities manager can sometimes seem curiously ineffectual. The problem is that it is not quite so obvious to him or her what everyone should be doing at any given time. With fewer rules and more scope for initiative and judgment, life gets more complicated than before

What this underlines is the importance of assessing where you spend your energy and where you can make a difference. How long is it since you allowed yourself a little time to stop and think what your priorities are and how you could be most effective? One major reason for high stress levels and poor productivity in this kind of executive role is spending too much time fretting about things you can't hope to change and too little time analysing where you could really make an impact. Ideally, you should be directing as much of your energy as possible towards the points where you will get the best value for the effort you invest.

It's easier, in the short term, to spend half an hour a day searching for telephone numbers or lost invoices, but a lot more useful to set aside 30 minutes each day for the purpose of refining and updating your database and filing systems.

> **Great office managers should have the company's mission in mind and the means of achieving it under control.**

Even if it sometimes seems that no one else in the company can manage it, your view of the whole picture is vital. Keep it clear and up to date and don't lose sight of the priorities implicit in it.

People first, then things

That's the theory. Then there's the practice. It is an inescapable fact that the people with responsibility for facilities management in any organisation, at any level, are among the most likely to be unable to see the wood for the trees. The nature of the task carries with it a load of detail that anyone can easily get lost in and the way the scope of the job keeps changing makes it harder and harder to define.

Call it facilities manager or office manager – even general manager or admin manager, if you wish – the important point is to recognise that the job is not just to arrange things, but to manage and support people as well. People come first. But the people are more likely to be happy, motivated, productive and creative if they are put in a setting that is comfortable and efficient, where they can communicate easily, concentrate without distractions and find what they want without wasting their time.

Smart Office | 11 Steps to a User-Friendly Office

> ## Type Casting
>
> Less than 150 years ago, not one British worker in a hundred worked in an office. When writing machines first appeared, in the 1880s, a new word was needed for the staff who operated them. Naturally enough, these people were called typewriters.
>
> Becoming a typewriter was one of the first respectable careers for middle class girls. Two lady typewriters were taken on by the Inland Revenue in 1887 and put in an isolated office, with a hatch so that documents could be passed in to them for typing. Once a week, the ladies emerged, flanked by two messengers, to pick up their wages.
>
> It was World War I that really brought women into the office for the first time. Before the war, there were 600 women in the civil service. By 1920 the figure was 170,000.

Doing it in a big way

The role of the office manager can vary greatly. In the High Street banks, for example, the Administration Manager usually takes on this responsibility, as part of the burden of being No. 2 to the Branch Manager

The Administrative Manager of a big corporation might have a number of other office managers reporting to him. He could easily be responsible for organising (for example):

- Sales Office Manager
- Computer Manager
- Production Office Manager
- Organisation and Methods Manager
- Accounting Office Manager
- Office Services Manager

Doing more on a smaller scale

The office manager of a small company, on the other hand, will usually have to do everything, from putting the heating on in the morning to recruiting and training office staff and from organising computer systems to turning out the lights and setting the alarms at night. It's not unusual to find one harassed individual in a company of up to 50 employees who is totally responsible for:

Step 2 | **Who Needs an Office, Anyway?**

- Ordering stationery and supplies
- Selecting, purchasing and maintaining equipment
- Supervising cleaning and security
- Organising communications and filing
- Making tea, answering phones and typing letters
- Bookkeeping, invoicing and bill paying
- Personnel matters

Personnel and bookkeeping responsibilities are the most likely to be farmed out or done by someone else in the company. But even without these areas to worry about, the role of the office manager is a complex and vital one.

An incompetent office manager is one of the worst disasters that can afflict any business, regardless of its size. The job itself is one of the most difficult and most rewarding of any of the key administrative roles. The days when the role was structured and routine are gone. The modern office manager needs to be the most flexible and well-informed member of any team.

He needs to update himself all the time on the latest technology, changes in European regulations and current thinking on health, stress, archiving systems and coffee machines. And he, of course, is increasingly likely to find that he's a she. Despite some sporadic rearguard actions by the more dyed-in-the-wool leftovers from the Dickensian era, this is an area where women are rapidly moving towards 50 per cent representation.

Most important of all, male or female, the office manager must be both mother and father to everyone in the company – strong enough to control unreasonable demands for new software and balance the petty cash, warm and sympathetic enough to spot incipient nervous breakdowns and disastrous interdepartmental affairs and sharp enough to get the company logged on to the Internet if there isn't an IT department to take care of it.

MANAGING THE OFFICE

Managing an office means balancing people, technology and systems in a relatively small environment. Management scientists with an ecological bent talk about the office as a living organism. But organisms need to be able to do more than survive. They need to be ready and able to grow. The business has to be able to interact effectively with the outside world of its market and its suppliers. An office can only be effectively managed by someone who has a clear overview of what the whole operation is about and where the strengths and weak points are.

Smart Office | 11 Steps to a User-Friendly Office

> ## Potted history
>
> - The paper clip was invented and triumphantly patented in Germany in 1900. The Norwegian inventor is commemorated by a 25-metre statue of a paper clip in his home town, near Oslo.
>
> - Fluorescent lights – originally bright green and not very durable, but soon vastly improved – arrived in British offices 50 years ago. Supporters keen to prove the new technology's virtues had installed London's first fluorescent tube at Piccadilly Circus tube station in 1945.
>
> - Chester Carlson, the patent lawyer who invented and patented the Xerox process in 1937, took ten years to come up with a commercial machine. Even then, it was almost unusable. His first really practical "automatic" copier wasn't seen in offices until 1960, though its instant success went on to make him a millionaire many times over.

GETTING DOWN TO THE DETAIL

So you've created an efficient, comfortable, elegant environment. The burglar alarm works and everybody knows where the fire extinguishers are. But once they've made their cups of coffee and settled down at their ergonomically correct desks – where do they go from there? How well do they communicate – in fact, *how* do they communicate? Can they easily find the information they need? Do they know how to use the software in their terminals?

COMMUNICATING EFFECTIVELY

Running an office is all about communication. A successful facilities manager is always a great communicator and organiser. This means being able to communicate with people at all levels, particularly in small to medium offices, where the manager will have to deal directly with everyone from the chairman to the restroom sanitiser. In very small companies, the facilities manager will also have to be prepared to cover for all the other administrative staff (if any) and may have to act as receptionist as well as make the tea for staff meetings.

    A good facilities manager is able to get the best out of everyone, influencing people and events without being unduly manipulative.

DELEGATING

Like all management skills, delegation is partly art and partly science, part wisdom and part technique. In a very small office there may be no one to delegate to. But even in the smallest office, it's worth keeping a checklist of people who are experts in everything you might need help with. This could range from plant care to databases and from insurance to electrical testing. You need to be aware of everything you might need to know. What you don't necessarily have to do is actually know it all.

In larger offices, where the manager may have anything from one to 50 people to delegate to, the most important thing is to be absolutely clear about roles. This doesn't mean fostering "not my job" attitudes and demarcation disputes. It does mean that people will have their own areas of expertise, for which they are ready to take responsibility.

EXPANDING THE ROLE

In some organisations, the role of facilities manager has developed entirely in line with the personality and capabilities of the person who first took it on. A highly computer literate person, for example, may have turned the office management job into something close to a one-man IT department. An office run by a person like this is likely to be run electronically, with e-mail, shared databases and networked diary systems and the most sophisticated forms of communication with the outside world. On the other hand, an office run by a "people" person is more likely to rely on direct communication and personal contact. It may be more idiosyncratic and less consistent in its filing and recording systems. But it may also be warmer and happier to work in and full of highly motivated people whose energy and commitment drives them on to deliver business miracles.

You can't have it both ways. Or can you? If you care enough to be excited by the idea, it's certainly worth having a damned good try. The key is to expand your role. We're not just talking about self-serving empire-building here, with the usual boring goal of world domination. The aim is to grow your role subtly, usefully, balancing your needs and ambitions with the needs of the business and the people who make it work.

CLONE YOUR OWN MEMORY

The typical old-fashioned office manager has always been depicted as a (semi) human filing cabinet, a walking data bank, the person who exists to make the system work at the expense of the people working in it. There's some truth in this and a good reason for it.

The first thing any efficient FM or OM should do, once he fully understands what is required to make this particular office run smoothly, is to turn that knowledge into a system that will run without him. If the efficient facilities manager is run over by a bus, it should make very little difference, in the short term, to the running of the office systems. Bills will still be paid, mail will go out on time and everybody will know where to find whatever's needed. The inefficient manager, however, will leave a legacy of chaos. Nobody else will know exactly how much is in petty cash, whether the toner has been ordered or how to recharge the franking machine.

It's nice to be missed, but not to be cursed for your absence. The effective facilities manager is much more likely to have a good turnout at her funeral, simply because the office will be running so smoothly that a temp can be left to man the reception desk for a couple of hours.

Clone your own memory by setting up a system that is as pervasive as a computer virus, unavoidable and self-perpetuating, but working on the side of the angels. Make sure the system finds the people, not the other way around.

SETTING UP THE SYSTEM

Once the business is up and running in the optimum location, the most important task is to set up a system that is as effective and as efficient as you are. It should be as visible as you are, too, so that anyone who doesn't know exactly where to find something can work it out quickly if you're not there to ask. Most important of all, it should also be as easy to communicate with as you are, so that everyone can put in and get out of it what they need, without damaging or weakening the system for anyone else.

THE PAPER TRAIL

Every order your firm generates, every receipt for payments, every invoice that goes out and every bill that comes in will eventually find its place in your filing system. Indeed, every scrap of paper you produce should end up in one of just two destinations – the filing system or the bin. The offices that cannot make up their minds whether to scrap or file marginal bits and pieces of paperwork are the ones that slowly sink into chaos under the accumulated weight of piles of nearly-important bumf.

So someone – and it is probably going to be you – has to draw the line about what is to be kept and what should be ruthlessly discarded. Once that decision has been made, it should be self-evident to everyone using your filing system where each type of document should go. But just as important as knowing where to put things is having a standard route for them to follow.

Don't lose track of the "live" paperwork

There are plenty of offices that can boast immaculate and almost up-to-date filing systems but have no visible system at all for "live" invoices, delivery notes and requisitions that are not yet ready to file. This is known as living on the edge. It guarantees regular panics and crises, or, at the very least, a thoroughly unhealthy dependence on the one key person in the office who stands a remote chance of being able to track down any particular piece of paper in the course of a 15-minute phone call.

If the system is no system at all, nothing is routine. Everything is an exception. And exceptions are hard work.

But there are sometimes clearly identifiable reasons for this apparently accidental state of affairs.

- **Nobody's responsibility.** The bookkeeper probably thinks it's the receptionist's job to collate all the bills. Or the facilities manager might decide that accounts don't need to be part of the main system, whatever that may be.
- **Easing the cashflow.** Responsible organisations don't do this, but it happens nevertheless. If you leave the financial paperwork floating around, you have a seemingly legitimate excuse for not being able to find it when your creditors phone to ask why they haven't been paid. Unfortunately, this kind of thinking usually clogs up the whole system – companies who practise it often find their own invoicing is delayed and inaccurate as well.

There should be a "virtual conveyor belt" for tracking every incoming and outgoing invoice that passes through the office. If you actually visualise this conveyor belt and see the image in your mind, it will help to remind you of the essential principles underlying a workable system. It must keep moving the paperwork along, however slowly, in the right direction. It must keep grouped items together, unless there is a very strong reason for splitting them. It must not allow anything to be sidetracked. The final destination will have to be linked to computer accounts, as well as ledgers, and will also need to be tied in with the main filing system. The route things take to get there, however, is an all-important part of the way the process operates.

Smart Office | 11 Steps to a User-Friendly Office

Drowning in a sea of paper

- Filing goes back a long way – at least to Shakespeare's time. It originally meant stringing papers onto a thread (*filum* in Latin) for storage. Samuel Pepys wrote in 1666 about "all the unnecessary letters which I have had upon my file for four or five years backward".

- British offices generate one billion pages of paperwork a day. Much of it ends up filed away in the country's 13.5 million filing cabinets.

- Current estimates put the proportion of business information stored on paper at 95 per cent. Despite all the talk of revolution and the increasing use of electronic document imaging systems in the banking and financial services sectors, just one document in 20 is held in digital form.

THE TRUTH ABOUT "FINDING" SYSTEMS

If you can't keep your information system up to date, you'll be exposed to the outside world as not knowing what you're talking about, whenever a query crops up.

Fifteen years ago, the one thing you could rely upon in most offices was the monotonous predictability of the filing system. Creativity was not seen as a desirable personality trait in either office juniors or facilities managers.

But all that has changed, due to two main factors. One is a general change in thinking, so that people now place more value on the accumulation of accessible information. The second is the pace of recent hardware and software advances, which have affected document storage and categorisation, as well as diaries and record-keeping. Management, too, is constantly moving the goalposts and redefining what it wants from its information store.

Trying to operate any kind of rigid, paper-based system in today's office is often like sweeping leaves in a whirlwind. And, to make it worse, the facilities manager is not even in control of all the information any more. Many firms pay lip service to the "paperless office". But paperless offices are rather like abominable snowmen – just about technically possible, but nobody has ever seen one.

In any business, there will be some individuals who try to do everything via their electronic mail, their networked diaries and their databases of information. They rarely print out. At the next desk will be someone doing the same job who writes memos by hand and sticks Post-it notes on everything. What happens to a central filing system in an office like

Step 2 Who Needs an Office, Anyway?

this? How can the facilities manager know what is going on and where everything is, let alone control it?

The answer is to compromise and survive. The office manager needs to be master of all systems, but dogmatic about none. Today's office manager or facilities manager can no longer impose order on chaos. These days, the job is to know exactly what kind of chaos each executive likes to dump his information into and work out some way of co-ordinating and keeping tabs on them all.

Let's hear it for the all-purpose database

Routine commercial filing is one area where computer power – and particularly the flexibility of loosely structured relational databases – really is a blessing.

Manual filing has always been uncomfortably dependent on the commitment and intelligence of the filer. In places where fast information retrieval is of vital importance, such as newspaper cuttings libraries, filing has long been recognised as something approaching an art form. A clever filing clerk can anticipate requirements and cross-reference documents so thoughtfully that whatever information is needed always seems close to hand. But it is probably unrealistic to expect junior staff in a run-of-the-mill sales or wages office to match the skill and enthusiasm of the people in the *Daily Telegraph*'s famous cuttings library.

Where efficiency is more important than imagination, computerised filing is a godsend. Don't spend too much time worrying about whether to categorise your files by subject or product line, geographically, or by customer's name. This used to be a critical decision. These days, your computer's relational database can cover all the options simultaneously and sort for you according to what you need at any given time.

Seven plus or minus two

The information you can actually use to run your business better is no longer limited by your own brainpower (research has shown that seven chunks of information, plus or minus two, is about the limit most people's heads can cope with, at any one time). The sales team can now record just about everything about every potential customer from his dog's name to her golf handicap (not forgetting the size of the last order) and call it up in seconds during the course of a telephone conversation. It's time to start thinking big about what you could do with power like this at your fingertips – literally.

FILM your customers now

You don't have to generalise any more. You can focus right in on your clients' real needs and position yourself to meet them before they even know what they are by recording what's known in the trade as the Full Inside Leg Measurement for each customer.

33

Every name, number and snippet of background information your sales force is likely to need for every foreseeable purpose, from talking through the second order to chasing up the first invoice, should be right there. And the database isn't just for managing your clients. It's just as important to tailor it to the needs of your staff and your company objectives. Most of today's standard armoury of business tools and techniques, like loyalty management, niche marketing, even the obvious applications of the good old 80/20 rule, wouldn't be viable without a database. And the most famous common-sense concept of all, networking, undoubtedly works best when it's underpinned by a comprehensive database (see Step 10).

There are some famous (even notorious) rich and successful entrepreneurs of the old school who always give the secret of their success as "applied common sense". What the new generation of top earners will tell you is that you need adequate, accurate data before you can start applying the common sense to it.

You don't need an MBA – just focus on your MVCs

One simple way to start using the leverage that comes with a usable database is to identify your MVCs or most valuable customers. You need to know who your MVCs are, not just so that you can be extra polite to them on the phone, but because the chances are that they are really only spending less than half their budgets with you.

Don't just be nice to them. These are strategic targets for your business. They are people who already trust you enough to buy from you regularly, yet they still spend money with other suppliers, who may be your direct competitors. Your aim should be to capture some of that cash. You could increase your share of customer spending by using a bit of extra, focused salesmanship – and if you don't, somebody else will. Treat your MVCs as a major growth opportunity or you might just find them gone.

Your database can help you work smarter, instead of working harder, all the time. Analyse what it's telling you and put more attention, service, products and incentives in the way of the MVCs. The rewards can be spectacular, yet it is one of the most reliable low-risk strategies you can adopt. As one leading wholesaler put it: "Focusing on our MVCs brings rewards very quickly and cheaply – for one thing, we don't have to market the world."

The value you derive from the software and hardware that runs your database could be higher than from any other business investment you make. And it's not necessarily the most expensive set-ups that do the best job. Moderately sized businesses can get good value out of standard software, without employing armies of programmers to adapt it to their applications.

Big players lead the way

The types of hardware that will support the large-scale record-keeping and database systems of the future are already taking shape. Companies such as Canon, Xerox, Kodak and

Panasonic have worked for years to develop powerful document handling systems which scan everything in, store it all on searchable optical or magneto-optical discs and make it available very fast when you need it. They are, however, ferociously expensive, and people are always finding exceptions that such equipment cannot be used for, making it necessary to run two parallel systems in the office.

Many big corporations now use this type of equipment, particularly in large offices where the volume of paper is potentially overwhelming and traditional archiving and storage would be prohibitively expensive. About a third of Britain's banks and building societies are using imaging systems and they claim major cost and space savings, as well as the ability to boost productivity and deliver better customer service. Since one optical disk can hold as much information as five four-drawer filing cabinets (at least 40,000 images, compared with a mere 13,000 on a magneto-optical disc), the cash value of the floor space savings can be spectacular, particularly in city centre locations.

Smaller firms watch and wait

In the smaller office, no one is likely to suggest investing in one of these electronic filing systems yet. The entry costs are simply too steep. Even entry-level systems are a major investment (Canon's Canofile 250 costs £10,000 and others from Kardex and Lanier start at £12,000 and £13,500), once the half-hidden costs of training, maintenance and reorganisation are taken into account. Everyone keeps looking longingly in the direction of the PC on the desk, with its ever-increasing power and flexibility, and hoping that a cheap and magically simple solution will appear. It may, but not for a while.

The problem is that your PC can't easily file your incoming letters and invoices, booklets of technical specifications from other companies, charts and photographs – not yet, anyway! In fact, computers are quite capable of doing all these things, but only if all the other companies and people who exchange information with you are thinking along the same lines. You need to be using open systems and adhering to common conventions, such as the Edifact electronic data interchange standard, and you must obviously be linked by modem. Even the open system software developers predict that mass take-up of this kind of technology is going to be ten years in the future, which, of course, means it will really be either three years away or 20.

In the meantime, some offices have more or less accepted the inevitability of chaos. This is a tempting stance, but unduly defeatist. The solution is to take positive action, step by step. (See Doing It Right – Finding the Right Finding System.)

IN A NUTSHELL
1. OM or FM, the job's getting bigger
- Support the work team
- The whole picture, not just the paper clips
- Underpinning the growth of the business
- Define your own role (how many things *should* you try to do at the same time?)

2. Communicating effectively
- Making sure everything runs smoothly and everybody knows what is going on
- Delegating effectively
- Expanding the role – fitting your skills to the needs of the business
- Building your expertise into the system, so that it can run without you
- Get the paper trail right – setting up a virtual conveyor belt so that you (and everybody else) can locate anything quickly and easily
- Four steps to sanity and keeping the finances straight
    - requisition
    - logging in
    - payment
    - filing

3. Filing systems and finding systems
- Coping with paper until the paperless office arrives
- Getting the new to work with the old
    - making sure the computer files don't duplicate or contradict the ones in the cabinets
    - prepare for a smooth transition from pages to bytes

4. Database management
- The advantages of an electronic database
    - takes the limits off the data you can control
    - makes it possible to tailor your operation to the needs of your clients and the skills of your team
    - enables you to focus your efforts on key targets, such as MVCs
- Making sure you use it to maximise your marketing and sales operation
- Databases of the future – planning ahead

STEP 3
LOOK AFTER THE POUNDS AND THE PENNIES DON'T MATTER

Step 3 | **Look After the Pounds and the Pennies Don't Matter**

TAKING CONTROL OF THE OFFICE
DON'T GET WORKED UP – GET SMART

Every office in the country has room for improvement. Everyone knows it. But the improvements that need to be made over the next few years are not just improvements in efficiency – doing the same things better, more quickly and more cheaply. The changes that are already beginning to take place in individual offices scattered throughout Britain have been made possible by recent and dramatic advances in computing and communications technology, ergonomics, office product design, management theory and industrial psychology.

These factors are leading to process re-engineering that can be just as radical as anything taking place on the factory floor. They are physically reshaping the office environment and the components that define it. And they are taking us away from the old, dull view that the office is a necessary evil, an overhead that drags down the performance of other parts of the firm.

The new office – the smart office – is designed and run to be very close to the centre of what the company is all about. It is a brainy, in-touch, creative contributor. It initiates ideas, rather than dragging along behind, because it knows how to use the energy and ingenuity of the people who work there. They are the people who make it work and make it different. And they are sharp, motivated and enthusiastic, because they see, at every turn, how valuable their contribution is and how much effort the business is prepared to put in to give them the right tools and opportunities to do a good job.

Every office needs processes and procedures. But these are not ends in themselves. In the smart office, people look beyond the immediate task and focus on larger, more ambitious goals. That means taking a more complete, holistic view of their activities. It's the kind of approach that makes buying supplies for the office, for example, a much more interesting and challenging business than it ever was in the days when price seemed to be the only thing that mattered.

Smart Office | 11 Steps to a User-Friendly Office

The Age of the Machine

What would you rate as the most important invention or machine in the development of the modern office?

The typewriter doesn't seem such a strong candidate these days. The lift (the big 19th-century breakthrough, because it made buildings over ten storeys feasible) and the telephone have obvious claims. And some fans of today's technology would point to PC clusters linked by Ethernet LANs, or, perhaps, to the yellow highlighter pen.

But if you look at a list of the devices that are used most in ordinary, everyday offices, the most striking point is how much of the technology is new.

The list below shows 25 items of equipment, ranked roughly in order of price and costing from a couple of thousand down to a couple of pounds.

A manager who is 55 now will have started work in an era without computers and faxes, obviously, but also without calculators, shredders, answering machines and even photocopiers. More than half the items on this list either did not exist or were unavailable for office use at the beginning of the sixties.

Almost without thinking about it, office managers have assimilated new tools and technologies year in and year out. They have learned how to make them pay their way by eliminating many mindless routine tasks and speeding up many more.

Yet the overall office productivity gains of the last ten years have been disappointingly small, considering the investment that has been put in and the technological firepower that is readily available in 486, Pentium and Apple computers. So far, the manufacturing industry has succeeded in harnessing recent technologies far more effectively, in terms of crude output productivity.

The challenge in offices is to make this raw power count, to channel it into places and tasks where it can assist people to do more and do it better.

That is partly to do with softening the edges of high technology, through the use of smarter, more intuitive software and better hardware designs.

But it is also to do with the bigger picture. It involves better management and motivation, clearer goal-setting, a positive office environment and a closer fit between people's capabilities and the jobs they do.

The machines and devices will keep on getting better all the time. But hardware will only take us so far. In the end, it's people that make offices work.

Copiers
Computer systems
Electronic whiteboards
Phone systems
Franking machines
Overhead projectors
Printers and plotters
Scanners
Shredders

Dictation systems
Fax machines
Word processors and typewriters
Slide projectors
Laminators
Labelmakers
Comb and thermal binders
Electronic organisers
Coffee machines

Adding machines
Guillotines and trimmers
Answering machines
Calculators
Rubber stamps
Punches
Staplers

Step 3 | **Look After the Pounds and the Pennies Don't Matter**

SNOPAKE STRATEGIES

Nothing you can win at the negotiating table, however hard you lean on your suppliers, is ever likely to match the cost savings that can be achieved by changing your approach or rethinking the way your company tackles its workload.

You might persuade the salesman to pare his margin to the limit. But there will still be a certain irreducible price level on most items below which he would be dumb to sell, unless he is completely certain that what he is giving away with one hand can be quickly clawed back with the other. No one is in business to make a loss.

Being hypnotised by percentages and pennies is a mistake that most of us fall for, from time to time. We look at the 50p price we have been quoted for a bottle of Snopake and get it into our heads that we have seen it cheaper somewhere. So we start badgering our supplier to get the price down to 49p.

We use up time. We use up energy. We use up goodwill. And when we eventually get our own way, what have we saved? Well, how many bottles of Snopake do we buy each year? A hundred? A thousand? Ten thousand? Even if it is 10,000, saving a penny per bottle only adds up to £100 in a full year.

Cutting the order from 10,000 to 9,799 bottles and paying the full 50p would save us more than fighting tooth and nail for our 49p price. But if the supplier, working with us, could come up with some smart way to help us cut our Snopake usage to, say, 7,000 bottles a year, that would release real savings, rather than petty cash – £1,500, rather than £100.

Where do you find the big savings?

How you make that kind of nifty trick work will depend on specific circumstances and on what the product involved is. With something like correction fluid that is handy around the house, as well as in the office, it might simply be a question of cutting shrinkage by keeping stock levels tighter, so that employees weren't tempted to take bottles home on the "they'll never miss it with all these stacked up here" principle.

Like felt-tip pens and many other small consumable items in the office, very few bottles of correction fluid are ever completely used up. But suppose that the supplier is aware that a fractionally better bottle or brush design has been introduced by one of the manufacturers, making it possible to use the fluid right down to the last drop. Just suggesting that the buyer should try this product could lead directly to a smaller volume order and the kind of substantial saving that could not be achieved by trimming a penny or two off the unit price.

From the supplier's point of view, that might not look like good business. But if the office manager or buyer has an ounce of sense, he will realise that this kind of thoughtful, well-informed supplier can be worth thousands of pounds a year to him directly – and possibly a great deal more through suggestions where the payoff comes indirectly, in the form of better work or higher productivity.

Smart Office | **11 Steps to a User-Friendly Office**

You're paying a lot for your people, so get the best out of them

Payroll and other people costs are overwhelmingly the largest cost element in running any office. You are paying people to be there, so their salaries can be regarded as a fixed cost – the entry fee you pay to be in the game. But what you get back, the return on that investment, is largely up to you and your senior management.

The traditional British approach to increasing productivity is straight out of *Mutiny on the Bounty*. Keelhauling and the lash may be out of fashion, but far too many managers still believe their job is to threaten and urge, urge and threaten, in what is usually a doomed attempt to make their people work harder.

Smart managers demand smart offices

Unfortunately, working harder is seldom the key to sustained improvements in productivity. What matters is working better, smarter, more intelligently. The productivity of American office workers is roughly one third higher than that of British workers – and it is hardly likely that the reason for that is anything much to do with a whole population working harder.

But it is almost certainly tied in with the greater investment in office equipment and better office products in the USA. American firms spend an average of $500 a head on office products to support their workers each year. The equivalent figure in Britain would be $300, roughly £200.

The Americans spend more on filing systems. They spend more on PCs (despite paying less per machine), on labelling systems, on dictation machines, on practical, ergonomically designed office furniture, on almost everything that goes to make work easier, faster and less frustrating. As a result, they have offices that work better, day in and day out, without having to rely on whipping their people into working harder.

UFOs seldom sighted

In Britain, some of the more forward-looking office supplies companies have made a sustained effort over the past few years to direct attention to the idea that investing in better offices would pay substantial dividends.

The theory is that the traditional British way of putting an office together is so haphazard and unplanned that a considerable chunk of the wages bill just slips away down the cracks. Compared with the factory floor, where material flows and movements of people are planned and monitored in minute detail, the average office is a very primitive machine for getting work done.

Step 3 Look After the Pounds and the Pennies Don't Matter

The return on investment from doing something about it can be calculated in exactly the same way as the ROI on any other project and will usually compare extremely favourably. Yet the idea that the UFO, the user friendly office, is worth this kind of commitment of funds and management attention is still seen as fairly revolutionary. In most companies it's certainly a great deal easier to make a case at board level for a new production or processing plant than for a radical reworking of the office.

Creating the UFO

Just how user-friendly the office can be depends on many subtle, intangible factors concerned with management styles, company cultures and personal dynamics. But it also depends, crucially, on much more concrete, controllable factors.

Do the people in the office have the tools they need to do a good job? Are they sitting comfortably when the working day begins? And, if so, are they still comfortable seven or eight hours later? Are the lighting and temperature right? Are the filing systems appropriate for the information they're storing and the way they have to be used? Are the printers fast enough, quiet enough and reliable enough? Is the stationery suitable?

There are a host of products that go to make up the physical side of the UFO. No one – office manager, facilities manager or in-house Superman – can keep track of all the relevant factors, new products and specification changes. But you need access to pretty good information, if you are to make good decisions about your office environment.

You could go out looking for this information, but it would be hard work. Instead, why not let the information come to you? Why not start with the people who are going to be falling over themselves to give you product information, whether you like it or not? Why not make full use of the reps, who will eventually be selling you most of the tools and equipment your staff will use to run your business?

REPS ARE NOT REPTILES

All kinds of eminent and perfectly respectable companies employ representatives to sell their products for them. In fact, only a small proportion of the total volume of business supplies in Britain will ever be purchased over the counter, like clothes and groceries, from retail outlets, despite the best efforts of chains like Ryman and Office World. Without reps, there would be a lot of useful, and occasionally innovative, products we might never even hear about.

Most people fall into one of two traps in dealing with calls from reps. Either they are rude and slam the phone down or they pretend to give buying signals and then put the information straight in the bin when it arrives.

Why not give this much-maligned profession some respect and tell them the truth? If you're not in the market for a new computer system, tell them so – nicely! A recent survey showed that people who are polite to unsolicited callers actually waste less time on the phone with them than people who are rude. They also feel less stressed after replacing the receiver.

Respect the caller's time as well as your own. If you're not a real buyer, it's much better for the rep to save a few seconds and get on with finding some genuine prospects.

One way of working out who you need to talk to and who you don't is to divide your office purchases roughly into two.

1. **Things you buy regularly,** such as stationery, consumables and maybe even some software, furniture and computer equipment, if you are in a large organisation. It's worth staying in touch with a range of suppliers and asking the reps to send their literature and keep you updated on their latest prices and products. You should have a file of this information, revised and cleared out annually, so that when you hold your regular price reviews you will find you have quite a bit of information ready to hand.
2. **Things you rarely buy** and which constitute major budget decisions. Unless you are actually in the throes of deciding on a new photocopier, the chances are that by the time you are ready to think about it either the literature will be out of date or the firm will have gone out of business. That means you may well be starting more or less from scratch each time, identifying your needs, collecting the brochures and reports from *Which?* and the trade press and eventually talking to selected reps.

Make friends with your reps

Doing business with people you like and trust is as good a way as any to ensure that you will get a fair deal. Making instinctive judgments about people gets a bad press in the esoteric world of business theory, but it's coming back into fashion in real life.

If the record shows you habitually pick the wrong spouse or the wrong golf partner, it may be that you need to pay more attention to your feelings – not less. Try giving your gut feel a trial run in a few insignificant situations. There are some good people out there and all the reputable suppliers are busy teaching their salesmen that the second sale is the one that counts.

Crystal vases v filing trays

Purchases you make for business usually have to perform better than things you buy for fun. There are fewer purely decorative items around the office than in the home. Even the plants and sofas in reception will have to look good for a long time, while being subjected to considerable wear and tear.

So it's a good idea to check out the quality of what you buy and the reliability of your sources. OK, a paper clip is a paper clip – but that's about it. Bin liners can split and chairs can become threadbare in under six months. If the veneer peels off the chairman's walnut desk, it's going to look just as embarrassing in reception. The office environment doesn't have guest bedrooms to hide your mistakes in.

Moths in the carpet

Stay in control of what you buy. The larger the purchase, the more solid the paperwork needs to be. Ironically, the larger the purchase, the more likely you are to be approached by salesmen making unsolicited and momentarily tempting offers.

Get it straight, though. There are only two reasons for something being offered on the cheap.

1. **A reputable supplier is using it as a loss leader** to keep your custom or secure it in the first place.
2. **The item is not what it appears to be.** Because most offices are open all day, and there's a fair chance that there will be people around who are less discriminating about how they spend their employers' money than they would be with their own, they tend to be a happy hunting ground for people with all sorts of things to sell.

Carpets are often a case in point. A man (usually) pops into reception and explains that he's carpeting a prestigious new office block down the road and happens to have some good quality carpet left over. It's not worth taking back to the depot, so he'll offer it to you at half price for cash. He'll take a look around and ask how many square feet you have. Amazingly enough, that's just the amount he's got left!

Of course, it's not really that surprising, because he'll measure it out in the van and hack off the appropriate length before dumping it on the floor by the lift.

> *Whatever you are told, this is very unlikely to be high quality Berber left over from the flashy development next door.*
>
> *It might just be stolen carpet of reasonable quality. But it's much more likely to be highly inferior stuff that he buys in bulk and sells door-to-door. One excruciating example of what can go wrong occurred when a training company in Surrey paid cash for a pure wool offcut which, coincidentally, fitted their reception area perfectly – but which turned out to be full of holes.*
>
> *On closer inspection, it became evident that herds of tiny moth grubs were still in occupation and grazing away. The carpet came up almost as fast as it went down. But before it was out of the door, some of its occupants had migrated into the office curtains and stair carpet. It was an elegant rural office development in a picturesque village and the firm concerned suffered the embarrassment of having the council's pest control van parked outside the office for several hours the following day.*

Smart Office | 11 Steps to a User-Friendly Office

The simple truth is, that if you're going to spend hundreds or thousands of pounds (and, apart from staplers, you don't get all that much for less than three figures nowadays) it's worth spending a few hours setting up a safety check procedure that you can use over and over again. It might seem like a lot of effort to design your computer tick list and assemble a good range of comparative products and maybe even take a little legal advice about what an acceptable contract should contain. But you can set all this up as a standard procedure that will make life much easier for years to come. And it could not only save your business money – it could save your business.

See the Doing It Right section at the back of the book for a checklist and format you can adapt to your needs, insert into your Office Bible (you do have one, don't you?) and photocopy to re-use again and again.

READING THE LITERATURE

As a general rule, it's a good idea to do a bit of unpressured research before you expose yourself to the sales reps. Reading brochures is an underrated activity, but you should bear in mind that manufacturers and suppliers have to be a lot more careful about what they put into print than what they say. Make sure you know what they are offering in black and white and be prepared to challenge anyone who seems to be implying they can bend the rules *just for you*.

A DAY OUT AT THE SHOW

Taking in a trade show can be a fun day out, with useful and productive consequences. It can also be a complete waste of time, if you don't know what you're looking for or are insufficiently knowledgeable about the particular items or services you need. Cost your time carefully, and take account of wear and tear – walking around Earls Court rates alongside Christmas shopping in terms of physical and mental exhaustion and there's a much higher chance of coming away with the wrong thing or (less disastrously) nothing at all.

There's no doubt that it's a great way of seeing a wide range of comparable products side by side. But that's no use unless you go armed with the right questions to ask, or accompanied by a technical expert who knows what's what.

The three golden rules for exhibition visits, apart from wearing your running shoes, are:

- don't accept drinks until half an hour before you plan to leave
- don't sit down on a stand
- don't take a cheque-book

Step 3 | Look After the Pounds and the Pennies Don't Matter

PURCHASE EVALUATION

If your time is valuable and there's plenty to do back at your own desk, you might ask yourself if there is someone else in your organisation who could be spared more easily and is competent to report back on the latest ideas and technology.

You may even be able to kill two birds with one stone here, because this kind of delegation can be more than just a time and energy saver for you. It could be a nice little perk, a morale booster or a motivator for someone whose time is less valuable than yours back at base, but whose loyalty and commitment may need reinforcement. There's nothing like a bit of recognition and responsibility to give a relatively junior member of the company a feeling of belonging and empowerment.

PROJECT EVALUATION

The way you plan your capital expenditure should be in line with the way you run your business. It's good practice to think in terms of managing projects rather than managing people and buying or leasing an expensive piece of equipment can be a pretty significant project. Provided you have taken the time to draw up the company guidelines for this kind of exercise, it makes a lot of sense to give someone specific responsibility for overseeing the operation and checking all the details.

But it's not just a question of getting people used to the idea of taking responsibility and seeing something through from start to finish. Project management from the bottom up is the best way of developing expertise that will come in handy in a lot of different contexts. One of the most useful areas for fine tuning during a purchase evaluation exercise is, of course, negotiating skills. A lot of people pay lip service to the currently accepted win/win theory of doing business, but still behave as if they are swimming in a sea full of sharks and have to eat the competition in order to survive. Some people are naturally good at getting the best possible deal in all situations, but most people aren't. Fortunately, everyone can learn.

And once your people have learned those skills, they can apply them to selling as well as to buying!

NERVELESS NEGOTIATION

Oddly enough, negotiating manages to be one of the easiest *and* one of the most dreaded tasks the office manager has to tackle. There is a mystique that is reinforced by films like *Wall Street*, full of steely-eyed men snapping their braces and being ruthless, and even by the fawningly uncritical business press on both sides of the Atlantic (hands up all those commentators who denounced Robert Maxwell before, rather than after).

Yet you can learn to negotiate. It's not an inherently magical process and there are some straightforward ground rules for successful negotiators. Follow them and you won't go far wrong. The problem is that most people refuse to believe it's a simple skill, with a set of rules that can virtually guarantee success.

1. BEGIN WITH YOUR END IN MIND

The best way to be a successful negotiator is to keep your goal in mind right from the start.

In fact, successful people in every field usually have fixed ends and variable means to achieve them. But the rest of us battle through life with characteristically vague goals and rigid behaviour patterns, which are typically effective in 50 per cent or less of all our transactions. We are all firm believers in Sod's Law – on the grounds that at least you know what to expect. But we could live under an easier regime, if we chose to.

The killer salesperson who arrives to negotiate with you will always be flexible. Resilient ingenuity is the hallmark of good sales technique. Your recipe for getting what you want and doing yourself and your company credit in the tussle is simply to be equally supple and fast on your feet, while keeping your mind fixed firmly on your goal.

> Step 3 | Look After the Pounds and the Pennies Don't Matter

Change the size of the cake

One of the fundamentals of successful deal-making is that whatever you think you are negotiating, it can probably be changed.

For example, if both sides are stuck in entrenched positions while negotiating a deal for desktop PCs, that is not necessarily the end of the story. If you are the buyer and the seller's price is just too high to contemplate, try bundling up.

Go for a price including the software packages you want, plus an extended on-site guarantee. You will need to pay for these anyway and your opposite number may be able to source them more cheaply than you could. An all-in deal may well be possible at a price that suits both of you, even though you could not strike a bargain based on the hardware price alone.

Alternatively, try unbundling. You've already got good SVGA monitors coming out of your ears and your licence from Microsoft covers more users than you have on the system. So explore the possibility of a smaller cake – a deal that gives you new processors and keyboards but utilises the screens and software you already have. If the seller has a ready market for the spare monitors and software packages, this may be the key to a workable bargain.

Bundle in maintenance cover or paper supplies when you're buying printers. Unbundle the handsets when you buy a phone system. Think positively and don't assume that what's good for you must be bad for the other party.

The secret is your refusal to accept that the cake is a fixed size. That would mean you were just negotiating about where the knife should cut. Free up your thinking and change the size of the cake and all sorts of new possibilities emerge.

2. DRAW UP BUDGET MARK 1

Most sales people these days have been trained to a pretty high standard. Sales technique has changed and developed, and some of the new approaches are remarkably ingenious.

Smart Office | 11 Steps to a User-Friendly Office

The best way to ensure you stay in control of the situation is to write down *in advance* what you really need and what you can afford.

To do this successfully, you need to start with a budget. The practical end of this area of company planning is often left to the office manager and it's one of the major advantages or disadvantages of the job — depending, of course, on your point of view.

The only way to cope with this responsibility and survive (and it may be the company's survival, as well as your own, that hangs in the balance here) is to sit down at the start of your financial year and work out your budget. If you do this, and stick to it, you are unlikely to be an easy touch for sales people of any kind and negotiating will suddenly become less of a trial of strength.

Start by locking yourself away and drawing up a draft budget. You will need access to your company's business plan and year-end figures. These may be projected or real, but you have to start somewhere. Try using the following questions to help you impose some structure on the information that's available to you.

- What is the company aiming to produce or sell over the next year — and how much of it?
- Can this be done with your current staff and equipment? Does it need more or less than you have already?
- How much of your equipment that's good enough now will become inadequate before the next financial year comes around?
- Is your use of consumables likely to rise or fall over the next year?
- Are any of your costs likely to change substantially over the next year? (utilities, rent, consultancy fees?)
- Are major capital outlays required?
- Are there any other external factors you may have missed?

This will probably take you quite a while if, like most office managers, you don't go through this exercise regularly. When you have drawn up your own list, cost it out. Try to work out what the next year is going to need, in terms of funding, and where the money will go.

When you have a model that seems close to satisfactory, put it into your spreadsheet program, if you haven't done so already. You don't want to have to start again from scratch next year.

3. GET SOME NEGOTIATING PRACTICE

A good place to start flexing your negotiating muscles is with your own people, rather than in the external arena. The chances are that the way you've allocated next year's spending won't be as obviously equitable and fair and reasonable to everyone else as it is to you.

TOO BUSY
Working Hard,
to take a *HARD* look

at the *Real Cost*
of Office Supplies?

Don't Work Harder - Work Smarter with

The *Personal* Office Supplies Specialists
to Growing Companies
Tel: 0181 893 4488   Fax 0181 893 4466

PEOPLE
LOVE
WORKING
WITH

Office
SMART

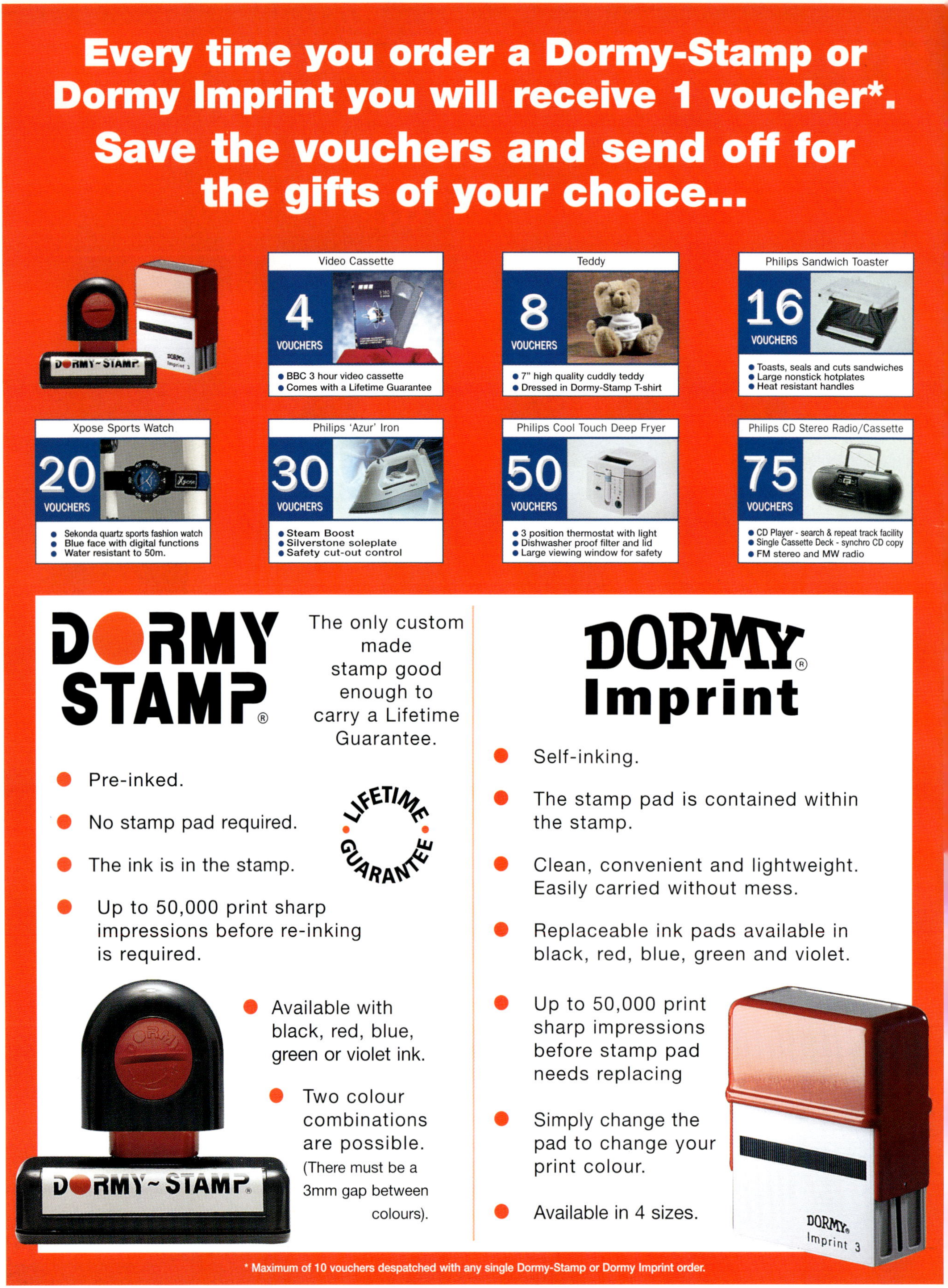

Every time you order a Dormy-Stamp or Dormy Imprint you will receive 1 voucher*. Save the vouchers and send off for the gifts of your choice...

Video Cassette — 4 VOUCHERS
- BBC 3 hour video cassette
- Comes with a Lifetime Guarantee

Teddy — 8 VOUCHERS
- 7" high quality cuddly teddy
- Dressed in Dormy-Stamp T-shirt

Philips Sandwich Toaster — 16 VOUCHERS
- Toasts, seals and cuts sandwiches
- Large nonstick hotplates
- Heat resistant handles

Xpose Sports Watch — 20 VOUCHERS
- Sekonda quartz sports fashion watch
- Blue face with digital functions
- Water resistant to 50m.

Philips 'Azur' Iron — 30 VOUCHERS
- Steam Boost
- Silverstone soleplate
- Safety cut-out control

Philips Cool Touch Deep Fryer — 50 VOUCHERS
- 3 position thermostat with light
- Dishwasher proof filter and lid
- Large viewing window for safety

Philips CD Stereo Radio/Cassette — 75 VOUCHERS
- CD Player - search & repeat track facility
- Single Cassette Deck - synchro CD copy
- FM stereo and MW radio

DORMY STAMP®

The only custom made stamp good enough to carry a Lifetime Guarantee.

- Pre-inked.
- No stamp pad required.
- The ink is in the stamp.
- Up to 50,000 print sharp impressions before re-inking is required.
- Available with black, red, blue, green or violet ink.
- Two colour combinations are possible. (There must be a 3mm gap between colours).

DORMY® Imprint

- Self-inking.
- The stamp pad is contained within the stamp.
- Clean, convenient and lightweight. Easily carried without mess.
- Replaceable ink pads available in black, red, blue, green and violet.
- Up to 50,000 print sharp impressions before stamp pad needs replacing
- Simply change the pad to change your print colour.
- Available in 4 sizes.

*Maximum of 10 vouchers despatched with any single Dormy-Stamp or Dormy Imprint order.

Step 3 | **Look After the Pounds and the Pennies Don't Matter**

Unless you're a one-man band, there are probably a few significant others who may have strong views about whether you should buy a cappuccino machine or a colour printer.

Only you will know whether you would do better to call a meeting of these significant others or pick them off one by one. The important thing is to have your own numbers and opinions written down in black and white first and to be fully prepared to talk them through.

4. DRAW UP BUDGET MARK 2

Take it as a bad sign if you didn't find that people made some helpful criticisms and suggestions which you are prepared to accept. Either your draft budget was perfect in every particular, or your colleagues and staff, for one reason or another, declined to point out what they saw as its weaknesses.

Do not be the person who attracts comments like: "It was riddled with mistakes, but I can't be bothered – let him go ahead and hang himself." The smart office is the interdependent office and you need the feedback. If it doesn't flow naturally, it's well worth going out of your way to draw it out.

Buy a key person a drink, provoke an argument or lock the door and shout "Nobody move." Do whatever it takes. You really do need to know, at this stage, what people are thinking.

Once you know, you can take their suggestions or leave them. That's part of your managerial responsibility. Incorporate what seems useful into your planning and figures and draw up Budget Mark 2. You'll feel better already, because once this is in place, you are ready to start negotiating with any salesperson who knocks on the door. Although it's better if they don't.

5. DEAL WITH UNSOLICITED SALES CALLS

If you have optimised your time management practices, you won't be available to casual callers anyway. It is *never* good use of your time to interrupt what you are doing to think about buying something you didn't plan to buy that day. If you do feel like sparing an on-the-spot moment, invite the salesman to come in, sit down for just one minute and summarise his USP, his unique selling point.

This may sound brutal, but it doesn't mean that you should rule out new recruitment agencies or office supplies companies, who may be leaner and keener and much more competitive than the people you've been using for years. Simply tell them that you are not available to talk to them on the spot and ask them to send you details, accompanied by a short note giving a contact name and their key selling points. You should have a place in your filing system for this kind of information, so that you can check every so often and be confident that you are getting the best deals from all your suppliers. Making sure your current contractors and suppliers know you do this keeps everybody's eye on the ball.

Smart Office | 11 Steps to a User-Friendly Office

6. PRACTISE YOUR NEGOTIATING SKILLS AGAIN

- Decide what you want and get a selection of quotes. For larger items, you should:
  - clearly specify the format you want for quotations
  - list the information you need

Reputable suppliers don't object to this. It actually makes their job easier, because you are telling them in advance what you want and that saves them a lot of time. All that is left then is for you to decide on terms and conduct final, detailed negotiations.

- Take the initiative. Ask the questions. Don't wait to be told the benefits:
  - Do comparable items or services – do the same job?
    - work at the same speed?
    - last the same length of time?
  - If you are buying in bulk, how many pence are you actually saving, spread over the length of time it will take you to use (and store) the product? Will you actually have used it before its sell-by date, or before somebody has invented a better system?
- Rework the salesperson's costings. Don't forget to add in any relevant variables that may have been missed out, either by accident or design. Ask a few more questions:
  - Is it energy efficient (compared with . . .)?
  - Is there another way of doing this? (You might want to share an electric binding machine, a shredder or even a copier with other firms in your building, for example.)
  - How much maintenance is it going to need? And is that costed in?
  - Can any competent engineers maintain it?
  - If it goes wrong, can we buy the bits and fix it ourselves?
  - If it has to go away for repair, what will it cost us to be without it?
  - And when it comes to consumables:
    - do I have to buy at top price from the equipment supplier?
    - can I buy suitable generic products from a cheaper supplier?
    - do I have to pay extra for delivery from either of them?
    - can I do a deal to share bulk deliveries with anyone else?
  - Is it a lease purchase or just a lease?
  - What happens at the end of the agreement?
- Should I be buying, leasing, or borrowing this equipment from a neighbour?

Put yourself in the salesperson's shoes. The first rule of sales technique is to sell the benefits of a product, rather than its features. Benefits can be very subjective and very individual. That's why good salesmen are always keen on getting to know you and tend to remember your golf handicap.

Check out your own weaknesses, prejudices and blind spots before the salespeople home in on them. Ask yourself the cruel questions. "Am I buying this software because:

- my company needs to communicate directly with all the major plastics industry databases,

or because

- I am the only member of the Huddersfield Soroptimists who doesn't have an Internet address yet?"

Be nice to your suppliers

Shouldn't that be the other way around? No. Because, as long as you make it clear that you will get competitive quotes from time to time and that you will only ever buy what you need, you'll get consistently better service if you take the trouble to build positive relationships with your suppliers.

Pay your accounts on time, be clear and reasonable about your requirements and pleasant in your dealings and you will get that little bit of extra service that makes the difference. The after-hours delivery, the special effort to get the blue window envelopes, the free advice and the inside intelligence about your business sector all have real commercial value, as well as reducing stress levels within your office. And it's easy. It just depends on treating your suppliers as real people. After all, they make a living by selling their products and services, just like the rest of us.

Win/win

The win/win cliché is just as relevant when you are negotiating to buy as when you are negotiating to sell.

If you are hoping your new supplier will become a regular and reliable source of products or materials, it is obviously short-sighted to try to grind him into the dust. He won't like it and he, too, needs to make his margin somewhere. Do you want him to write your firm off as not worth the hassles?

If the purchase involved is a one-off, you and the salesman may both feel hit-and-run tactics are all that's needed. The fact is, though, that having a satisfied customer he can come back to for repeat business, even a couple of years on, is of some value to someone selling you big-ticket items such as your main copier. And you have more of a vested interest in the relationship than meets the eye. If the copier salesman has been screwed down to his last £100 of commission, you can be sure he won't be easy to reach on the phone if there's a problem after delivery.

Time to take a break

Unless you are certain it comes naturally to you – and you've got plenty of past experience to back up your belief – try to avoid having to think on your feet in negotiations.

Right at the top of the tree, among the peace brokers and powermongers of global politics, negotiators simply refuse to be stampeded into thinking in real time. One of the accepted conventions of high-level negotiation is that anyone can call a break at any time, for any reason or none.

If you are involved in complicated talks about serious issues, do the same. You can indicate that it's time for lunch, or that you need to phone your office for more information before replying on that last point, or that the two of you on your side of the table need to confer.

If you are feeling backed into a corner, take a break from the pressure. If the other side has just dropped a bombshell, retire to review your options. If you need to work out some new figures, break off to make sure they stack up right. If you've just had a bright idea that might resolve everyone's differences, cool off for ten minutes before you blurt it out.

Successful negotiations should ideally produce win/win results. Failing that, they should breed useful compromises. But there's nothing in the rules that says they should be a test of physical stamina or psychic endurance. So if you want a break, take one. Believe it or not, the people you're talking to will still be there when you come back.

BE READY TO WALK AWAY

If the deal isn't right, or it isn't the right time, always be prepared to walk away from it.

There is no such thing as a one-off opportunity to buy anything *legitimate*. And if it's the very last nuclear weapon from Kazakstan, the UN may well impound it before you get a chance to use it. The risk is never worthwhile.

The worst you risk by walking away from a deal is usually a delay in getting what you want. The down side of going ahead can be catastrophic – not least because suppliers who hold guns to the heads of potential clients often don't do good after sales service.

Step 3 | Look After the Pounds and the Pennies Don't Matter

CONTRACTS AND AGREEMENTS

When it comes to larding contracts with small print, conditions, exceptions, loopholes and pitfalls, you can't hope to beat the lawyers – or the determined and professional con-man. Be warned. Con-men can be expensive and lawyers may leave you broke and disillusioned.

Your best bet for ordinary run-of-business contracts is to rely on plain language and common sense, in the hope that any court that comes to consider the contract will apply principles of common law and natural justice. The more verbal tomfoolery there is, the more scope exists for sleight of hand and perversely exotic interpretations. The basic rule is that everything should be written down, clearly, at the time and in the most straightforward, unambiguous and commonsensical words you can find.

KEEP IT SIMPLE

Planning comes into this, yet again. If you are a small company, you won't have your own legal department and you may not even retain a law firm. Start by investing a little time in working out what kind of formal documents you are likely to need in the course of your business. These will include contracts or agreements:

- with employees, partners or shareholders
- with suppliers
- with clients
- with contractors and consultants

Draw up your requirements for each, as clearly as you can state them, and then find yourself a solicitor who specialises in servicing your particular business sector. The chances are that there are already some standard formats for what you want, which means you might only have to pay for amendments.

Arrange for some standard contracts to be drawn up which you can load onto your computer when required. Insist on simple language which you can understand and explain yourself. If special circumstances arise in a particular area, you can always ask the lawyers to provide you with an amendment to fit the situation. You will cut back on legal fees by doing it this way and you will also find your contractual arrangements much simpler to administer, because you will quickly get to know exactly how they work.

WRITE IT DOWN

Even in situations where a legal contract seems like overkill – if you are thinking of working informally with another group, or hiring an office cleaner for a few hours, for example – it's still worth writing down what the intentions of both parties are and what ought to happen if

Smart Office | **11 Steps to a User-Friendly Office**

problems arise. It may not be watertight, but if it's signed by both sides it will certainly carry weight in court as evidence of intention.

In fact, if you are involved in any situation which seems to have taken a turn for the worse, where the relationship with an employee or a contractor is no longer amicable, start writing down what happens. Keep a diary record — handwritten is best — summarising every conversation, incident and phone call, dated and timed.

These records *are* taken into account by the courts, so don't leave it until it's too late. The other side of the coin is that they must be genuine and contemporaneous. Do not try to fool the system by faking such a diary the evening before the case comes up. If you were rumbled, you would then be in deep trouble — and rightly so.

Movie mogul Sam Goldwyn summed it up once and for all in his memorable line: "A verbal contract ain't worth the paper it's written on." Always get something down on paper and you'll always have some ammunition if the situation turns bad.

GOLDEN RULES FOR BUYING EQUIPMENT

Before you talk to a salesman or delve into the brochures, make sure you know what you want to do with whatever it is you're buying. If you're a one-man band and your business plan depends on staying that way for the next five years, don't get talked into paying for a switchboard that will expand up to 100+ extensions.

- Never buy or lease machines that do things you do not fully understand
- Never buy or lease anything if the salesman cannot satisfactorily explain its function

Before you sign on the dotted line, ask yourself:

- Does this piece of equipment have any functions I don't need right now?
- Will I definitely need those functions for business purposes in the next two years?
- How much extra am I paying for the privilege of having them?

Never buy or lease anything until you have talked to a couple of other people in a business like your own who are already using it. Unless you are a Richard Branson, you cannot afford to do someone else's R&D.

Even if the answers to all these questions are satisfactory, do not sign on the dotted line until you have checked out the following:

- What is the relationship between
    the supplier
    the manufacturer

> Step 3 | Look After the Pounds and the Pennies Don't Matter

   the maintenance engineers
   the finance company?
- Who takes responsibility if the equipment doesn't work?

SERVICE IS A MAYBE – PRICE IS NOW

These days, business supplies firms all want to build a relationship with your company.

If that means they go out of their way to track down unusual items you need and rush them to you at short notice when you're under pressure, this relationship may be of some significance to you. If it just means sending you catalogues and ringing up now and again to try to sell you a PC or an extra ream or two of paper, it's hard to see how your business benefits.

One cynical manager in a family-owned West London manufacturing company says the only sane way to assess service as an "added value" element is to ask yourself just how valuable it is to you, in cash terms.

"Put a figure on it. How much extra would you be prepared to pay for the intangible bonus of personal service, or the promise of fast equipment repairs?

"I'm always aware that the extra cash you pay is definite and today, while the gold-plated service quality is a maybe – and a maybe that's some way off in the future."

A jaundiced word in your ear

Copiers can be a boon and a blessing. But buying or leasing them can be the kind of convoluted business that'll make you grow old before your time.

One otherwise confident and assertive businesswoman still trembles at the thought of her own photocopier saga. Two years after selling her office services company, she was still battling through the courts to untangle the copier contract. Her advice is obviously jaundiced, but none the worse for that.

"If you are not good at maths, never take the salesman's word for it about how much you are paying per copy," she says. "You probably forgot to add in the compulsory paper purchase scheme or the maintenance charges or failed to notice that for that price they only take call-outs every other Thursday."

> **Smart Office** | **11 Steps to a User-Friendly Office**
>
> There's seldom any real hurry to buy, she points out. So slow things down and don't be stampeded into a commitment.
>
> "Before you decide whether it's a good deal or not, get someone with a vested interest in your financial survival to go over the figures with you," she advises.
>
> "Register in advance with the Photocopier Users Association – and ideally go for a personal counselling session before taking this major step in your life."

PAY LESS FOR YOUR MACHINES

Further tips from the same source include always asking for and insisting on reduced bank charges, buying major items like copiers by defining the exact model you want and then going ruthlessly for the lowest price, and looking out for two particular clauses in machine maintenance agreements.

"With copiers, I make perhaps 20 calls, getting quotes from every supplier in the Yellow Pages. I note the best price, then call the first supplier again and ask if he can beat it. And so on, round the loop. You get some flak and abuse on the way, but it's worth it for a small firm.

"When we buy copiers, we are quoted prices of £2,100 or so and end up paying £1,400. They are a specific model, from a leading Japanese maker, so we know what we're getting. If the dealers can afford, under pressure, to cut that much fat out of their margins and still sell to us, I have no compunction at all about going for the best price they'll give me."

This sceptic's other advice concerns the conditions in copier maintenance contracts. He says you should stipulate that no price increases may be brought in that are above the level of inflation and, above all, that the agreement must specify a minimum period of 12 months between price increases.

IN A NUTSHELL
1. The office as a business tool

- The office is an opportunity – not an overhead
- Make the office work for the business
- Choose the right tools for the job
- Getting the best from your people
- Working smarter, not harder, in the **U**ser **F**riendly **O**ffice
- Go for a good working relationship with your suppliers

Step 3 | Look After the Pounds and the Pennies Don't Matter

2. Finding the information you need to set up your UFO

- Work with the reps and save everybody's time
- Know the difference between a bargain and a rip-off
- Set up a company system
- Checklists for getting it right
- Read the literature
- Keep an eye on trade shows and exhibitions

3. Project evaluation and purchase evaluation

- Applying good business practice to buying, as well as selling
- Purchase evaluation as a training ground for tomorrow's top salesmen

4. Negotiation skills

- Principles of successful negotiating – a checklist
    - keep your goal in mind
    - know your limits
    - be flexible within your limits
    - practise, practise, practise
- Business needn't be a battleground
    - go for win/win
    - look at the long-term relationship

5. Contracts and agreements

- Keep it simple
- Write it down

6. Golden rules for buying equipment

- Break it down so that you know exactly what you'll be paying for and when
- Make sure you know who is responsible for the working of the equipment up until the time you finish paying for it
- Be absolutely certain about who you are contracted to (it may not be the company you think) and what their responsibilities are

STEP 4: MAKING IT HAPPEN

Step 4   Making it Happen

THE IMPACT OF COMPUTERS ON OFFICE MANAGEMENT

"If business is the engine of society, computers are the bearings that keep the wheels going round."

Tony Buzan

AFTER ALL THE PROMISES, HERE COMES THE REAL THING

Falling prices, soaring performance levels, affordable worldwide communications links and today's enormous range of specialised off-the-peg software have made the opportunities offered by information technology available to every company in the land. The question now is what will ordinary businesses up and down the country make of these opportunities?

The first wave of the computer revolution was all about control. Computers were used to collate and manipulate figures and to enforce rules about business practices, as laid down, more often than not, by the accountants. Better records and faster access to data meant tighter controls and inevitably tended to elevate measurable facts and figures to the top of every agenda. When people asked if you were computer literate, you could bet your boots they really meant computer numerate – because the figures ("the numbers", as people suddenly began to say in the mid-eighties) seemed to be all that mattered.

What has changed now is an explosion in the use of information technology to store, handle and communicate non-numerical information – text, photographs, details of customers' addresses and buying habits, sound and video, X-ray images or whatever else is needed for a particular business situation. It's true that the processing is always in digital form, but no one in his right mind gives that a thought as he creams off the most promising names from his customer database or settles down to knock out a report on the PC.

Smart Office | **11 Steps to a User-Friendly Office**

The old pillars of business, the economist's three agents of production — land, labour and capital — are being joined after hundreds of years by a fourth, in the form of knowledge or ideas.

Ideas will be as much the business currency of the future as capital. Those who have useful knowledge will also have such power that they will be able to translate knowledge into cash almost instantly. And it is IT, with its ability to deliver knowledge to any point on the planet, inexpensively and in usable forms, that has given ideas the value of currency. You can see early examples of the knowledge = money equation in automated share price services run by Reuters and other information providers, in on-line charge card validation and in company credit check services.

Even when the information is not traded externally to generate revenue directly, it still becomes a valuable asset. The bar-code readers at the supermarket checkouts are not there primarily for short-term stock control. They are there so that Tesco and Sainsbury's and Safeway and the rest can collect a mass of fine-grained customer information to help them plan new lines and get the footwork right to match the slightest shifts in public preferences.

The barriers to entry into this wonderful world of IT-driven opportunities are virtually negligible. If you have an idea that will really help your business, it is highly unlikely that the cost factor alone will be what stops you forging ahead. Yet there are still many small and medium-sized firms that are uncomfortable with information technology and regard it as more of a challenge than an opportunity. For the office manager or facilities professional with even a modest amount of knowledge and confidence in this area, this can offer the chance to make a noticeable and wholly positive impact.

TAKING CONTROL OF YOUR SYSTEM

The trouble is that people still associate computers with control — or lack of it — rather than expansion. What unnerves people most about computers isn't the cost or the complexity — it's the loss of control. You can't see where the machine has put your data. You can't see what it's doing with it. And if you have ten or even 100 people all inputting in their own idiosyncratic ways, how are you ever going to organise it?

The facts and figures inside your office computers may well be the lifeblood of your company. Whether it's the accounts, the details of overdue invoices, the client database or the technical specifications of the latest design, it's all vital stuff. But the same set of chips which contains and organises this crucial information may also be used, perhaps simultaneously, to play battleships, conduct flirtations via e-mail or even download information to your business competitors.

If someone put you on the spot right now, could you give a satisfactory answer to each of the questions in this list?

Step 4 | **Making it Happen**

- Do you know exactly what hardware and software is currently in use in your office? How long would it take you to draw up an inventory? How accurate is your update when the insurance comes around for renewal each year?
- If you have a network, or just a lot of assorted equipment, do you have an up-to-date floor plan of what is plugged in where and what is connected to what?
- Do you know who has access to your computer network or to individual PCs? Can anyone with a working knowledge of Windows log in from cold?
- Do you have an office protocol for logging in and out and protecting work? How do you make sure everyone sticks to it? Do people pop out for lunch in the middle of a spreadsheet (with or without saving) and come back to find the motorcycle courier playing solitaire on their workstations while he waits for a package from another department?

Do you know how much time is wasted in your office just looking for data?

- Do you have an office system for tagging, identifying and retrieving files, particularly word processed documents?
- Could you retrieve all the data stored in the system in the event of damage or breakdown, minus, at most, a few hours' worth of current work?
- Do you have a working overview, not necessarily detailed, of all the applications in current use?
- How standardised is your software? Does everyone use the same WP, spreadsheet and graphics? Or are some people wasting time translating from one system to another just because of minor personal preferences?
- Do you have a security system for checking illegal access and damage, including viruses?
- Do you know exactly what you would do if you suspected something was amiss with your system? What are the warning signs that might alert you to damage, loss or illegal entry?
- Do you have spares of all the little basics, like plugs, mice, cables and connectors? Are they all kept in one place (like the stationery cupboard), with a system for logging in and out that people actually use when no one's standing over them?

How many of these questions did you have positive answers for? It's unlikely that you are absolutely perfect in all respects. If not, now is the time to face up to it, get organised and take control. And the good news is that it's much easier now than ever before. You don't need anything like the kind of expertise you would have needed even ten years ago to be able to cope.

Smart Office | 11 Steps to a User-Friendly Office

WHO DO YOU TRUST?

Once upon a time, large companies had IT departments and small companies relied on whichever member of staff (not always the office manager) had a particular interest in computers and had read a few magazines. There was always one in every office, though you were in trouble if there were two because they rarely agreed and that would usually be the first step towards computerised chaos.

For far too long this kind of hit-and-miss, anorak-driven scenario was accepted as part of the natural order of things. And that was an unsatisfactory situation, when you consider what large chunks of companies' budgets were sunk into all this equipment and what vital information it could contain. No wonder people distrusted small company computer systems. And no wonder salesmen who traded on this fear often had a field day among the small firms.

It's not quite such a jungle now. There's no reason to be intimidated either by salesmen or ill-informed friends and colleagues. The biggest software companies are at last coming up not just with applications, but also with the means to manage them – and your hardware, too. Some basic standards are finally being laid down.

The manufacturers are on your side (at last)

A lot of the hard work involved in managing a computer system can now be done by the computer itself. Office management software has been bitty and unreliable until quite recently. But all that is changing fast. For example, a body known as the DMTF (the Desktop Management Task Force) has now developed a specification that provides a standardised way to inventory computer equipment over a network. The DMTF has come up with DMI (Desktop Management Interface) specifications that are already being adopted by equipment manufacturers and will make this kind of housekeeping task quicker, easier and more consistent. Over 150 leading companies in the US have pledged support for the standard, making its adoption in the UK a virtual certainty.

You can now install software (from mainstream manufacturers such as Microsoft, Symantec and Intel) which will effectively enable you to operate an IT department singlehandedly, from the comfort of your own desk.

These programmes will inventory your hardware and software (so that you will know straight away, for example, if someone has loaded a game that needs 50 per cent of the system's memory to run). They can also give you a great deal of control over what's going on, through a series of integrated security systems which will:

- block unauthorised access to computers
- prevent loading of illicit applications (games and non-standard programs)
- provide an audit trail record of all log-ins, applications used and user times

- perform on-the-fly transparent cryptography of material on the hard disk
- detect and disarm viruses automatically
- identify many hardware and software faults (though the diagnosis is sometimes completely incomprehensible)
- protect your vital files, such as CONFIG.SYS and AUTOEXEC.BAT

You may not be quite as fully automated as all this seems to imply. And, in any case, control software is only as effective as the controller who installs and uses it. To use it well you don't need great technical skill, but you do need to be organised and efficient – basic qualities for any successful office manager. Before you go out and buy any control automation program, read through the following process and decide what you can do manually and what really needs to be automated.

EIGHT STEPS TO HAVING CONFIDENCE IN IT
1. KNOW WHAT YOU'VE GOT

Establish a system now, if you haven't got one already, to maintain an inventory of all equipment, cabling, software and peripherals (printers, modems, scanners and so on). This means noting models, serial numbers, dates of purchase and guarantees – on average, it takes about half an hour per PC to run this kind of check from scratch. You may not need a computer program for this if you are a relatively small office and are prepared to be meticulous about updating your records.

2. KEEP A LOG BOOK

Just like a car, every part of your computer system should have its own performance history. You can save a lot of time and money by noting bugs, failures and steps taken to repair or reinstall. If the worst comes to the worst and you withhold payments on a piece of unsatisfactory equipment, you are in a much stronger position if you have kept a timed and dated log of all the failures and downtime.

3. ESTABLISH A FILE IDENTIFICATION SYSTEM AND MAKE IT STICK

Work out a simple system for naming files. If possible, tie it in with your regular filing system. If there are project or customer numbers, as well as names, for example, these should be consistently used. Most software (particularly WP) can be customised so that every time a document is saved, its file name is inserted into a footer (which should also include the date and page number). At the very least, you can build in a screen prompt to remind users to do this manually.

4. DECIDE WHO HAS ACCESS TO WHAT

Even if your company system is only used as a typewriter substitute, there will certainly be some information (like client addresses and order details) which would be of interest to someone else, if it went astray. Gone are the days when typists in the civil service had to put their ribbons in their handbags when they went to lunch. But it is absolutely true that the average small company doesn't take its data at all seriously until it's lost or stolen. Most people assume that because their computer system is a bit of a mystery to them it will also confuse the determined rival or saboteur. But it ain't necessarily so. In a small firm, everyone may be using everything. The larger the office is, the more likely you are to need some controls or access restrictions (in terms of competence, if nothing else).

5. MAKE SURE PEOPLE DON'T STRAY OUT OF THEIR TERRITORY

Do you have a password system? Do you use encryption? And, if so, can anyone lock anything away from anyone else – or do you have a master key? These are all practical possibilities for even the smallest firm nowadays. It just depends on the level of security and control you need. In a small office with three or four chiefs and no Indians, it's probably not important. But if you have split responsibilities and different status and accountability levels, or even if you just have a lot of users on your network, you might benefit from a security control software system. If you decide to install one, though, remember to let everyone know that Big Brother is watching them and make sure you check it regularly. Otherwise you are taking up quite a bit of space and memory for nothing.

6. EXTEND YOUR INFLUENCE BEYOND YOUR OFFICE

Modems have made everybody potentially more powerful and more vulnerable, too. We may all eventually be tangled in the Net – and some people aren't even coming to work any more, though there is a lot of hype and nonsense about all this, of course.

The US "Work at Home" market was alleged to have reached 40 million in 1994 (according to LINK Resources, a respected, though, in this case, probably deluded, NY-based market research firm). This is the sort of statistic that cries out for a quick reality check (*Total US workforce = 124 million. Does one worker in three work from home? Next*

Step 4 | **Making it Happen**

question, please). But it is true that access technologies are getting cheaper, more powerful and more reliable all the time. So how can you protect your system from both your own people, when they are away from the office, and from unwanted visitors as well? Is modem access limited? Or can anyone slip through the door?

7. ESTABLISH SOME RULES

Who is allowed to load and customise new software? Do you have a procedure for authorising what goes onto the system? Some companies physically block or remove floppy drives from every workstation except the system manager's. This may seem rather drastic, but business is a serious business. Games take up a lot of memory and can slow the system down, while disks can carry viruses which could bring it grinding to a halt.

8. GUARD YOUR DATA

This means thinking in advance about what could go wrong and taking practical precautions to prevent loss or recover data after damage has occurred. Everyone instinctively wants total, watertight, belt-and-braces security and you can get pretty close to it. But there's always a price to pay, both in cash and in terms of complicating the office routine. What you end up choosing inevitably depends on the size and complexity of your system, the money that's available and how truly critical the loss of the information you hold would be.

How do you back up your files – and how often? Consider the alternatives of back-up systems, tape streamers or disks. Tape streamers are quick and easy to use and much cheaper than they used to be. For small systems, the brand new Iomega Zip Drives (100MB on a small disk, not much fatter than an ordinary floppy) look cheap and practical.

Do you keep copies of your back-up tapes or disks *somewhere else*, away from the office? If so, congratulations. Now, tell the truth, how often do you update them?

Snap, crackle and pop – it's all a question of power

How many times has an office you were working in been struck by lightning? It is easy to react cynically when people whose job it is to sell Uninterruptible Power Supply (UPS) equipment or surge protection devices start telling you horror stories.

As they wax lyrical about what would happen if the hard disks with all your data on were fried by a lightning strike, you might wonder about their motives. They would say that, wouldn't they? But, unfortunately, they do have a point. How much you worry about it and how much you are prepared to spend to ensure clean, regulated and uninterrupted power to your computers is a decision only you can make.

One recent survey did claim, though, that 70 per cent of PC malfunctions were linked to electrical supply problems. And some insurers are now recommending the use of surge protectors.

There are actually three main types of electrical supply problems to bear in mind – spikes and surges, noise and power cuts.

- Spikes are short but overwhelming voltage pulses, caused by lightning or sometimes by bad switch contacts in heavy electrical machinery, such as lifts and air conditioning units. Surges are longer, slower, but equally unpleasant. Both can inflict permanent damage on PCs and hard disks. Relatively easy to guard against, though the response has to be quick – most devices boast a response time of about ten nanoseconds or less. Surge plugs for your power cables start at about £8, a three-way adapter is about £15 and surge strips with varying degrees of protection for a bank of four or five sockets will cost anything from under £25 to over £100.
- Noise is a type of mains-borne interference made up of two elements, RFI (radio frequency interference) and EMI (electromagnetic interference). We hear it as the crackle when a fluorescent light is turned on or an electric drill is in use. It can cause puzzling data losses and infuriating, intermittent hard disk problems. A four-outlet combined surge/noise strip costs anything from £40 upwards, but surge/noise filter plugs, adapters and other filtering devices start at £20 or so.
- Power cuts are more tricky to deal with. They take us into the realms of the UPS, though, needless to say, there are several different levels of uninterruptibility. All UPS units filter and smooth the day-to-day power supply, protect against spikes, surges and noise and give you some defence against power cuts by providing battery back-up. The cheapest (from just under £100) are off-line or "line interactive" designs that give you a few minutes of battery power to allow you to shut down your applications without losing data. The other end of the spectrum extends to on-line units that can look after a whole network, using automatic shutdown software to save current work and close the system down safely without human intervention. Life gets complicated towards the high end of the range, but for standalone PCs and workstations you can work out the size of UPS unit you need by checking the VA rating of your equipment. To do this, look for the amp ratings shown on the metal plates on your PC and monitor. Add these figures together and multiply by 240 to get the VA rating. You will find sophisticated UPS units from firms like APC, Emerson and Tripp Lite that even compensate automatically for over-voltage or voltage sags in routine use.

Step 4 | Making it Happen

Where do you get help? What's the minimum you need to know?

If you've read this far and you still feel your computer system is getting the better of you, where do you go to find out what kind of control software you need, or what kind of modem? Here are the options.

Source of advice	advantage/disadvantage
The IT manager	If your company is big enough to have one, you probably don't need to worry about software or hardware. It's unlikely to be your responsibility.
Friends in anoraks	Unreliable and difficult to understand. May not be sufficiently aware of your business needs or your technical capabilities. Tend to recommend things they want to try out but can't afford themselves.
Big computer dealers	The salesmen probably don't know much more about their product than you, but are unlikely to admit it and can be very convincing.
Manufacturers' or specialist salesmen	Even if they sell more than one brand, you will be lucky to find one who isn't offloading his product of the month. They are usually disinclined to take the time to understand what you really want or can cope with.
Computer magazines	There are so many of these now that they are a bit of a minefield. Some of them are so specialised as to be incomprehensible. For example, the summary paragraph on networks in a recent issue of *BYTE* began, jauntily: "Network operators can minimise management overhead through WAN devices that support SNMP, Telnet and TFTP . . ." Pick and choose. If a journalist can't make you understand what he's writing about, he's either incompetent or writing for a totally different audience. UK magazines that might help are: *Computer Shopper, PC Pro, Personal Computer World, PC Magazine, Internet, The Mac* and *Mac World*. Try reading them for a few weeks to get an overview of the current situation. Don't force yourself to focus on bits you can't easily understand. Skip to a bit you can and be prepared to buy plenty of them.

Smart Office | **11 Steps to a User-Friendly Office**

Newspapers — Most newspapers have a regular weekly computer feature and some of them are excellent. Get used to reading the one in your regular daily and try some of the others too.

Exhibitions — Computing shows are an excellent way to do some hands-on browsing. Exhibitions (as long as they're not too specialised) are much better for this purpose than the shops, which are usually too eager to shift the boxes and maintain the salesman's commission. On the stands you find people prepared to talk about their products at length and, better still, plenty of punters who are there to contradict them. So it's less of a one-sided debate.

Manuals — When you've bought your software and hardware you will usually find that the biggest box that's delivered is the one that contains the instruction books. And when you get them out and read through the first few chapters (which often tell you how to open the other boxes), they are often not very helpful. Some of them explain in laborious detail the functions which are obvious and the ones you don't want to use, while others assume that you do indeed have an IT department to set it all up for you.

Idiot Guides — The software guides you buy in ordinary bookshops are often far more useful than the information supplied with the product. It may cost you £10 to £20, but it will save you more than that in time and phone calls to the helpline. These books are usually easy to read and do focus on some of the things you might really want to do with your equipment.

Helplines — These are occasionally staffed by benevolent mind-readers who probably work with the Samaritans in their spare time. But you may also be stuck in a queue for 40 minutes listening to Herb Alpert, only to find, when you do get through, that the person on the other end has been trained by the Fawlty Towers school of customer service and thinks anyone who hasn't got a degree in computer science has no right to use the stuff anyway.

In the end, the best method of educating yourself just enough to avoid disaster is to use a combination of methods. The best approach is:

1. Skim through as many magazines as you can for a few weeks (beware of addiction).

2. Start reading newspaper supplements.
3. Talk to other people who use computers. Make sure you talk to more than two or three. A broad spectrum of opinion is crucially important.
4. Try other people's systems – ask to spend a few hours using the applications they are familiar with when they are on hand to help you out.
5. Go to an exhibition (optional).

THE COMPUTER REVOLUTION

Computers don't just make it possible to do more work faster. They affect the way you work, the environment you work in and the way you interact with your colleagues.

APPEARANCES MATTER – WHAT IS IT GOING TO LOOK LIKE?

Computers have changed the look of the office and even the design of its furniture. For 300 years, a desk was pretty much a desk – a flat surface, a knee hole and some drawers. Now it often looks more like a set of shelves, with ledges that slide in and out of view carrying keyboards, printers and stacks of paper. Monitors, instead of sitting on the desk itself, can be suspended above it, with the possibility of tilting, lifting, gliding, swinging and rotating to give the perfect viewing angle. Channels concealing all the cabling will soon be as much of a standard item as inkwells were a century ago.

Seating is now a matter of safety (avoiding RSI – repetitive strain injury – and back problems), rather than simply comfort. Office chairs are now so adjustable that some seem to need manuals to operate. Yet a lot of smaller companies (and even some larger ones), for reasons of habit or finance, are running 20th-century automation in a Dickensian environment. This doesn't work well from the point of view of safety, or comfort, or aesthetics. Spaghetti coils of cables, inaccessible switches and adjustment panels make it difficult to move around and unnecessarily hard to identify faults or isolate problems.

As you trip over your cables and tip coffee on the keyboard because there's no logical place for it, you might sometimes wonder if computers were such a great idea at all. You may not be able to replace all your office furniture and re-wire your system immediately. But when you do replace things, think carefully about what you buy. There is a lot of expensive and elegant looking woodwork on the market that is really still designed around the needs of the clerk with the leather-bound ledgers. And while you are at it, you can make out your ideal floor plan (including the cabling), even if you can't put it into practice yet. You may be surprised at the improvements you can make merely by thinking about the whole area as one working environment, rather than just letting it happen.

Smart Office | 11 Steps to a User-Friendly Office

WHAT IS IT GOING TO BE USED FOR?

Having thought about how your computers change your working environment, think another step further about what they should be used for, and, more importantly, what they *shouldn't* be used for.

When you've worked out what you've got, it's worth taking a moment to think what you are going to do with it. If you are clear about what the office computer system is for, and who it belongs to, you will be in a better position to control it, use it effectively and tell your people how to do the same.

E-mail is an interesting example of the limitations of a computer system in the office. Like many other applications, it was meant to reduce paper and increase security. It was never intended to replace words that should never have been written and it is actually not even as secure as a piece of paper, which can, at least, be shredded or burned.

Whispered words round the coffee machine about the latest office scandal, or even the incompetence of the MD, cause less trouble and fewer repercussions because they are spoken. The courts have recently supported a company which sacked a member of staff for sending unwise words about the management to her colleague by e-mail. Both the medium she used and the time she took to type it were deemed to belong to the company and she was considered to have used them inappropriately.

Remember that even deleted e-mail messages can be retrieved by experts. Hardly anything you have typed into a computer is lost for ever – it just seems like that when you are in a hurry and something vital evaporates off the screen.

DATA PROTECTION ACT 1984

Business people sometimes get very jumpy about the Data Protection Act, which requires you to register as a "data user" if you hold any kind of personal data about individuals in your computer files.

In theory, the Data Protection Registrar could come down on you like a ton of bricks and you could even end up going to jail if you failed to comply. But the registrar's office spends more of its time talking to companies and giving them helpful advice on what they can and can't do with their data than taking database villains to court. In the year 1994/95, only 69 businesses were prosecuted, mainly for non-registration.

There are sensible exemptions, anyway, for information in certain categories, such as payroll details, material relating directly to sales and financial information which has to be kept for inspection by the auditors.

Rather than try to find ways round the regulations, though, it is best simply to register and be done with it. If you don't use a prospects database as a major marketing tool now, you probably will in the near future. And the 200,000 businesses that are already registered don't seem to find it cramps their style unduly. You can order the registration pack and forms

Step 4 | Making it Happen

from: The Data Protection Registrar, Wycliffe House, Water Lane, Wilmslow, Cheshire SK9 5AF (01625 545 745).

Individuals are entitled to see the information about them that is being held on business computer files within 40 days of making a request. They pay a small fee each time, up to a maximum of £10.

IN A NUTSHELL
1. Computers offer virtually limitless opportunity

- Take control of your system and use the power it offers you
- Checklist: are you getting the best out of your hardware and software?
- Diagnose your problems
- Where to get help if you need it
- What you can do to help yourself
- Safety, stability and comfort
- Why systems are more user-friendly than ever before

2. Eight steps to IT confidence

- Make sure you know what it can do and what it is doing
- Establishing a consistent, easy-to-follow system

3. How computers affect the way you work

- Computers set the pace – you need to run faster to keep up
- Computers change the shape – desks, seating, lighting, human interaction – nothing will ever look or feel the same again

4. The Data Protection Act 1984

STEP 5 TOWARDS THE UFO

Step 5 Towards the UFO

MATCHING THE WORKPLACE TO THE PEOPLE

There have always been good offices to work in and bad ones that made people feel that coming to work was some sort of penance. So what is so special, and uniquely modern, about today's user-friendly office?

The answer is that it could never have existed, in anything like this form, at any previous stage in history. The office has changed forever, literally in the last ten years, taking a lunge forward in its evolution that's on a par with our distant ancestors' decision to get up and totter around on two legs, instead of scurrying about on four. After a watershed move like that, there's no going back. And it is the arrival of cheap, networkable computing power that has changed the whole landscape.

Because computers are suddenly so cheap and powerful, every firm that sees a use for them can have them. Because computers can store and search enormous quantities of information, internally or on floppies and other external storage media, records and information can be put at people's fingertips fast enough to be used in real-time situations, such as during a telephone call. Because spreadsheets and word processing use the clerks' and typists' skills, backed up by electronic memory and computational power, whole days of repetitive work have been flushed right out of the office routine.

But the chief difference that real computing power makes available has hardly been exploited yet, except in the one world-beating case of Microsoft's Windows operating system.

Soft front ends make all the difference

What goes on deep inside computers and their software is a closed book to most of us. As long as what's spat out at the far end is useful information, we aren't usually too bothered about how it got there. But, as Microsoft, Apple, Xerox and one or two others realised, the

Smart Office | **11 Steps to a User-Friendly Office**

interface between the person and the machine is hugely important to us – infuriating when the designers have got it wrong and almost unnoticed when they have done a good job.

The big difference with computers, compared with any other tool, is that the interface, the front end, is customisable. It can be fiddled about with so that the screen, for example, is coloured, configured and patterned to suit the user. And that can make a great deal of difference to a person's relationship with both the computer and the work.

Try this. If you use Windows and are used to staring at a grey screen with blue markings, save and close what you are working on, find your way to the Control Panel and the Color option within it and arrow down through the Color Schemes menu till you get to Plasma Power Saver. Now click on the OK button, go back to your work and you will be writing in white on a jet black screen, with bright mauve menu bars and blue trimmings.

The question is not "Is it art?", but "Could these startling colour combinations provide useful options for some people under some circumstances?" And the answer is a definite yes. Shocking your brain out of its rut could be a very good move if, for example, you were struggling late into the night to finish a report.

The existence of "soft" interfaces which can be tailored to individual needs and preferences – on fax machines, telephone equipment and many other devices, as well as computer terminals – is a crucial factor in raising productivity and creating the user-friendly office. So is the ability to use new materials and advanced computer modelling to design furniture and equipment that not only looks purposeful but also provides comfort and ease of use in real office situations.

Given these advantages, we have the opportunity to create the first generation of truly user-friendly offices. And if we pay the right sort of attention to the motivational aspects of the office, too, to fostering initiative, ideas and teamwork, the productivity gains that will follow will soon convince even the most hardened cynic that it's worth believing in UFOs.

Motivation means more than money

Good communication as the key to successful performance management is all very well, but managers are beginning to realise that buzzing coffee areas and regular team meetings are not enough. Organisations of all sizes are increasingly manned by staff whose jobs are constantly on the line. Yet their levels of motivation may determine not only their own survival but the survival of their companies as well. Matching the workstyle to the job and the person seems to be another vital ingredient in the ultimate recipe for motivation.

Motivation is the Philosopher's Stone of the twentieth century. People may have stopped trying to turn base metal into gold, but for 60 or 70 years now employers have been pumping money into research to try to crack the secret of how to turn less staff into more creative energy.

The results of this research have been interesting and widely published, though usually ignored by the people who paid for them. Anyone who ever came close to doing an MBA knows about Maslow's hierarchy of needs, Herzberg's theories about job satisfaction and Douglas McGregor's tough Theory X and cuddly Theory Y companies. Most people who didn't contemplate an MBA understand the broad outlines of all three concepts, as matters of intuition, experience and common sense, but manage to get by without wallowing in the textbooks.

Few managers these days would be proud to claim they were running out-and-out red-in-tooth-and-claw stick-and-carrot organisations. But how many companies still work on the fixed assumption that what really motivates people is nothing more than the size of the pay packet and the sniff of promotion?

The answer is more than 50 per cent. So much for the moral victory Theory Y seemed to have secured, with its emphasis on initiative, participation and worker satisfaction.

The problem is that the problem disguises itself. People don't ask for what they really want, because they know they won't get it. So they ask for money instead.

Ask ASLEF why the train drivers are in militant mood and they will tell you that they are striking for 6 per cent. In fact, though, they are striking for 100 per cent — not wages, but work content, recognition and respect. Underground train drivers over the past ten years have been given increases in salary in a crude trade-off to compensate for decreases in satisfaction. Unfortunately, though, they are intelligent people who enjoy a challenge. What they really want to do is drive trains, not just sit in the cab making announcements, in a monotonous routine broken only by the occasional gruesome diversion of what is known in the business as a "one under".

HOW MUCH OF WHAT YOU DON'T WANT WILL MAKE YOU HAPPY?

If you give people something that's not what they really want, you will never be able to give them enough of it to satisfy them for long. If you try to bargain with people who have never been allowed to take responsibility for what they produce, or to invest anything of themselves in their daily grind, the only bargaining counter that will come into play will be money. And because that's not what they really need, they won't value it as much as you do and are likely to make arbitrary and unreasonable demands.

If you use only carrots and sticks to motivate performance, what generally happens is that innovative, creative risk-taking decreases, to be replaced by a more cautious and conservative approach. Fear of failure replaces the will to win and you are back to the cowed, sullen workforce of the nineteenth century. It sounds like an obvious recipe for disaster, but you don't actually have to go back 100 years to find grotesque examples of it. Older managers will remember that the atmosphere in most British firms was totally Victorian, in this respect, right up to and through the 1950s.

Smart Office | 11 Steps to a User-Friendly Office

CHANGING WORKSTYLES

The user-friendly office may not be an office at all, or at least not all of the time.

Enlightened employers who realise that they have to offer something more than money and discipline to keep the best people, who recognise the need for respect, involvement, peer group support and a friendly environment, may also feel that this kind of working heaven on earth is more than they can manage.

THE ROOTS OF TELEWORKING

One outcome of this employer anxiety syndrome is the move to get rid of the workers from the office altogether and give them responsibility for setting up their own environment of support, comfort and motivation. All that's left for the employer to provide then is the work and equipment. If the employee is out of the office a lot of the time, it reduces spending on all kinds of overheads, from floor space to biscuits. It's called teleworking and we'll be discussing the ins and outs of it (mainly outs, of course) later in this chapter.

CHANGING THE GEOMETRY OF JOBS

Before we get to the nitty gritty of how and where you work, however, it's worth taking a passing glance at how we got into the present state of flux and uncertainty. And there are plenty of symptoms that can be identified. Role definitions and status lines are becoming blurred. No one seems to have a definable sense of place or function any more. Sales executives are printing out contracts in their clients' offices, switchboard operators are working from networked PCs set up in farmhouse kitchens and MDs are chairing policy teleconferences from their health spas.

Apart from the recognition that it takes more than money to keep the modern workforce running at full strength, there are other subversive forces at work. Not least of these is the explosive chemical reaction caused by the combination of technology and imagination.

It has, for example, blown apart the romantic notion that for every creative inventor or salesman you need an army of dull, worthy clerical support staff. From the time the first clerk was made redundant because a comptometer could add a column of figures faster than he could dip his quill in the inkwell, the number of layers in every organisation has been set to shrink and go on shrinking.

The company of the future won't need many support staff at all. What it will need is motivated, innovative people who not only sell the product or service but channel feedback and develop products on towards the next generation as well. This means that the office organisation is typically getting flatter and permanently occupied desks are rapidly becoming fewer.

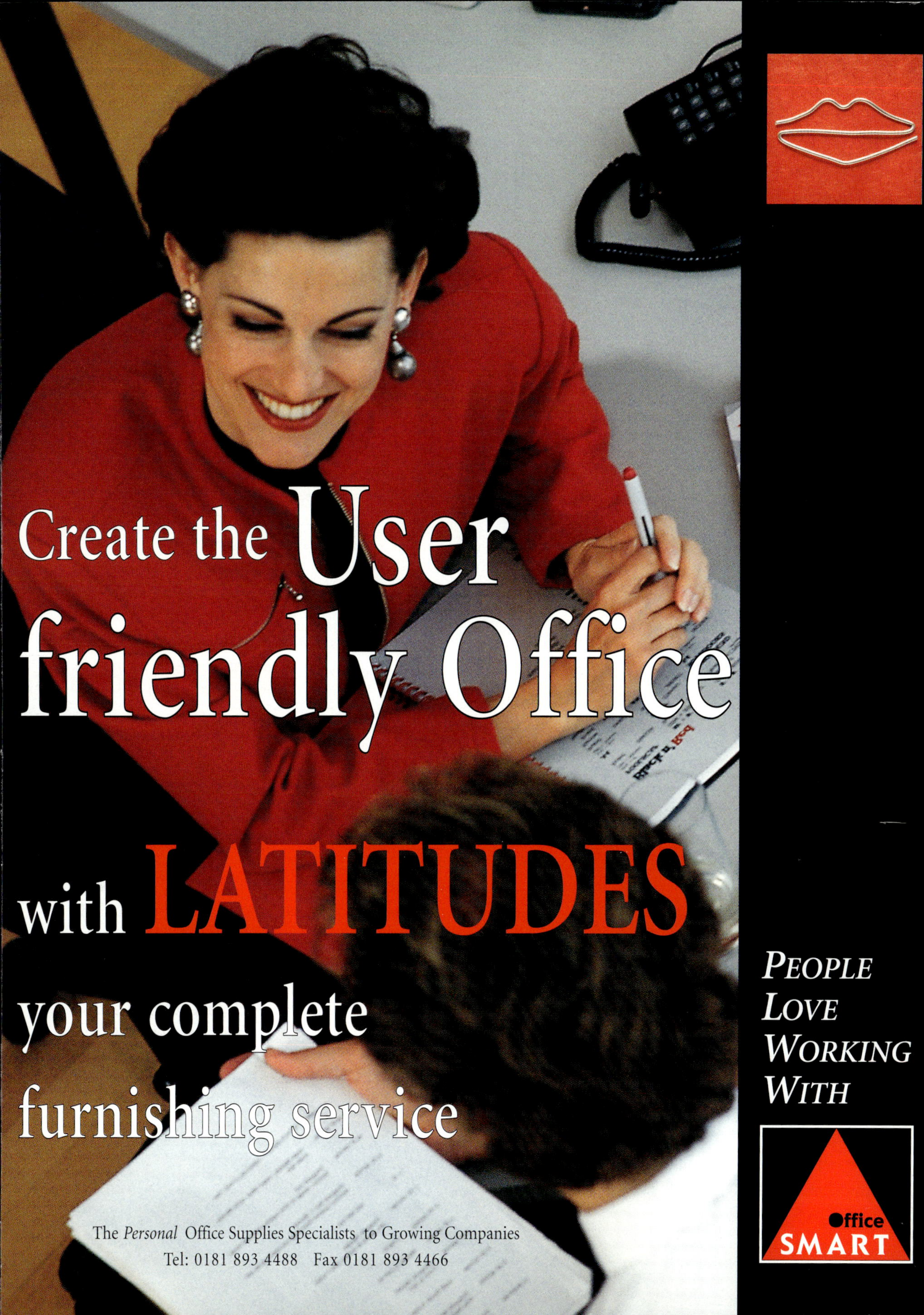

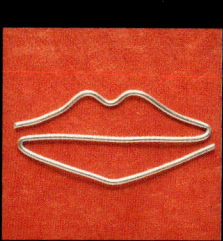

Create the User friendly Office with LATITUDES your complete furnishing service

The *Personal* Office Supplies Specialists to Growing Companies
Tel: 0181 893 4488 Fax 0181 893 4466

People Love Working With

Freeing **you** to work more **effectively** is **our** job

ACCO UK

"I don't have the **time** to **worry** about my mouse dropping **dead**"

"When I'm up against **deadlines** I need access, fast"

"I want my whole **presentation** to run **perfectly,** and **look** great"

Everyone of our brands is a familiar sight in the workplace. Their daily presence is so reliable you take them for granted. But when you need them, you know they will work for you.

Press your Rexel stapler and click your Accodata mouse, delve into your Twinlock Crystalfiles and project your views in a Sasco presentation layout. For thousands of everyday operations, from planning to shredding, you can rely on the breadth of our product portfolio to maintain smooth office management. As market leaders in office products, we free you to work even more effectively.

Since the early 1900's we have been helping to shape the work environment with reliable products and practical innovations. Our brands continue to give you the best range of choice and quality. If you would like to know more about any area of our product range, please write, or call us free on 0800 252359.

Acco UK Limited, Gatehouse Road, Aylesbury, Bucks, HP19 3DT

Step 5 | **Towards the UFO**

	Old	New
Managers		
Professionals		
Clericals		

THE VISION WILL BE WHAT HOLDS THE VIRTUAL OFFICE TOGETHER

We are constantly being told that members of the working section of the population 20 years from now will have several careers in the course of a lifetime. We have to be prepared to acquire new skills and master new technologies, time and time again. People who work will be doing more complete jobs, rather than contributing bits to a process, and the professionals in a company will be both their own managers and their own clerical support.

It's possible now, and it will soon be easy, to carry a whole office around with you in a pilot's case – computer, phone, fax, printer and copier. You can do everything you need to do from wherever you happen to be. And as we get nearer to the time when each of us will have a telephone number for life, which will accompany us onto aircraft and on treks through the jungle (just use your voice mail option if you don't want to answer), the very idea of an office building may start to seem limiting, rather than supportive.

When organisations have gone through all these changes and convulsions, the support staff and managers who are left will need to be at least as flexible and highly skilled as the people they are providing structure and back-up for. They will need to have a realistic overview of *how* their organisations run, from the production line to the last distribution point, and they will certainly need to be technically ahead of their professionals, in order to be able to anticipate and meet their needs.

A LEADING ROLE FOR SUPPORTING PLAYERS

The best support staff will make it their business to be clairvoyant. They will predict and track the significant trends in every kind of support, from software to furniture, to make sure that *their* people and *their* organisations can gain the competitive advantages they need, in terms of tools to do the best possible job.

The distinction between office managers and general management has been crumbling for years. It is already as good as dead, because of trends which have meant that well over half of Britain's workers now work in offices. In the next few years, office managers will be seen as very much a key part of the team, valued just as highly as the specialised professionals they work with and just as likely to end up shaping the firm's future.

What we are talking about, of course, is the flat hierarchy office. No chiefs. No Indians. No nonsense and no status symbols. Just a shared commitment to playing a team game for the common good, to setting and achieving challenging targets and to creating an environment in which skill and talent – and, ultimately, profitability – can thrive.

CHANGE THE OFFICE AND YOU CHANGE THE WORK

This has implications for more than floor space. People need to be on the move. They must be close to their clients and aware of their needs. There will be more consultants and engineers and salesmen in the future and few of them will need to occupy the sort of static, permanent desk space that clerks, accountants and typists needed in the past.

These people will input their own data as they go along, on laptops, PDAs (personal digital assistants) or whatever workstations are available to them when they do touch base. Their loyalty and productivity will be major management issues, because they will operate on quite a long leash. At the same time, one of the key elements in making them feel and remain committed, involved members of the team will be the quality and appropriateness of the support provided for them.

MAKE OR BUY

It is becoming more and more common to buy in the support services that a business needs. External caterers replace the canteen and the tea lady, while contract cleaners pass silently through the office at night, so you never even meet the person who glued your keyboard together with Mr Sheen. Instead of a training department, there are consultants who come in as required, while employees whose presentation skills need polishing up are sent out for half a day to get the boost they need.

The end result is that the core people who are left – the ones with the unique skills needed to make, develop and sell a company's products or services – will usually be working closely together, often in smaller units than before, sometimes in isolated locations, but always very close to the customer.

WHERE DOES TQM FIT IN?

Total Quality Management is not quite the buzzword it used to be. But that's partly because many of the good ideas it incorporated are now largely taken for granted. TQM was based

Step 5 | **Towards the UFO**

on a vision of the company of the future working pro-actively rather than reactively, thinking creatively and, above all, grinding failure out of the system.

Organisational studies had shown that too many jobs were built on the acceptance of failure in the workplace. Too much time was spent sorting out mistakes, tracking things down, finding out why deliveries were late, checking suspect data, rectifying and re-working, dodging blame and apologising to customers for poor quality and lateness. It was estimated that one third of all working time was spent in these grossly non-productive ways. And that is a very provocative thought.

If one third of people's working time is wasted, it follows, arithmetically, that workers could potentially do half as much again.

If the costs of poor quality could be eliminated from the system, managers could capture productivity gains that would transform companies overnight. And while it would take a magic wand to do it completely, even a partial release of that wasted 33 per cent of people's time and effort held out the possibility of a huge payback.

Many important TQM-related concepts and slogans – the notion of the internal customer, quality circles, zero defect production, right first time, designed-in quality and so on – have filtered through to help firms that would never dream of instituting a formal TQM programme. And the idea of a chain of interdependent links adding up to consistent excellence in a product or service is one that can be used in almost any business to focus people's minds on what needs to be done to achieve success.

Using the chain of excellence

The basic idea is to consciously build chains of excellence into the organisation, ensuring that, at every point in the product cycle, perfection is achieved and the customer is satisfied.

Even in the kind of office where TQM theory would not get a sympathetic hearing, mapping out the failure factors that hold things up and make life frustrating and unproductive is a first step towards reducing the waste of time and effort.

Your van drivers may think all management theory is bunk, or worse. But you can bet they take no great delight in having to do trips twice because people have made a mess of things. No one wants to haul themselves back out onto the M62 or the M25 because someone in the office left an item or two off a delivery list.

Taking the organisation of your office as a discrete unit, try keeping a section at the back of your day book to note these patterns over a six-week period. Record all instances of the following and how long they took to solve:

- chasing up an unpaid invoice, in or out
- putting in a special stationery order because something was forgotten

Smart Office | **11 Steps to a User-Friendly Office**

- apologising to customers or clients
- apologising to suppliers
- apologising to members of staff
- hunting for data of any kind
- changing appointments because of double bookings
- running out to any kind of supplier for urgent items
- chasing up incomplete or missing paperwork (requisitions, holiday forms, etc)
- searching for anything (stationery, equipment, information or people)

The easiest way to do this is to draw a grid (or print one off from the computer). It will cost ten minutes of your time to prepare and print, and a few minutes a day to jot down the examples of wasted effort. But the chances are that six weeks' worth of carefully logged results will shock you – and your colleagues – into wanting to make some fairly radical changes in the way the office is run.

The acid test for mission statements

Whether or not you could actually claim your chain of excellence is securely in place, you at least know where your organisation is aiming to be, because of your mission statement. You know exactly how everything is done and when and so does everyone else. And it's all bound together by your mission statement. After all, everybody has a mission statement these days – don't they?

While we're about it, what's yours like?

- Who thought of it?
- Does everybody in your office know it by heart?
- Does it mean something to your people?
- Does it greet the visitor in reception – and does it mean anything to him or her?
- Does the way you run the office itself reflect the spirit and intention of the mission statement?

If your mission statement doesn't mean anything, or is so bland that it could apply to any size of firm in any one of half a dozen industries, it won't be doing much good. If it is warm and meaningful and completely ignored, its motivational power will be nil.

If it spells out, in a few well-chosen and evocative words, to staff and customer alike, why you're here and why the firm is worth taking notice of, it will be doing a useful job.

Without customers, you haven't got a mission

If the mission statement tells you why you're here, your customers are the best people to tell you why you need to keep changing if you want to continue to be here in three or five or ten years' time.

Step 5 | Towards the UFO

Listening to customers is a key part of the sales function. But it is not just a job for sales people.

Everyone who ever has any contact at all with any part of a customer's company or an individual consumer has to be tuned in to pick up whatever feedback is available. That's another good reason to abandon the cosy camaraderie of the head office canteen and get out to where the people who count are waiting to talk to you.

The customer is not your enemy. Business is not war. And it is amazing how often people will tell you what you want to know, if you wait for the right moment and then ask them a straight question. Once you know what your clients really want, you can turn that knowledge into a competitive advantage. Could you supply it to them cheaper and faster than your rivals? Or maybe what they really dream of hasn't been invented yet, in which case your R&D department needs to know that there's an unsatisfied demand waiting out there.

Benchmarking

If taking a critical look at your mission statement raises some awkward issues, another useful question to ask yourself and the people around you is whether you have a measurement and improvement cycle. How do you know how your business is doing and whether you're getting better or worse? Is anybody taking that kind of measurement across the company as a whole?

If you actually have a Quality Unit somewhere up on the 35th floor, but all you know about them is what kind of hanging files they use, it might be an interesting exercise to pop up and ask them what they do and whether they have any strategies that might help you with your office management responsibilities.

If, on the other hand, you suspect that you *are* the TQM department, now would be a good time to think about how you run things, whether you could do it more efficiently and what you would need to make that possible. Do you have an office manual? If you were hit by a runaway tram tomorrow, could your boss, or even the agency temp, find out where to order some new paper clips, the right fax rolls and toner cartridges for your equipment or the vegetarian sandwiches for a buffet lunch?

This documenting aspect of TQM isn't about writing down your job so that it happens without you. It's about finding out how it's done now, writing down the best possible way it could be done and implementing that and then using that set of procedures as a stepping stone towards developing the organisation of the future.

Finally, try asking yourself:

- What would happen if your firm grew 25 per cent larger than it is now?
- What if it downsized by half?

- What if you had to move offices in a couple of months? How would you cope and what would you change and improve when you moved?

CAN YOU HAVE AN OFFICE WITHOUT WALLS?

If companies are changing in so many ways, what are the knock-on effects? What's happening to all this office space that's not needed any more? And what is the role of the office manager or facilities manager in a shrinking office world?

The answer to the last question is that the office manager's primary task of keeping the wheels of industry turning and co-ordinating everything from stationery to mission statements is very far from disappearing. The office may be on the way out, but the office manager isn't. In fact, the more invisible and fragmented the actual office becomes, the more crucial the job is turning out to be.

Continuity, structure and control are needed more than ever now. When they are not imposed by rows of desks and a time clock, or the looser framework of the modern open plan office, they still have to be provided somehow. You can – and should – put onto the computer system all the information that is likely to be needed about where everyone and everything is. But experience shows that an electronic office diary is not enough.

The organisation needs one person with a real overview of the situation – someone who knows what's going on, who's doing it and what needs to be happening next. There has to be somebody to make sure that everyone is in the right place with access to enough of everything that's needed to do the job.

TELEWORKING

Teleworking originated in Scandinavia, as a response to bad winters and sparse population, and became popular in the USA as a way of saving on travel time and tapping into the pool of qualified and experienced working women – programmers, researchers, salespeople and even bond traders – who were tied to their homes by the need to look after children.

In broad, over-simplified theory, teleworkers need no centralised office, because the office is wherever they happen to be. They are at the end of a phone or fax line and contactable by e-mail. They could be at home, or with their clients, or out on the road. But not in the office. Teleworkers don't necessarily have to travel, either, because they can send their work unaccompanied, down the line, thus saving on time, fares and subsistence claims.

Because teleworking is a relatively new phenomenon, there are almost as many teleworking styles as there are teleworkers. For every teleworker who is happy to see his colleagues annually at the Christmas party, there is one who has tried and failed to make it work, and another one who struggles miserably against loneliness, lack of stimulation and the insecurity brought on by dependence on high-tech gadgetry.

The rosy image of the executive at her workstation by the window overlooking a sunlit lake, hens clucking in the yard and a toddler playing contentedly on the rug, is not always matched by reality. In practice, the hens find their way in and start clucking on the rug, while the toddler gives the teleworking mum ten seconds to open a file or start a vital phone call before making a bid for freedom and a beeline for the lake.

The theory is that the lack of interruptions (apart from the children, the neighbours, the pets, the housework, the spouse and the hobbies) is bound to promote productivity. But Murphy's Law operates just as effectively at home as in the office. Anyone who has ever decided to spend a morning catching up on domestic chores in between calling clients will know, with absolute certainty, that when the phone rings as the washer goes clumping into its final cacophonous cycle, it will be your biggest and most demanding customer on the other end of the line. You will hear next to nothing and he will mutter irritably all the time about how there must be something wrong with your phone.

The electronic village hall

A few years ago, the UK government picked up on the idea of teleworking and, with some input from BT, decided to set up telecottages or "electronic village halls" to help in the regeneration of some remote rural communities.

The telecottage idea has grown and is reckoned to have made a real contribution towards stemming rural depopulation in some areas. There are now more than 100 of these electronic cottages scattered around the British Isles, providing high-tech tools and practical training facilities for people who want to run their businesses from where they live. Almost as important as the facilities and expertise they provide is the camaraderie and support of other telecottage users.

Big Business works from home, too

But it's not only individual entrepreneurs who work from home. Increasing numbers of large organisations (most obviously, of course, BT) are now employing teleworkers. BT has telephone operators, marketing planners, salespeople and a whole range of senior managers working from home for three to five days a week.

Some firms are doing it on a small scale to solve short-term problems – for women wishing to extend their maternity leave for an extra six months but still keep their hand in at work, for example. Others have an active policy of encouraging as many of their staff as possible to opt for working from home.

Smart Office | 11 Steps to a User-Friendly Office

Handle with care

There are 101 ways of organising teleworking, from both the company's and individual's points of view. The Telecottage Association has published a set of useful guidelines on how to make it work successfully. But too many companies undoubtedly see it as an easy way of getting the work done without the inconvenience of having workers cluttering up the premises. Not surprisingly, the organisations that approach it this way are the most prone to disaster and breakdown. Despite the unreliability of some of the estimates quoted in discussions about teleworking, it is unquestionably here to stay and growing fast – so it really is time we found out how to get it right.

The key to success with teleworking, from the office manager's point of view, is simply to follow four basic rules.

1. Check that all equipment is working, correctly configured and tested on site.
2. Make sure that all rules and responsibilities on both sides are clearly spelt out and detailed in a contract that is signed by both parties.
3. Ensure that the teleworker knows what is involved and is of a sufficiently strong and self-sufficient personality type to survive and enjoy the experience.
4. Check that the teleworker has an appropriately supportive home environment, in terms of both facilities and relationships.

In other words, don't just give them a computer and a modem and tell them to get on with it.

There will almost certainly be a transitional period in which productivity will dip. For a time, people new to teleworking may need even more support than workers in the office. If correctly handled, with home visits as necessary, this period is usually brief. Once the system is running and individuals feel comfortable with it, teleworkers typically produce more work per hour with lower overheads than their office-based colleagues.

Be clear about what youre doing

Teleworking works worst when there are loose ends and uncertainties that leave the teleworker and his firm unclear about their rights and obligations. A detailed contract may seem harshly formal, but it is the best way to clear the decks, once and for all.

Use this 16-point checklist to make sure all the vital areas have been covered.
1. Ownership and maintenance of company-supplied equipment
2. Use of company-supplied equipment by anyone other than the teleworker
3. Use of company-supplied equipment for any purpose other than company business

Step 5 Towards the UFO

4. Return of equipment
5. Maintenance of teleworker's own equipment used for the work
6. Telephone lines – ownership and payment
7. Insurance: teleworker/equipment/public liability if applicable
8. Arrangements for visits to base office by the teleworker
9. Arrangements for visits to or inspections of the teleworker by head office
10. Job description and workload commitment
11. Working hours: specified, numbered or self-determined?
12. Supply of stationery and other consumables
13. Performance reviews, training and professional and personal support
14. Cover and access to information in the event of accident or sickness affecting the teleworker
15. Terms and conditions
16. Community charge and business rate (it is unlikely that liability for business rate would arise on any premises which normally revert to domestic use after work has finished)

NESTING BOXES FOR FLEDGLING BUSINESSES

Business centres sprang up like mushrooms during the boom in small business start-ups in the late eighties. One-man bands and micro businesses often found it easier to have someone to answer their phone, do their typing and frank their mail for them, while they concentrated on selling or developing their products. They paid a premium, of course, but it was cheaper and much more convenient than having their own copiers, fax machines and receptionists.

More importantly, the business centre offered a support network of sorts when all else failed. The office manager of these establishments was usually an agony aunt as well as a rent collector. You could talk to other businesses that were also struggling to get off the ground, learn from other people's mistakes and sometimes even discover mutual interests and generate business ideas.

There was usually a conference room which the small businessman could pass off as his own if he had to entertain important visitors. The most flexibly sympathetic business centres kept a pile of brass plates tucked away under the reception desk and would display whichever one was appropriate on a particular day. No one was to know that the other people hurrying around, answering phones and looking busy were running completely different organisations. It gave the start-ups substance, confidence and practical support.

You may even be running one of these worthy establishments yourself, in which case you could probably write this book in your spare five minutes every other month. However, there are fewer of them around now than there used to be – mainly because the small start-up business of the 1990s can get away more easily with seeming real on the end of a telephone line. PC, fax and modem technology is cheaper and more usable, so the one-man

Smart Office | **11 Steps to a User-Friendly Office**

band can probably do his accounts, his word processing and his spreadsheets on his own computer, print them out, make rough and ready copies on his fax when needed and connect himself to his clients across the Internet.

Instant offices – by the hour

There could hardly be a better symbol of the nineties than the instant office. These are real business dream machines – the shell of an office that can be anything you want, any time you need it. One of the best is in Bond Street, in the heart of London's West End and, as any Monopoly player will tell you, a street of real class. You can use it for a day, or just an hour, and it will appear to be totally, convincingly yours.

This is a far cry from the old-fashioned poste restante business addresses, where you called in once a week to collect your mail and messages and wondered whether you were the only customer on their books. E-mail and teleworked answering services connected directly to your home PC have more or less put that idea out to grass. The instant office is different. It's slick, it's plausible, it's expensive and it's there all the time – yet it only exists for you when you are in it with your customers.

STRATEGIES FOR THE ALTERNATIVE OFFICE

Big international organisations, cutting back on their floor space, are experimenting with some new ways of providing for the needs of the semi-invisible work force.

Before you rush into decisions about whether to try out approaches such as mobile pods, multifunctional cockpits or the fashionably pastoral idea of creating common space around a crackling fire, it's worth spending some time analysing your company's actual needs.

What is your workforce like now and how will it function in five years' time?
- How many people are in the office all day, every day?
- How many people spend some of their time out of the office (salesmen, consultants, on-site engineers and so on)?
- How many people spend most of their time out of the office?
- How many of these people could actually do their job just as well, if not better, if they worked from home or spent more time with the clients?
- How much more equipment and head office support would they require to do this?
- Has anyone in your office tried teleworking?
  - Did it work? What were the advantages?
  - If it failed, what went wrong?

How well used is your current office space?
- How many desks are empty every day?

Step 5 | Towards the UFO

- How would people react if you asked them to share?
- Do you have voice mail and other back-up systems which can cope with messages if people aren't in one place all the time?
- How mixed is the usage of space in your office? (Do you have people who need to talk a lot on the telephone sitting next to people who need to concentrate on detailed analytical activities?)
- Is the one-to-one communication between people at their desks actually useful for your organisation as a whole?

Just answering these questions will have given you a pretty good idea of your own best guess about the future. Now that you know what you need, here are the options so far.

A problem shared is a problem doubled

Office sharing is the compromise solution that doesn't work. Two people, or even three, share an office. What happens if two or more are in on the same day? Whose job is it to co-ordinate who has the desk on Tuesday and who uses it Wednesday? (Answer: Isn't it always? The office manager's.)

It gets worse still if they also share a PC and a telephone. Every time a different person is in, the IT department has to re-route e-mail and voice mail. Of course, they never do that until nearly lunchtime and then, if they get it wrong, you can't get them until the afternoon.

One small, highly specialised and prestigious computer company in the East End of London had just this problem. There were 30 consultants, four directors and one office administrator. It was agreed that the administrator should have a permanent work area (she was also lucky enough to be the receptionist as well) and the directors pulled rank and had desks of their own. Although they pointed out that they were still being democratic because they didn't have separate offices, everybody knew that this was because they were not well liked and preferred to be able to hear what everyone was saying about them.

But the consultants were a problem. Each of them was out of the office for at least 50 per cent of the time, sometimes for months on end. A rational system was therefore introduced, under which the 30 of them shared 17 desks. Unfortunately, only three desks were in natural light, 10 of the 17 terminals had better screens than the others and some of the desks had two banks of drawers rather than one.

This town ain't big enough

These men and women were highly intelligent programmers, charged out by the company at £800 per day to the clients. But whenever they got back to base, much of their time and energy would be spent arguing with their colleagues about whether they had left vital disks in a particular drawer or whether they were entitled to one of the large screen computers.

Smart Office | 11 Steps to a User-Friendly Office

Eventually such a violent argument erupted one day over a bag of boiled sweets (allegedly "disappeared" during the six-week absence of one of the programmers) that the administrator felt forced into making some radical changes.

The company was doing well, so she was able to demand — and get — a substantial refurbishment budget, which was spent on temporary partitioning, tables and mobile drawer units which rolled under the tables to make them look like desks. Each consultant had his or her own, identical three-drawer unit in which all personal possessions were locked away when the programmer was out of the office. These mobile units were shunted off into a back room and the owner was responsible for both storage and retrieval.

The partitioning delighted everybody and all the consultants began by building themselves boxes, into which they disappeared for the first few days. Interestingly, after six months, the partitions had virtually all gone into the back room and were rarely used. But at least everyone had had the choice.

TREATING THE PLACE LIKE A HOTEL

What the office manager in the consultancy had actually done was find a compromise between office sharing and what is now known as "hotelling".

The office of the future probably won't involve people sharing particular spaces, which seems to cut across our territorial instincts in a way that courts disaster. No, the floor space in the office of the future belongs to everybody. But it is furnished and partitioned according to who is using it at any particular time.

There may be small "cockpit areas", or it may be open planned or partitioned. But most people who are not permanently office-based will have their papers, files, photographs, monogrammed paper clips and so on in a mobile "pod". In practice, a pod can be anything from an under-desk unit to a wall unit with terminal connections, telephone and printer. It all depends on the status and working style of the individual and the company.

The motel

You arrive at your building. It won't necessarily be a particular building in a particular city. It won't necessarily belong to (or be leased by) your company. It could be any office block, owned by a development company, in which any particular organisation (including yours) rents space for no particular employees.

You arrive. You check in, pick up a coffee from the machine and a telephone extension number and find the workspace you've been allocated. Once you've re-routed your voice mail and plugged in your laptop and fax, you're up and running.

Step 5 | Towards the UFO

The Dorchester

You phone or fax ahead and specify how much space you need for how long, what equipment and software you need, and how you like your coffee and doughnuts. When you arrive, you'll be escorted to your cockpit or conference room (depending on your budget) and offered personal help, if you need it, for anything from word processing to booking dinner.

The pied à terre

This will be the place your company owns and you use regularly. You will have your own mobile pod with your files, photographs and maybe even your own computer and printer in it. When you check in, you will be told who else is in the building and asked if you have any preference as to location. You will then collect your pod and tow it to your designated area, which will be your home until you go on your travels again. You call the IT department as you hook up to the network and should be on-line, with your usual configuration of equipment and software, within half an hour.

The village green

What worries a lot of people about all these new ideas is that everything ends up seeming so bloodless and impersonal. One of the main reasons that people go out to work at all, once the need for an income has been satisfied, is for companionship and social stimulus. The architects of the future, still in shock from the big mistake of the twentieth century – the tower block as family dwelling – are anxious now to build in the human factor.

Their solution is to have plenty of common space – even, as one Californian suggested, a real hearth with a real fire. At the very least, there will be oasis or sandwich bar areas, with informal seating, but still with the kind of table space and access to communications that facilitate business talk and the exchange of ideas.

Even the corridors and passing points in these new offices are going to have a secondary function for people in a hurry. Instead of just being wide enough for two pods to trundle past each other, they are to have niches with leaning points to encourage busy professionals to stop for a chat. More than that, there will be whiteboards at regular intervals, in case someone feels the need to sketch a diagram to make a point. The idea is that you can compare notes, chat, gossip a bit and generally stay human, without wasting too much time.

Territorial disadvantage

In the 1990s, the profit-making activity of any organisation takes precedence over status. But questions of position, status and structure, as applied to individuals and whole departments, are permanently under scrutiny.

Smart Office | **11 Steps to a User-Friendly Office**

- Why do we do things this way?
- Why do we do them here?
- Is he (or she) the best person to do that?

These are all good, searching questions and asking them is becoming more acceptable all the time.

Right through the first half of this century, a monumental building was the sign that a business was successful. Even factories, like Hoover's Egyptian fantasy on the Western Avenue at Perivale, were built with this kind of megalomaniac flourish. Apart from the occasional development bank and a few other dinosaurs, the legendary corporations of the future will be investing less in marble-lined reception areas and more in technology, training and innovation.

No more presidential privilege

Even the person at the top of the heap isn't safe, it seems. Because the Chief Executive's office tends to be well lit and elegant, it makes sense to get more use out of it. In future, his or her trophy cabinets and bookcases will be closed off, like a massive roll-top desk, when the CEO is travelling. Then the big conference table, those elegant plants and that inspirational view may be enjoyed by those involved in client meetings, small conferences and team brainstorming exercises.

The office of the future will have function-based, rather than status-based, design features. Survival and growth are more important than any individual. Everything is up for change and challenge.

THE USER-FRIENDLY OFFICE

So what is a user-friendly office? Everyone knows the UFO is a rare phenomenon. But does it exist anywhere? Have you seen one? Could you pinch any useful ideas you've come across in other people's offices?

Or do you just have to follow your own dream?

A book like this can alert you to a few ideas you may not have considered before. But only you can answer the question. Here are some factors you might take into consideration in deciding whether the kind of office set-up you have now is really right for you.

Your Business	What kind of business is it? Do you manufacture a product, run a railway, sell a service? How big an infrastructure and how many support staff do you really need to make it work?

Step 5 | Towards the UFO

Your Customers	What do your customers expect? Do they visit the offices and see the company as a whole? Do they form relationships with individual consultants or salesmen and care little for the corporate image?
Your Personality	Could you manage a scattered workforce of self-organised individuals? Do you find it easier to have everybody in one place, where you can see them? Or would you happily trade your empire in the interests of efficiency, new challenges and the chance to visit your home occasionally?
Your Buildings	Are your current offices too large, too small or just right? And what will they be in five years' time? Would it make sense to start thinking about doing things differently – *very* differently – now, before you order the new desks and bookshelves?
Your Budget	If you now have an image of your ideal office and how it would run, does this involve much up-front expenditure? Do you have the budget to make those changes now? In five years? Can you make some small changes right away that would make a difference?
Your Staff	Are your people mostly consultants, salesmen, engineers, accountants? Where do they need to be to do their jobs? Do they spend too much or too little time in the office? What could you do to get the balance right?

IN A NUTSHELL
1. Computers and customised offices
- For the first time, almost unlimited processing power is available to all
- Manpower capacity is no longer a limiting factor
- "Soft" interfaces mean computers can be tamed to suit individual users
- The office environment can be customised to suit the needs and the people in every organisation

2. Build your own UFO and make it fly
- Offices used to be there largely to provide a mailing address and keep staff and equipment dry

Smart Office | **11 Steps to a User-Friendly Office**

- Modern offices are supposed to provide motivational, stimulating environments – but must still be warm, comfortable and safe
- To achieve this, the office must be more flexible, designed around people and the projects they manage
- Quality management concepts have become mainstream ideas, though TQM doesn't get spelled out so often

3. Choose the right work style and design a matching environment

- Offices need to be flexible and designed around the needs of the workforce
- As organisations get flatter, fewer admin staff are needed to run them

4. Teleworking

- Moving data instead of people is growing as fast as technology to support it
- Despite teething troubles (loneliness, power failure, lack of support), savings in time, travel and pollution make teleworking a major option for the future

5. Business centres and other shared resources

- For individuals and companies that don't need an address to themselves
- For people who need
    - offices in a number of locations
    - an office only one day a week
    - access to expensive equipment they can only afford to share

6. Hot desking and pod rolling

- For flatter firms that don't have many people chained to desks from nine to five
- Cuts down on space and encourages workers to get out and see customers

7. Criteria for working out what works best for you

- How many of what sort of staff does it really take to make your business grow?
- What *exactly* do they do and where and how do they need to do it?
- What sort of structure would work for your business and support your employees best?
- How close can you get to a UFO?

STEP 6: HEALTH AND SAFETY FIRST FOR PRODUCTIVITY THAT LASTS

Step 6 | **Health and Safety First for Productivity That Lasts**

LOOKING AFTER YOUR MAJOR ASSETS
THEY WALK, THEY TALK AND THEY MAKE IT ALL HAPPEN

When it comes to the crunch, it is always going to be the people who make or break your company's success. Even in industries with very sophisticated equipment and high capital costs, it is the human factor that makes the difference. So how do you create an environment that makes it likely that you will get the best out of your human capital?

First, of course, it must be safe. That means complying with the explicit requirements of the fire and health and safety regulations. But it also means taking to heart the important legal concept of "a duty of care" to all employees – an idea that is being extended and refined all the time.

Last year (1995) saw Britain's first action in which an employee successfully sued his company for health damage caused by stress at work. The employer was held to have neglected its duty of care in putting the man in a situation of unremitting stress. There are now reckoned to be hundreds of similar cases in the legal pipeline.

So the dividing line between what is a safety problem and what is tolerably comfortable for workers, in terms of physical conditions or stress, is becoming increasingly blurred. But anyone responsible for getting the best out of the team in an office needs to look well beyond any minimum requirements that might be legally enforceable.

By setting up a working environment that is not just safe but warm, comfortable, well lit and equipped with the furniture, equipment and fittings to encourage productive effort and focused attention on the job in hand, the facilities manager or office manager can make a positive contribution to the business.

If he or she can also encourage the kind of informal contact and communication of ideas that lays the foundation for real teamwork, the results may be startling. The biggest change you are ever likely to see in an office is the change that crystallises when members of a group suddenly begin to see themselves as a team and start to work unselfishly for each other.

You're better off with a flourishing grapevine

Internal communication always takes the line of least resistance. Information and gossip, facts and myths swirl around the place, whether managers like the idea or not. Short of shutting people up in isolated cells, there's no way to stop it happening – and even prisoners traditionally find ways of banging on the pipes and tapping out messages to each other.

Every workplace has its rumour mills and watering holes. Every firm has its grapevine, and it's better to be on it than off – even if you don't always like what you hear. If you're not on it, you have no way of monitoring what's being passed around the company. The Victorian boss who stalked round his offices snarling in at every doorway and shouting "Silence" at his cowering staff was doing himself no favours at all. By treating his people as cogs in a machine, he trained them to give him nothing but their time.

In the smart office, there is thinking to be done and teamwork to be fostered. Most of the jobs that needed cogs can now been done faster and better on a PC. Productivity is harder to measure when what you are producing is ideas. But ideas are the currency that matters. And if you want to encourage new thinking and new ideas, you have to create an office that will help them take shape.

Create a focus

Once managers accept that they do want people to talk and swap news and views in the office, there's a lot they can do to support the process in subtle, informal ways. Photocopying machines, lift lobbies, washrooms and stairwells have all traditionally formed focal points where people can bump into each other – by accident or on purpose – to exchange everything from the most trivial gossip to hair-raising Chinese whispers about rumoured redundancies.

Minor changes can wreck this fragile communications network before anyone even notices. Things may be rearranged on what seem like perfectly sensible, logical grounds. Yet the change that places a copying machine in a narrow, inaccessible place where it's difficult for people to wait and talk together may have quite far-reaching consequences.

The consultant and the coffee

In one London office of a major UK communications company, a particular coffee machine was removed, at a time when change and uncertainty was in the air and the department was abuzz with stress and rumours. The senior managers who had always traded news and

Step 6 — Health and Safety First for Productivity That Lasts

comment around the coffee machine retreated into their own offices with electric kettles, mugs and teabags and more or less stopped talking to each other during the day. Morale sagged visibly over a matter of weeks and no one was quite able to put a finger on the reasons why.

The answer, pointed out by a £1200-a-day management consultant, who had known the office for some time and was alarmed to see the jumpy state people had got themselves into, was simple.

"Bring back the coffee machine," he said. "The coffee was always lousy, but that thing was doing a lot more for you than just supplying drinks."

After the usual cries of "You cannot be serious" and "You mean we're paying consultants £1200 a day for advice like that?", the company did as he recommended and the grapevine quickly re-established itself. There's no happy ending, of course. The axe fell and there were redundancies and readjustments all round. But it was admitted, by very senior management, that the low point of the department's morale had been when the chatting had to stop, rather than later, when the bad news about people's jobs came out. Bad news is bad, by definition. But suffering uncertainty in isolation is often even worse.

There's a place for us

What's entitled to a column of space roughly seven feet across and ten feet high – or the equivalent in some slightly different shape?

The answer, surprisingly to those who don't spend their lives planning out office accommodation, is a worker.

Forty square feet, to a height of ten feet, is the minimum space each individual should have in any office. Which means, for example, that the standard start-up business format of three people, two phones and a filing cabinet, crammed in a broom cupboard somewhere, should not really be operating out of a room measuring less than twelve feet by ten.

So if 400 cubic feet is the volume a person can lay claim to, what other entitlements does a worker have?

As far as the other sort of volume is concerned, the noise level should not be higher than 70 decibels. The European Union's current proposals state that 55 decibels – roughly as loud as someone talking quietly about three feet away from you – should be the limit for work that requires mental effort or concentration.

Smart Office | 11 Steps to a User-Friendly Office

People in desk jobs have a right to be kept reasonably warm. Although there is a bit of leeway covering the first hour of work, after that the temperature should not fall below 16 degrees Centigrade. Workers must also have adequate lighting, based on a standard of 500 lux for most office tasks, 750 lux for drawing and design offices and 1,500 to 3,000 lux for any work requiring minute concentration.

The premises must be safe, with proper fire precautions, equipment and drills. Nominated staff must have had appropriate fire and first aid training. Furniture must be comfortable and supportive. Volatile or hazardous materials, such as correcting fluid, solvent cleaners and toner refills must be stored safely and kept tightly sealed. Guillotines must have guards, filing cabinets should have anti-tilt mechanisms and, of course, every item of portable electrical equipment – from kettles and desk lamps to computers, projectors and shredders – must be inspected and tested.

It is round about this point in the list that directors of small and medium companies tend to turn with a smile to their office managers or facilities managers and say things like: "But you know all about this stuff. You take care of it all for us, don't you?"

In cases like these, once the almost irresistible urge to hit the speaker has passed by, the correct answer is usually "Yes." Because, astonishing as it may seem, office managers and others with similar roles but different titles do succeed in coping with this challenging set of responsibilities, day in and day out, in the majority of British companies.

One of the goals of this book is to provide a useful source of up-to-date information and practical ideas for all these unsung heroes and heroines and help them do a good job even better. But there is so much relevant legislation these days that this section cannot hope to give comprehensive coverage of all the legal ins and outs – no book that would fit in your briefcase could.

Instead, the aim is to try to clear some of the fog surrounding subjects like lighting levels, the rules about VDU and furniture design, Sick Building Syndrome and RSI. The idea is to help you take sensible, practical business decisions that will move your firm along the road towards the smart office – and the contact points for more detailed regulatory information are all listed at the back of the book, just in case you should need them.

Step 6 | **Health and Safety First for Productivity That Lasts**

PLAYING IT SAFE

Work can be a dangerous place. Despite people's best endeavours, despite better equipment and working methods and despite a mountain of European and home-grown health and safety regulations, every couple of weeks someone dies in an accident in an office in Britain.

Dying to take control?

Latest results from a long-term study of 30,000 UK civil servants have pinpointed a clear connection between people's heart attack risk and the amount of control they feel they have over their working lives. Feeling out of control at work isn't just uncomfortable – it can kill you.

The civil servants who were studied were divided into four groups for the 20-year research project, ranging from the bottom group of messengers and clerks to an élite top group of senior mandarins.

The amount of autonomy and control people felt they had was periodically assessed and related to various physiological measurements.

The telltale conection appeared when the researchers looked at levels of the blood clotting agent fibrinogen. This determines susceptibility to heart attacks and is affected by smoking and drinking. The unexpected news from the survey is that feelings of being out of control at work affect fibrinogen levels almost as much as habitual smoking.

As a result, the top civil servants, dealing with the pressure of weighty affairs of state and, of course, paid and pensioned accordingly, suffer far fewer heart attacks than their minions. Nobody said life was fair. But it will be interesting to see how long it is before the family of some harassed low-ranking employee who has died from a heart attack brings an action for appropriately substantial compensation.

A hundred serious accidents a week are reported to the authorities. But for every person who suffers an accident, there are dozens whose health and well-being are affected in more subtle ways by factors such as a poor office environment or badly planned working procedures.

From an employer's point of view, this is a costly business. It translates directly into increased absenteeism, disappointing output, frequent mistakes and low national productivity. So it is not just altruism that makes governments introduce new health and safety laws. Investing in a smart, purposeful, stimulating working environment can pay off in the crudest and most direct financial terms, as well as making people's working lives better and more satisfying.

WHO'S READY FOR A SIX-PACK?

The two long-standing pillars of British health and safety legislation are the Offices Shops and Railway Premises Act 1963 and the Health and Safety at Work Act 1974.

They have been joined, over time, by many more specialised bits and pieces of regulation affecting aspects of the office environment, including regulations about Control of Substances Hazardous to Health, Noise at Work, First Aid at Work and the Reporting of Injuries, Diseases and Dangerous Occurrences.

But the real, sudden rush of legislation has come in the last few years. And the most comprehensive bundle of nightmares and headaches for office managers has been the famous "six-pack" of new regulations which came into force in 1993. This consisted of:

- The Management of Health and Safety at Work Regulations 1992
- Manual Handling (Operations) Regulations 1992
- Display Screen Equipment Regulations 1992
- Workplace (Health, Safety and Welfare) Regulations 1992
- Provision and Use of Work Equipment Regulations 1992
- Personal Protective Equipment at Work Regulations 1992

One of the major innovations the six-pack introduced was the requirement for employers to conduct formal risk assessments. These must cover work tasks and processes and the workplace itself, spotlighting potential hazards and proving that a systematic approach is being used in dealing with them.

That makes it radically different from most earlier regulation, because of the insistence that management must not just wait to see what goes wrong. Employers must now be much more forward-looking and methodical about health and safety, or face substantial penalties.

Time for a chance to catch our breath

The six-pack was enough to make many office managers reel, but it is not going to be the end of the story. The flow of further rules and legislation affecting the office environment will undoubtedly continue. We have recently had the new Fire Precautions (Places of Work) regulations, placing specific and sometimes onerous duties on employers, and there are still more regulations in the pipeline.

Step 6 | **Health and Safety First for Productivity That Lasts**

One thing employers and office managers might reasonably ask from the lawmakers now is a pause for consolidation. Just like our schools and the health service, where there have been waves of change sweeping through one after another, till no one can really be sure of his ground, offices could do with a chance to catch up.

A breathing space of two or three years would give professional office managers the opportunity to get on top of their subject again, instead of toiling along behind and having to look everything up in books or leaning heavily on computerised information services such as Barbour Index. At present, inevitably, there is not one office manager in ten who could claim to be confident about all the ins and outs of the latest rules. This has been made worse by the changing nature of the regulatory system.

COMMON SENSE IS NO LONGER ENOUGH

There has been a marked shift in recent years away from guidelines and codes of practice and towards more definitive rules and legislation. This is more than just a change of style. It is a change of philosophy – and one that creates its own problems for office managers. It also introduces a new financial factor, which we might call the cost of compliance.

> **It's tough to realise it, but just thinking sensibly, acting with goodwill and showing consideration for employees' comfort and welfare is not necessarily enough any more.**

Despite all the political rhetoric we're fed from time to time about freeing the entrepreneurial spirit and cutting back on bureaucracy, this is the way the wind is blowing.

And despite everything we hear about British opt-outs from the Social Chapter and other bits of European Union regulation, the trend is probably unstoppable. In terms of rooting out the worst practices and the most unpleasant and dangerous workplaces, this kind of regulation is certainly having a positive impact. But it can also have some very nasty unintended consequences.

When new regulations lay down stipulations in strict, measurable form, they have to be complied with, even if common sense dictates that the previous set-up was safe, reasonable and healthy – even if it was entirely acceptable to the people directly affected.

Compliance can be expensive. It can even, sometimes, be physically impossible. And that is how genuinely well-meaning officials and politicians in Whitehall, Westminster and Brussels, anxious to protect the health and rights of working people, can end up smothering them in red tape and even – in extreme cases – putting them out of a job.

PREPARE FOR THE WORST

Do you have a first aid kit in your office? And how often is it updated? In many offices the first aid box sits at the back of the cupboard, behind the biscuits, and is never opened again once

Smart Office | **11 Steps to a User-Friendly Office**

the TCP and aspirins have been used up. In fact, according to current advice from the St John Ambulance Association, there shouldn't even be any TCP in the kit in the first place – wounds should only be washed in water!

So what would you do if you actually had to use one of those long bandages? Would you know how tightly to apply it and where to tie the knot? Or should you use a safety pin? And what if there isn't one around? If you have a trained first aider in the office of course there's no problem. If you don't, then it's time you did.

The first thing to do is to get a copy of the office bible on the subject, the Health and Safety Commission's *Approved Code of Practice* (available from HMSO). This publication contains all the government regulations on the subject and some helpful advice as well, including a list of what to include in a first aid box.

It also specifies that, however small your office, there should be one person designated as the first aid officer and that he or she should have received at least one day's training from an approved supplier such as the St John Ambulance. If you have more than 50 people, you will need a first aider who has received four days' full-time training and that person should be on the premises at all times. Which, of course, means that you actually need at least two of them.

MAKE SOMEBODY RESPONSIBLE

First of all, decide who's going to help. You need to have a Health and Safety Co-ordinator, as well as the trained first aider mentioned above. This may or may not end up being you. But it's usually a good idea to look around first and check whether there are others in the office who have special interests or aptitudes in these directions. You may have a scout leader in the accounts department who's already massively qualified in the first aid skills. Maybe she could even run an in-house first aid course in the lunch breaks, so that other people would know what they were doing as well. There's often someone who's more likely to take a special interest in fire drills and different kinds of extinguisher – so this person might as well have some fun with it. The important thing is that *somebody* takes on the responsibility and that everybody's efforts are co-ordinated.

TAKING ADVICE

If you are unsure about your liabilities, responsibilities and hazards, it's best to take advice, and there's plenty of it about. Very small businesses may get away with applying common sense and hoping for the best. But if there are more than five people working on your premises, you really have to be sure you are complying with all the regulations. After all, when you get to six members of staff you have already reached the point at which you need to install a second (separate) water closet and washstation! You may also need to consider whether you are required to provide special provision for pregnant and nursing mothers.

Step 6 | **Health and Safety First for Productivity That Lasts**

Leaflets, summaries and forms are available from HMSO and from the Health and Safety Executive (see list at the back). You may also get help from some local libraries and chambers of commerce.

Your best form of help may be to commission a formal safety audit. It needn't be complicated and there are plenty of firms and consultants who will do this for you. Work out how long it will take you to read all the literature and run the checks yourself before you decide to save money by doing it in-house. Experts may charge a high hourly rate but they can do it a lot more quickly than you and they are less likely to miss something important. Once again the critical number five comes into play – because if you have five or more people in the office then the results of any risk assessment survey must be recorded and made available for inspection.

Internet information

While there's quite a bit of practical advice on how to exploit the Internet and the World Wide Web coming up in a later chapter, it is worth mentioning here, too, that the Health & Safety Executive has now put a lot of useful information on the goverment's World Wide Web site.

This means that it becomes part of a free electronic library which you can dip into any time you like. Contact numbers for enquiries to the HSE, plus a great deal of regulatory information, can be found at:
http://www.open.gov.uk/hse/hsehome.htm.

If your firm is not yet exploring the potential of the Internet and the Web, this may not mean much to you. But this is certainly a good example of an area where it is clearly better to be able to search someone else's electronic library than to have to collect and store mountains of regulatory bumf on your own premises.

Meanwhile, there are a few key areas to bear in mind as you make your mental checklist on the safety of your own environment. A relatively new hazard which has arisen over the past ten years is the computerisation of many high-tech offices. If not planned carefully, this can result in spaghetti piles of cables, overloaded sockets and greatly increased fire risks. Special extinguishers are needed for electrical fires and should be kept by the equipment, clearly marked.

Smart Office | 11 Steps to a User-Friendly Office

FIRE REGULATIONS

The local fire service is the best source to call on for advice on fire precautions and regulations. Every office should have:

- clearly marked fire exits
- a fire drill, with instructions posted at key points throughout the office
- an adequate number of fire extinguishers, clearly visible and annually serviced. The fire service will advise you about what you need and will also give you a list of reputable companies to provide you with the equipment. Be sure to check whether you also need a pressure hose, and, if so, where it should be placed
- regulation fire doors at key points. You will need detailed advice on the thickness and design of these doors and how many are required
- one or two designated fire officers who will take annual top-up training, pass what they learn on to others and take responsibility for ensuring all equipment is in order

All of this becomes more complicated if you share an office with other companies, as staircases, doors and fire escapes may be common property. It's vital in this situation to take the initiative, call a meeting and decide who is responsible for what and whether money needs to be spent on updating and upgrading safety facilities. Shared facilities, except in serviced offices which are professionally managed, always introduce an extra element of fire risk. Everybody is busy and hopes someone else will organise the necessary checks and actions. They won't, so take the initiative. It's worth half an hour of your time and you may make some interesting new contacts for your network.

Apart from their potential as a fire hazard, PCs and their peripherals can be bad for your health in a multitude of other ways, all of which are comprehensively documented and provided for in current European Union regulations.

THE STING IN THE TAIL: PCs AND THE EC

A few years ago, when the European Union was still the EC, a set of health and safety directives was thrashed out to cover PCs and computer terminals in the office.

At the time, everyone's eyes were on the rules about new workstations, which had to comply with the tighter regime from 1 January 1993. Manufacturers quickly came into line and the necessary design changes were made in all new equipment. Then the flurry of activity died down and most people soon forgot about the EC directives. But there was a sting in the tail. The EC, as such, may be gone, replaced by the enlarged European Union. But there is a legacy that is going to come back and haunt many of us during 1996.

Because while people tend to talk as if every office these days is stacked with Pentium-powered PCs running Windows 95, or at least Windows for Workgroups, that just isn't true.

Step 6 | **Health and Safety First for Productivity That Lasts**

1996 is your deadline

There is a PC in the London office of one major international newspaper that is still running, just, and still used, every day, that has been there since before Gorbachev came to power in Moscow in 1985. Countless small firms have old PCs or Apples they bought well before the 1992 EC directives and intend to carry on using for some time to come. For them, the delayed-action EC rules may bring some rude shocks.

These rules state that by the end of 1996, your equipment must conform to several clear health and safety standards.

1. PC screens must be free of glare and reflections likely to cause discomfort to users.
2. All radiation from workstations (other than light) must be reduced to negligible levels.
3. Screens must be able to swivel and tilt easily to suit individual users. Keyboards must be tiltable and separated from screens, so that workers can find comfortable positions and avoid fatigue in the hands and arms.
4. Copy-holding devices must be stable, adjustable and positioned to avoid uncomfortable head and eye movements.
5. Footrests must be made available to any members of staff who want them.

Only equipment manufacturers can do anything much about radiation discharge levels. But there is clearly going to be something of a rush throughout 1996 for accessories such as clip-on screen filters, copy holders, footrests, monitor arms and keyboard wrist rests.

Who's afraid of the big bad mouse?

RSI – Repetitive Strain Injury – is still not nearly as common as most people think. As more and more executives begin to do their own letters and the ergonomics of furniture and computer design improve, the increase in cases is showing signs of levelling off, though it hasn't gone into reverse yet.

Now that we have all got used to talking about RSI, the experts are trying to relabel it with an even less elegant tag, WRULD – Work-Related Upper Limb Disorder. Whatever you call it, it is a serious business, capable of progressing at a gallop from minor twinges to a crippling disability that can make work impossible.

No one denies that continuous pounding on the keys can trigger RSI – the first cases appeared during the early 1980s, well before the world's offices were invaded by mice. But the latest research, from the ergonomics laboratory at the University of California at Berkeley, has pinned the blame for most of the new cases on the mouse, rather than the keyboard.

Smart Office | 11 Steps to a User-Friendly Office

It's the click that does the damage

This tallies with the fact that most problems occur on the mousing side of the body, though keyboard use is more or less evenly divided between the two hands. The Californian studies showed that fast word processing and editing tasks could involve 250 mouse clicks an hour, while many people using graphics and design programs clicked 1,000 times an hour.

The particular danger seems to stem from repeated "button-down dragging", which requires the hand and arm to be kept in tension and not relaxed for several seconds. In graphics and desktop publishing work, constant repetition of this tiny strain — less than a tenth the pressure the finger is capable of applying — is what seems to trigger the problems.

Trackballs and trackpads, as used in laptop PCs, are thought to be much less likely to cause difficulties. One enterprising American firm is also redesigning the mouse to incorporate a lock button, so that the user does not have to keep pressure on with the finger.

Employers have been warned to insist that staff doing this type of work take regular and frequent breaks or switch to other types of work from time to time. But it has also been noted that RSI seems to be in the process of being privatised. The people who are most likely to appear in the doctor's surgery these days are freelances — designers, journalists, typesetters and entrepreneurs of all kinds — who often get into the habit of pushing themselves far harder than any employer would dare.

LIGHTEN THE MOOD

Has it ever struck you that many modern glass-walled office blocks are strangely gloomy inside? After all, we know that lighting is crucially important to people's moods and productivity. You would naturally think that abundant natural light from today's acres of window area would make for a generally cheery, upbeat and productive atmosphere.

But it's not as simple as that. Generally speaking, the people whose desks are nearest the windows get all the light they could wish for — and occasionally a good deal more than they'd choose. But the depth of many open-plan offices often causes problems.

In a fair-sized office floor of more than, say, 2,000 sq. ft, the innermost desks can be a long way from the daylight. If the lighting in this part of the office is not strong and positive enough, even the most jaunty individuals may find that working at these desks is unduly taxing and tiring.

A little light reading

Lighting can often account for over 50 per cent of the office electricity bill. The scope for savings can be substantial, since the energy efficiency of almost any office installation over five years old is likely to be low by modern standards.

Step 6 | **Health and Safety First for Productivity That Lasts**

> A fluorescent tube usually gives five times as much light as a bulb of the same wattage. Less energy is wasted by being converted into heat.
>
> The most usual cause of failure in strip lighting is the coating flaking off the electrodes or coils. These are only in action and heated up for a few seconds when the light is switched on. So what decides the life of a fluorescent tube is the number of times it is turned on and off, not the number of hours it is in use. With tungsten bulbs, it is the other way round – time is of the essence.
>
> Recent improvements in office lighting have focused on replacing twin-tube systems with single tubes and using reflectors so that less energy is wasted and running costs can be cut. High frequency control gear is claimed to give flicker-free light, longer lamp life and 20 per cent energy savings. Lighting systems which switch zones on and off automatically, under the control of photo-cells, infra red sensors or timers, have shown that they can reduce consumption dramatically and pay back investment costs in as little as two years.

Most experts recommend a general lighting level of about 500 Lux for ordinary admin work. Drop much below this and you start to run into problems of tiredness and glare caused by the contrast between screen illumination and ambient lighting. Large or complicated lighting problems should always be put in the hands of a specialist, who will combine practical experience of what works with a knowledge of the relevant legislation and the industry's codes of practice covering interior lighting.

Lighting design is a big subject, with plenty of pitfalls for the unwary. But there are several things you can do in an established office to make life more comfortable and improve productivity.

Arrange desking so that, wherever possible, people have a glimpse of the outside world, even if they are some distance from a window.

Consider buying extra desk lamps – task lighting, the experts call it – so that more individuals have more control over their own areas and their own pools of light on the desk.

If people are not entirely happy with the lighting, check whether you are using fluorescent tubes with high frequency ballast units. If not, try changing. High frequency ballasts produce less flicker, so many people find these lights less tiring over long periods.

Smart Office | 11 Steps to a User-Friendly Office

SHOULD WE BE WORRYING ABOUT SICK BUILDING SYNDROME?

There has been a lot of publicity recently about SBS – Sick Building Syndrome – which produces black moods, lethargy and quite disabling depression in some people. In extreme cases, SBS has also been blamed for allergic reactions, skin problems, aggravated asthmatic conditions and feelings of nausea or dizziness. All in all, it's distressing for people and costly for businesses.

Sick Building Syndrome has now been recognised by the World Health Organisation, even though it is still almost impossible to define. At long last, research has started to strip away some of the mystery about what causes it, focusing mainly on lack of natural ventilation and dust-free, pollution-free air.

But there are also a clutch of other elements, physical and psychological, that have now been identified as contributory factors. What is fascinating about recent research is the way it emphasises the interaction between the environment and the ethos in an office. Worldwide, there are no recorded cases of SBS in young, growing, rampagingly successful firms – though many of them operate for a time in cramped conditions and substandard premises. No one is saying it's all in the mind. But psychological factors obviously play a major role.

Sick buildings: the 10-point recipe for disaster

Here is the basic checklist of what every business needs to avoid. And though Sick Building Syndrome itself is relatively rare, the practical, common-sense points that are highlighted here are potentially relevant to every workplace. How does your office measure up?

1. **NO AIR:** Nothing beats an open window. In sealed offices, where ventilation depends entirely on the air conditioning system, this must be planned carefully and maintained in tip-top condition.
2. **BAD AIR:** Make sure the air conditioning doesn't recirculate a high proportion of return air and that the fresh air intake is not polluted. Materials that will be in the office, such as paints, carpeting, adhesives and inks, should be chosen with care, avoiding those which might give off irritating fumes.
3. **NO ROOM:** Overcrowding leads to frayed tempers and accidents and wears people down. Where space is tight, ventilation needs to be emphasised, with more air changes and air movement than elsewhere.
4. **NO TIME:** The dividing line between the physical atmosphere and the psychological atmosphere is hard to define. All undue stress affects performance, so that people work

DON'T BE GROUNDED BY BAD ORGANISATION AND PRESENTATION. TAKE OFF WITH CONCORD.

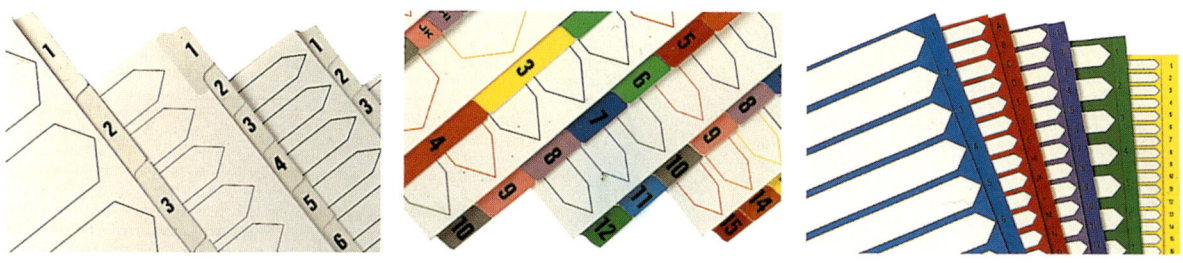

Even in the computer age, offices are prone to getting bogged down in paperwork. You can suffer in silence, pull your hair out, or get your nose in front with Concord filing products. We've indexes, dividers and files for every need, from organising your memos and computer print-outs to making presentations more professional. Don't waste time looking for lost letters and memos.

Use Concord indexes for easy retrieval and increased efficiency. In short the total solution to filing organisation.

So if you want your filing to be way out in front, make sure to ask for Concord by name.

I WANT MY FILING TO BE WAY OUT IN FRONT.
For a free copy of our informative, fun booklet on applications and products just fill in and send off the coupon.

Name..
Company...
Position...
Address...
....

Send to: The Jet Stationery Company Ltd., 163 Peckham Rye East, Peckham, London, England SE15 3HT
OR FAX: 0171 732 4963

EP3

Concord™
Quality that's way out in front

Think recycled

RECYCLED COPIER PAPER

RECYCLED ENVELOPES

RECYCLED LETTERHEAD

RECYCLED FLIP CHARTS

Think PANDA

If you want to show you care for the environment, the next time you need office stationery think about ordering PANDA from your stationery supplier.

PANDA is the only office stationery range developed in co-operation with WWF UK (World Wide Fund For Nature) – the international charity dedicated to the fight for nature.

That's because each and every product in the PANDA range is manufactured from recycled paper.

Which means you can order the copier paper, letterheads, note-pads and envelopes you need - and help conserve our precious natural resources at the same time.

PANDA from your office stationery supplier. Well worth thinking about.

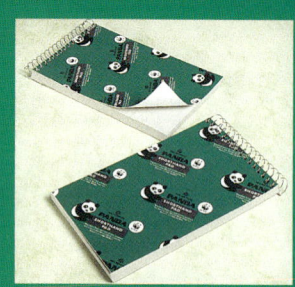

RECYCLED SHORTHAND NOTE P

RECYCLED A4 PADS

RECYCLED FILES

WIGGINS TEAPE
OFFICE PRODUCTS

Step 6 | Health and Safety First for Productivity That Lasts

less effectively and the jobs pile up and the pressure gets worse and their performance sags again and so on. High-stress offices are prime candidates for SBS epidemics.

5 **NO PEACE:** Irritating noises, even if they are not particularly loud, greatly increase the chances of SBS symptoms occurring. Jangling phones, clattering printers and abrasive bosses can all make their disturbing presence felt, even at a distance, and emphasise the absence of privacy in the office.

6 **NO QUIET:** Whether it's building work outside the window or people talking all around, the sheer volume of noise is frequently a factor in SBS. The use of screens and intelligent positioning of furniture can often make all the difference.

7 **HOTHOUSE ATMOSPHERE:** Poor temperature control can make anyone wilt. Roughly 19-26 degrees Centigrade is generally reckoned to be a reasonable working temperature. Oddly enough, though, the indoor plants that make some offices look like refugees from Kew Gardens can be more than just decorative. Many can absorb carbon monoxide from the air and some will even soak up formaldehyde molecules, which are given off by finishing materials and are often prime suspects in cases of SBS.

8 **POOR LIGHTING:** Lighting that is too dim or too bright and that flickers or distorts colours badly is often part of the story in offices where Sick Building Syndrome has been recognised.

9 **STATIC SHOCKS:** The wrong carpet and a dry atmosphere can lead to an office in which people walk on eggshells, half-expecting a crackle of static electricity every time they touch a door handle or a machine. This is exactly the kind of nagging, niggling, faintly unnerving irritant that is characteristic of SBS epidemics.

10 **LAB RAT FRENZY:** People need to feel they have some control over things in their immediate vicinity. In workplaces where there is no desk lamp to fiddle with, windows won't open and the furniture can't be adjusted, some people feel frustrated and put upon. Building in a little flexibility provides a vital safety valve.

DON'T RISK IT ALL ON A DISK

When disaster strikes, the fact is brutally underlined that the most valuable and irreplaceable assets of any business are its people and its information. Stock, plant and buildings can be restored or renewed on a like-for-like basis after a fire, a flood or a robbery. As long as your conventional insurance policies are adequate and kept up to date, the biggest body blow to the company is normally the time-lag before you get back to anything resembling business as usual.

But what happens if you are hit by the newly fashionable IT bandits? The problem is that these people break in to offices knowing exactly what they want. And what they want is a great deal more valuable to you than it is to them. They can no longer be bothered to steal whole PCs. So what they do is simply gut the computers and remove the chips and, far more seriously, the hard disks.

Smart Office | **11 Steps to a User-Friendly Office**

Chips you can replace – but anyone who has financial records, customer databases, survey data, membership lists or other vital information stored on a hard disk should take this as yet another last warning to back everything up regularly.

You can use floppies, tape streamers, data cartridges, mini-cartridges, Zip drives, CD-recordables, SyQuests, optical disks, magneto-opticals, removable hard disks or a blunt pencil and a lot of sheets of paper. Whatever technology you choose, the aim is to make sure your business does not skid to a halt if the hard disks go. And if you think it couldn't happen in your office, look what happened at the National Union of Journalists' London HQ recently. Thieves broke in through a security door in the underground garage and made a beeline for the second floor and the computers in the membership and finance offices, where they filleted the machines and walked off with their pockets full of chips and hard disks. It is a tribute to the NUJ's back-up systems that both departments were back in action within three days. But would your office be able to shrug off that kind of assault?

You may want to investigate the cost of a consequential loss or loss of profits policy or extension to protect you in this kind of situation (there may already be consequential loss cover in your fire insurance package). But premiums will be high and money, however welcome, will not instantly replace your lost data. It is far better to avoid the risk than rely on insurers to rescue you.

MISSING, PRESUMED EXPENSIVE

One of the most sobering experiences a manager can have in business is to sit down and work out who, in his or her company, is truly indispensable. Ideally, of course, nobody would be. In a perfect world, you would have trained and experienced staff able to slip smoothly into position to cover for any individual's absence, illness or abrupt departure.

In practice, there may be one particular sales negotiator, diamond cutter, centre forward, banjo player, midwife, software whiz-kid or Eurobond dealer in your organisation who possesses obviously unique technical skills. But there are also many businesses that revolve around one person with a different, non-technical kind of knowledge or expertise or an unrivalled network of close personal contacts among customers and suppliers.

People like this may have been with the company for many years, but they won't be there for ever. Mortality alone guarantees that. So if they are indispensable now, action should be taken to decant as much of their knowledge as possible into your databases or onto paper and spread it to others in the firm over a period of time. In the meantime, if their loss or absence would lead to direct and costly consequences for the business, it is realistic to consider taking out what is known (irrespective of the gender of the person insured) as a key man insurance policy.

This type of policy is particularly important in a partnership or a small limited company with only a handful of directors. If, say, 33 per cent of the equity is likely to be inherited and come under the control of a fairly distant relative as soon as the first of the three founding

Step 6 | **Health and Safety First for Productivity That Lasts**

directors dies, the firm has an interest in insuring all three. Rather than accommodate a powerful stranger on the board, it may want to have insurance cover on a scale that would allow the late director's shares to be bought in, coupled with a contractual arrangement giving the survivors that option.

IN A NUTSHELL
1. People are the greatest asset of every business

- Provide a safe environment for your most important resource
- Make sure it *feels* safe and comfortable, rather than just conforming to minimum standards

2. Find your way through the legislation

- Don't be daunted by the regulations – use them to help you
    - analysing the hazards in your own environment
    - reading the regulations that apply to you
    - keeping up to date with your legal responsibilities
- Organise the office with safety in mind
    - consider a safety audit
    - check whether your facilities are adequate
    - design a safety system
    - make somebody responsible for keeping it in working order

3. Check out the key areas

- First aid and accident prevention
- Fire regulations
- Computer system safety

4. Sick Building Syndrome

- What to watch out for
- 10-point recipe for disaster – prevention is better than cure

5. Cover for your vital assets

- Information resources
- Key people

STEP 7
TIME TO PUT ECO BEFORE EGO

Step 7 | **Time to Put Eco Before Ego**

GROWING GREENER GRACEFULLY
A CHANGE OF PERSPECTIVE

What's stopping every responsible manager and business in the country from going several shades greener, starting right now?

Generally speaking, it's no more than a lot of misguided and out-of-date ideas about cost and quality compromises, ignorance about how to go about it in ways that will make any significant difference and, unforgivably, the kind of caveman attitude that holds that only wimps and hippies care what sort of world our children will face 30 years from now.

Times have changed. There's a lot less guesswork about now and a lot more in the way of hard facts and authoritative advice. Many of today's eco-friendly products are strictly comparable, in quality and cost terms, with the items they are designed to replace. And there are certainly plenty of ruthlessly costed-out ways of making real cash savings by cutting back on the amount of energy your company uses or the quantities of raw materials wasted by inefficient production processes.

So what is really getting in the way is usually more to do with personalities than facts.

Just as some people won't give up smoking for the barmy and paradoxical reason that they have failed to do so in the past, some of those who seem most determined not to let environmental considerations get a look in are really trying to justify their past neglect.

It is just about possible to imagine the arguments an ingenious "conscientious objector" might put up (probably something along the line that says that individual actions at the micro level give governments, which should be taking radical action, the chance to slip off the hook). But most managers who refuse to take modest steps towards greener thinking have no intellectual basis for objection. They won't admit it, but they are digging their heels in mainly because they resent being told what they should do.

It may make a man feel tough and rebellious, like James Dean (and it is, almost without exception, male managers who take this line). But this personal contribution to making the

Smart Office | 11 Steps to a User-Friendly Office

world a worse place for everybody on it marks him out as a rebel without either a cause or a leg to stand on. It is a case of ego getting in the way of eco – and there's nothing very smart about that.

If green work means teamwork, there's a real payoff

Environmentalists are always telling us that "green" offices are more likely than others to be full of happy, healthy, shiny people. But which come first, the people or the policies?

Most people are more aware these days that the world environment is in danger and that they may be working in unpleasant and dangerous conditions which they can do something about. Twenty-five years ago, the average office worker had virtually no control over his working conditions. People are less willing now to put up with darkness, draughts, dirt and bad coffee. But does that make them feel more responsible about the rest of the planet, or just their own little eight-hour bubble on it?

A growing body of evidence seems to be indicating that it does lead people towards thinking in more global terms. Office managers who bother to provide air purifiers, good drinking water and a bit of greenery tend to set up a virtuous circle, an environment which is not just a pleasant background to people's routine jobs but a positive encouragement to recycling, co-operative working and posters of dolphins.

MUST WORK MEAN WASTE?

Awareness of waste and pollution, followed by action to counteract the damage, has generally been higher in people's offices than their homes. Offices use resources in a concentrated way. Waste paper, for example, tends to be more obvious at work than at home. People are more careless about throwing away partly used things which are not their own. They tend to take less care of equipment and products which they don't personally have to replace. The resulting backlash has made recycling easier to start in the workplace – and sometimes these attitudes get taken home. Good news and good habits can spread.

Awareness of environmental problems in the workplace is also high because many offices are in town centres. The most polluted and dirty parts of any country and every city are still, despite Telford and Milton Keynes, the industrial and business districts. People still commute to work in the kind of cramped and dirty conditions that make them very aware of overcrowding and environmental stress.

Step 7 Time to Put Eco Before Ego

IT'S THE SECOND STEP ON THE JOURNEY THAT COUNTS

But if awareness is the first step towards action, most people don't know where to step next. Many recent surveys of environmental awareness in the workplace have started optimistically with highly positive responses to questions about saving trees and recycling toner cartridges. Answers to the next question, about what is actually being done, make more depressing reading. Most people don't know how they can actually make a difference and can't be bothered to make much of an effort to find out.

But ignorance isn't a good enough excuse for inaction any more. There are a wide range of agencies offering advice, information and eco-friendly services. You can even call in a consultant (for around £100) to assess your office practices and environment and advise you about practical steps you can take to improve the situation.

BUY GREEN, DISPOSE CLEAN

Heightening awareness that you are all sitting on the same planet, using up the same finite resources, can be quite a team building exercise in itself. In one very important sense, every member of the organisation, from the chairman to the gopher, is ultimately in the same boat. So where do you start?

Being responsible about your environment in the office setting falls into two areas:

- being careful about what you purchase
- being careful about what you dispose of, and how and where you do it

Begin with what you buy. It's amazing how many recycled products are available now. Most office supplies catalogues cater for this growing demand and clearly mark their recycled and environmentally friendly products – though they often bestow upon them the honour of a premium price as well, with or without any cost justification.

The European Union has been slow to introduce a Europe-wide "green label" which would indicate compliance with high standards for both ingredients and recyclability. But the UK Ecolabelling Board now has this largely under control, with its own logo and a strict matrix of criteria which every product it labels must conform to.

Environmental Fields	Product Life Cycle				
	Pre-production	Production	Distribution & packaging	Utilisation	Disposal
Waste relevance					
Soil pollution and degradation					
Water contamination					
Noise					
Energy consumption					
Consumption of natural resources					
Effects on ecosystems					

Tackle the things you can change

It is worth taking a good look at this matrix chart and seeing how many of the products we regularly use actually measure up to it. You can never get perfection, but when you buy something – particularly a major item of equipment, try raising some of these questions, as well as the usual ones about efficiency and value for money.

- **Paper products** are what everyone thinks of first. But it's not just toilet rolls. Every paper product, from envelopes to hanging files, can be made from recycled materials.
- **Toner units** for faxes, copiers and printers can be refilled or recycled. In the early days, there was some controversy about whether refills lasted as long and were up to the same quality standards as new ones. This is less likely to be a problem now, but run your own tests and decide for yourself.
- **Office equipment** varies a great deal in terms of energy efficiency. If the salesman can't tell you how it measures up, the chances are that energy saving *isn't* one of its big selling points. Manufacturers usually make a feature of this if they have built it in.
- **Lighting** burns quite a lot of energy. But you can cut this substantially without losing

Step 7 Time to Put Eco Before Ego

sight of your safety exit sign. A conventional incandescent light bulb works by heating a tungsten filament until it glows white hot, which is an inefficient way of producing light. Far more efficient bulbs have been developed, known as compact fluorescent lamps or CFLs. These give the same light output from just 20 per cent of the energy, reducing pollution and immediate running costs by 80 per cent. They also last up to eight times as long. So although they are more expensive to buy, they work out cheaper in the long run. And that's not allowing for savings on labour associated with frequent replacement of bulbs in awkward places, over stairwells and in high roof fittings.

- **Tropical hardwood** is still used in making a lot of "prestige" office furniture. When you are revamping the chairman's office, try to persuade him to go high tech and use modern materials, rather than traditional mahogany (or even iroko and meranti if he has really exotic tastes). Avoidance is best, because even when manufacturers claim to insist on sustainable forest management, it's worth bearing in mind that only 0.2 per cent of tropical forests are actually managed in anything like a truly sustainable fashion. If only one forest area in 500 is managed sustainably, you've got to be very naive just to take the manufacturer's word for it that your wood comes from one of these rare and precious sources.
- **Consumables**. Cleaning materials, correcting fluid and pens vary in the way they are made and packaged. Look out for the Eco label and avoid anything which is over-packaged or uses ozone-layer-eating CFCs.

What can we start recycling?

One tonne of office waste will have been responsible for the creation of five tonnes of waste at the manufacturing stage and 20 tonnes of waste at the point of extraction of the raw materials. Manufacturers are slowly becoming more responsible, but you can speed up the process, from the consumer end, by thinking carefully about what you buy and what you do with things once you've used them.

Office recycling always needs a champion and it is often the facilities manager who can make it happen. Fortunately, it has never been easier than it is today. Waste Watch and some other organisations publish guides to recycled products, from adding machine rolls to water butts (useful for collecting water for the plants in the truly environmentally aware office). It is predicted that, in ten years' time, almost everything may well have to be recyclable. But, for now, the easiest places to start are with paper, drinks containers and plastics.

- **Paper**
  For every person in the office, an average of 3kg of waste paper each month is used but not collected for recycling. For a department of ten people, this would mean that three

Smart Office | **11 Steps to a User-Friendly Office**

large sacks of paper would be put in landfills every month. Make a contribution to lowering these figures by calling your local collectors and finding out:
- the minimum amounts they will collect
- when they are in your area
- how the paper should be sorted (some recyclers won't collect low grade paper any more, so you may need to take this to a collection point yourself)
- how to package your waste for collection
- whether the collection team will take anything else besides paper

If you can't find the appropriate names and numbers in your local directory, check the back of this book for contact points.

- **Aluminium and glass**
  Tailor your methods to your output. If you are a small office, all you need is a carrier bag on a hook for each type of material, so that it can be taken by hand to the nearest recycling point. Move up to separate, clearly labelled bins and then to regular collections if you really generate the stuff on a large scale.

- **Plastic**
  Many people don't think about recycling plastic. But it's a growing market and can now be made into a wood substitute and turned into garden furniture and traffic cones. It can also be broken down into materials which can be used to make duvets, quilted jackets and fleeces (thus neatly completing the cycle by saving energy use for heating somewhere else).

REDUCING WASTE

The less you use, the less you have to buy and recycle. The two main areas for cutting back on waste are paper and energy.

Six ways to stop wasting energy

- **1. Use what you need, but save some for later.**
  A UK government report published in 1990 showed that it would be practical and cost effective to more than halve electricity use for lighting in the UK, simply through improvements in lighting efficiency. You can start by switching off the power when it is not needed. But it's hard to train people to do this, unless you install speakers that say "Thank you" every time someone switches something off. It might be easier to take some of the human element out of the equation by installing one of the new energy-

saving systems. These combine the latest fluorescent lighting technology with sensor-operated control systems that switch off when there is enough daylight or when there is no one in the room.

- **2. Insulate the office.**
Avoid heating the outside world by closing doors, filling cavity walls with foam or fibreglass and draught-proofing windows and doors in older buildings.

- **3. Think things through.**
Would a solar panel on your roof (depending on your budget and location) pay its way and reduce your energy consumption? Incidentally, make sure you are plugged into the mains whenever possible. People seldom realise that batteries use up to 50 times as much energy to manufacture as they produce – and most of them leak mercury when they are scrapped, too.

- **4. Keep moving.**
Promote fitness, save on heating and increase sales by encouraging people to spend less time sitting down. Almost everyone knows now that if you want to sound convincing on the phone you should be standing up and smiling as you are talking. Some ultra-modern offices in California even encourage meetings on the move by cutting back on desks and seating and providing temporary "leaning areas" with whiteboards in corridors and communal rooms. Colleagues pause, exchange ideas, maybe sketch a diagram or two, and then move on.

- **5. Peddle your ideas.**
Sell the idea of a greener routine to others in the company and start a new cycle of energy savings by getting on your bike and encouraging your co-workers to do the same. A few enlightened organisations even have bicycle fleets and covered cycle sheds (possibly with designated smoking areas behind them). Shower cubicles can be added to restrooms for those who want to combine commuting with their exercise schedules. It generally costs less to add a few showers to a building than to pay inner city prices for rented parking spaces. A cycling magazine recently came up with the figure of 7p per mile all-in-cost for commuting by bicycle, including insurance, replacement of parts, regular servicing and depreciation.

This figure was hotly disputed by regular commuters, who claimed it was based on a top-of-the-line mountain bike (not really necessary in flat areas like the Thames basin) with all the latest gadgets. Their figure was more like 4p per mile. And if you deduct from that the cost of your annual subscription to the local health and fitness centre, it may well work out to be even more economical.

Smart Office | 11 Steps to a User-Friendly Office

- **6. Go public.**
  Encourage workers to use public transport by providing interest-free season ticket loans. If your offices are out of town, you can make car pooling easier by setting up schedules, notice boards and e-mailed rotas.

Six ways to stop wasting forests

Many thousands of trees have been sacrificed to the noble cause of writing about the paperless office that was supposed to follow on from the computer revolution. Unfortunately, computer manuals are still some of the largest unread and unrecycled waste paper items around. Until the day comes when you can recycle your wastepaper basket, you can, at least, try to put less into it.

- **1. Stop junk mail.**
  Nobble it at source by calling the Mailing Preference Service (0171 738 1625).

- **2. Re-use envelopes.**
  Do it whenever you can – starting, perhaps, with internal mail.

- **3. Use both sides of the paper.**
  At the very least, use the second side of old documents for your draft printouts.

- **4. Proof as much as possible on the screen.**
  Printing out early drafts that you know are nowhere near ready is almost a nervous tic.

- **5. Learn to use e-mail properly.**
  Start with the proper use of the delete key and print only as a last resort.

- **6. Don't go for disposable cups and kitchenware.**
  You know coffee tastes better out of your own mug anyway.

A GOOD WORKING ATMOSPHERE DOESN'T JUST HAPPEN

The differences between the kind of office that people feel comfortably at home in and the ones that lead to mutterings about possible cases of Sick Building Syndrome can be hard to pin down. SBS is still controversial. Despite the World Health Organisation view that it is a genuine medical problem, there are still plenty of managers who think it's just an excuse for skiving – and plenty of double-dyed sceptics who think it's just a symptom of bad

Step 7 | **Time to Put Eco Before Ego**

management. But there's no doubt about the effect the atmosphere in an office can have on people's productivity, so why take chances? Whether it's all in the mind or something in the air, try doing what you can to move towards a better office environment. Follow up with a survey to see how aware of the difference people are. Even if you're in the city centre or under a flyover, there are still several straightforward steps you can take to keep your own air clean and create your own oasis of calm, comfort and sanity.

- Buy some air ionisers (an ioniser costs less than a toner refill) and see if they have an impact on the number of coughs, colds and minor ailments next winter.
- Enforce a strict no smoking policy, if you don't have one already. This has also been proved to reduce absenteeism, though it may lengthen comfort breaks for the remaining smokers.
- Install screen filters on your VDUs. Quite apart from cutting out glare, they constitute a signal to your people that you care about the details of their welfare.
- Involve everybody. Most of us are closet hypochondriacs, so why not start a suggestion box, to generate ideas for making the office environment healthier and more pleasant?

If you can make some changes for the better, you will undoubtedly end up with healthier, happier and more productive people and a more profitable organisation.

GOING GREENER NEEDN'T BE AN UPHILL STRUGGLE

You may still face comments about being a hippy environmentalist, but most people will go along with any sensible green initiatives if you make it easy enough for them.

- Make recycling simple and routine by having bins, clearly marked, at all the strategic points – by the copier and printers, at the post sorting desk and in the kitchen for aluminium and glass.
- If you think your executives will object to the rougher appearance of recycled paper, make a feature of it by making sure every piece of paper advertises the fact that you are an environment-conscious company. After all, the Body Shop built its fortune that way. You may opt for the prominent green tree logo and go for deeper colours than you are used to. This is quite acceptable nowadays, particularly if you make a great play of your virtue in this area.
- Publicise the cause. There are some very professional-looking and convincing posters and information sheets you can get hold of for nothing (see list at the back of the book). Stick them up in places where they'll be seen: by the kettle, by the copier and on the backs of loo doors. You have so many captive audiences going to waste.

- Tap the power of peer pressure. If you are part of a large organisation, start posting up details of the recycling achievements of different groups or teams. You might even think about introducing competitions and prizes for the most ingenious ideas or the greatest weight of paper collected for salvage.

CLEANING UP YOUR OFFICE SPACE

Like the Teflon frying pan, the idea of using plants to mop up airborne pollution and remove specific poisons from the air in today's sealed, energy-efficient offices is one of those rare space race spin-offs that is making a useful difference here below.

It all started with NASA, America's National Aeronautics and Space Administration, and its attempts, over many years, to create self-sustaining life support systems for use in deep space.

NASA's top researcher in this field was Dr Bill Wolverton, a former chemical and germ warfare specialist, who is now America's leading advocate of plants for clean air.

Wolverton's experiments underlined the way bio-effluents (all the substances given off by humans, through the skin, by breathing and so on) can combine with chemical traces, micro-organisms, humidity and a build-up of carbon dioxide to create a polluted and uncomfortable working environment. But they also showed that many common house plants were surprisingly effective at grabbing toxins and pollution out of the air and cleaning it up.

Breathe green, breathe easy

The particular troublemakers are substances like formaldehyde, trichloroethylene (TCE) and benzene, which are present in many offices. Traces are given off by carpeting, copiers, computers, chipboard and fibreboard, foam insulation, paint and sealants and can lead office workers to complain of itchy eyes, headaches, blocked noses, sore throats and stomach aches. These chemicals are not good for your long-term health either – trichloroethylene and benzene, which are found in some inks, paints and adhesives, are both believed to be carcinogenic.

But the effects of introducing ordinary, familiar plants are remarkable. The NASA research showed that *nephrolepis exaltata* (an unassuming evergreen fern), pot chrysanthemums, philodendrons, English ivy, mother-in-law's tongue and weeping figs topped a long list of house plants that could quickly lower the level of formaldehyde in the air. Peace lilies, dragon trees and English ivy were all effective at removing trichloroethylene and benzene. Spider plants simply eat up carbon monoxide and formaldehyde and these and other plants can also remove other noxious chemicals such as xylene, chloroform, ammonia, acetone and methyl alcohol – all of which are quite commonly found in modern buildings.

Step 7 | Time to Put Eco Before Ego

Cool, comfortable and cold-free

The latest twist to this tale comes from very recent research at the horticulture department of Reading University, where the emphasis was more on the ability of common plants to "air condition" an office. Rather than looking at the question of removing pollutants, the researchers investigated how much help plants could give in terms of keeping temperatures and carbon dioxide concentrations down and stopping the air getting too dry (which makes workers susceptible to colds).

The weeping fig (*ficus benjamina*) again emerged as a star, though there were also promising results with hibiscus and rubber plants (*ficus elastica*). *Benjamina*'s high rate of photosynthesis made it very effective at lowering carbon dioxide concentrations during the daytime (though, logically enough, the effect was reversed at night) and boosted the relative humidity in the experimental office.

A number of experimental buildings, both in Britain and the US, are using large, heavily planted atrium spaces to minimise the need for conventional air conditioning. But Bill Wolverton and a handful of other pioneers are already daring to think about possible designs for large-scale buildings where plants could take over the whole job of keeping the air fresh, cool and clean.

For those working in more mundane surroundings, though, there's no doubt that having plants around can make a substantial difference to the office environment at very low cost. It is not likely to impose a great burden on the office management team, either, since almost all the plants mentioned above need an absolute minimum of watering and attention. The worst thing you can do with a mother-in-law's tongue is take any notice of it. Just leave it alone and it will repay your hospitality by improving the atmosphere in the office every day of the year.

IN A NUTSHELL

1. Wasteful, polluting office practices are a bad habit

- The macho attitude of getting on with business instead of fiddling about with recycling schemes can actually be counter-productive
- Good eco-practice produces short-term improvements in morale as well as long-term ones in air quality:
    - fitter, better-tempered people
    - a spirit of co-operation and teamwork
    - a wider perspective on the aims of the organisation as well as life and the universe
- It's easier to get recyclable materials collected in large amounts

Smart Office | 11 Steps to a User-Friendly Office

2. The office is a good place to start saving the world

- Waste is more obvious in the office
- Workplaces (not just factories) tend to be more polluted than homes
- Action taken by groups can seem more meaningful and satisfying than action by individuals or families

3. Buying eco-friendly products

- European labelling standards make it easy to see what you're buying
- Draw up a chart and check what you buy
- Foster product and resource awareness – stay up to date

4. Reducing waste

- Paper and energy are the main areas where savings can be made

5. Recycling

- Taking responsibility (or giving it to someone else) and getting it organised
- Raising awareness and creating a sympathetic climate
- Designing a system that people take seriously

6. Promoting a pollution-free office

- Clean air (using plants or ionisers)
- Reduced emissions (check your equipment)

STEP 8: TRUST TEAMS TO WORK

Step 8 | Trust Teams To Work

POSITIVE TEAM BUILDING
THIS IS NO TIME TO BE MANAGING PEOPLE

Of course you want to get the best out of the resources that are available to you. And the science of doing that is known as management. But in the smart office you really do not want to be spending your time managing people, in the old, controlling, disciplinarian ways.

Life's too short to waste it standing over people. You want to be able to manage projects and activities, at the head of a largely self-managing team of people who take responsibility for their own work. So how do you find the individuals who can make that kind of self-reliant system work for you? And how do you hold on to them, once you have trained them and taught them everything you know?

The right people are the key to a successful enterprise. Finding them is hard enough. But keeping them, once you have got them, is just as important. There are serious costs involved in hauling even the brightest newcomer up the learning curve and you cannot afford to have to restart and retrain people every few months. Apart from the cash costs, high staff turnover leads to low morale and damages both customer confidence and business performance.

Keeping people doesn't usually revolve around money, though that may come into it. What will usually count for much more is what used to be called, rather blandly, "job satisfaction" – a nebulous factor that generally boils down to questions about whether the individual feels stretched and flattered by the challenges of the job and whether he or she is really making a difference by being there. The facilities manager or office manager who takes these things seriously does not often have to resort to straight cash incentives to keep the team together.

How do you find the right candidates for the job?

In a large organisation, the human resources department (the artists formerly known as

Smart Office | **11 Steps to a User-Friendly Office**

Personnel) will usually have the hiring and firing documented and regulated down to the last application form and job profile. In smaller businesses, it may well fall to the MD, general manager or office manager to select all the people needed for success. This is tricky, because you probably won't know all the ins and outs of every job you are hiring people to do for you.

There are a number of options:

- Use an agency that you trust, that has been recommended or that has given good results in the past. Some of the most persuasive sales people in Britain work for recruitment agencies, but they may know very little about your business or the person they are trying to place.
- If you have the time and the expertise, do it yourself. You know your office and you know your staff better than anyone else. You have the vision of the future. You also know what your new staff member should look and sound like and what he or she has to be able to do. There's a word of caution needed here though – you also know yourself. If you have any soft spots that might make you less than impartial when faced with a certain sort of candidate, get someone else to give you a second opinion.

If you do it yourself, be aware of how long it is likely to take. Cost out your time and the advertising fees and balance them against commercial recruitment fees (£1,000 to £2,000 or more). The whole process is likely to work out like this:

Prepare advertisement and place in evening paper	Cost £30 – £100	2 hours
Typical response to advertisement for admin staff at any level	50+ telephone calls Each call takes just long enough to decide who is: • Unsuitable (anyone who cannot make themselves clearly understood or who is eating) • Worth looking at. Ask for CV, either faxed or posted. Give extra points to those arriving first • Be prepared to describe the job briefly to anyone who sounds interesting 5 minutes per call	4/5 hours

136

Step 8 Trust Teams To Work

Prepare lists of criteria and interview questions	You will need: – a profile of the person – a job description – a set of questions to ask on the phone – a set of questions to ask in interview – a set of questions to ask the references – a set of criteria for final selection	**3 hours**
Read through CVs. Interview approx. one in four	Eliminate anyone whose CV is not immaculate or whose letter is illiterate. You may not get through to people when you first ring. Allow 10 minutes per call.	**2 hours**
Writing to unsuccessful candidates	Some firms don't bother and just tell the ones who ring up. This is unacceptably bad manners – and anyway, you might need to call on these very same people again, if the appointment you make does not work out.	**1 hour**
Interviewing up to 15 candidates	Include simple aptitude tests.	**22 hours**
Taking up references	One written and one verbal, both business, from every person you seriously consider appointing – without exception.	**3 hours**
Calling 2 or 3 candidates in for second interview	The rest of the team should be present for at least part of this. Allow for debriefing.	**5 hours**
Writing to unsuccessful shortlist candidates	Brief, polite and amiable letter. Do not be patronising. Do not imply any commitment with respect to future vacancies.	**1 hour**
Total time spent	**At least one 50-hour week**	

This may seem like a huge investment of time. But weigh it against the time you would spend trying to teach the job to an unsuitable candidate, working out how to get rid of one if you didn't succeed and patching up the damage to morale among the remaining workers. Hiring

Smart Office | 11 Steps to a User-Friendly Office

the wrong person is not only a waste of time and resources. It's actually detrimental to the way your business runs, affecting other staff and, possibly, even clients as well.

INTERVIEWING

Even if you get an agency to make you a shortlist, you still have to make the final choice yourself. At least one software company in the US has now developed recruitment programs so that companies can get their computers to do some of the interviewing for them. They found that prospective candidates are less likely to lie to computers than to real people when asked questions like "How long do you plan to stay?"

This only goes to show that interviewing is a subtle skill which few people take the trouble to master. It's probably better to rely on a well-written computer program than a poor interviewer. But it would be better still to improve your interviewing skills and use the computer programs for back-up and comparison. What would you do if, when you printed out the interviewee's answers to the questionnaire, they contradicted the verbal answers he gave you in the interview?

Some people have a natural gift for seeing through whatever human facade is presented to them and understanding the real person behind it. The rest of us, however, can muster about 90 per cent of the skill with careful preparation and plenty of practice. This may well mean interviewing far more candidates than you need, for the first few years, until you find that you are able to predict with increasing accuracy the kind of person who will fill the post the way you want it filled. Don't be afraid to do that. It may take time, but getting the right people is almost priceless. Provided you are courteous and respect the candidate's interest in your firm, you will be benefiting him or her as well by providing live interview practice.

Conventional wisdom is that the time and effort you spend on an interview should match the status of the job. In fact, firing someone because you made the wrong choice rates only a few notches below being fired yourself on the stress scale. And most people feel more distress when firing a person lower down the scale than they do about firing someone at their own level.

So don't skimp on the interview. And if your record for hiring the right people doesn't improve, get someone else to do it. There are some things you will never find out from a CV and a form.

The best place to start in an interview is with a cup of tea or coffee. It relaxes people and lowers their guard. Making people comfortable before you give them the third degree also ensures that you don't disqualify an excellent but superficially nervous candidate, so everybody has a better chance of getting what is wanted.

Step 8 | **Trust Teams To Work**

FIRST IMPRESSIONS

Yes, appearances do matter. Whatever your profession, the chances are it will have a dress code of some kind, whether it's casual, outrageous, or designer suits. Most people who apply for a job are well aware of what is expected in the kind of business they are in. If candidates are serious about an administrative post in a firm of accountants they are going to come to interviews looking smart. If they arrive unwashed and in jeans it may mean they have very little experience of that particular working environment. It may also mean that they are making statements about their individuality or lack of self-esteem, which might make it hard for them to cope in an office where traditional roles and responsibilities are taken for granted.

START WITH THE CV

Read the CV carefully *before* you sit down with the applicant. It's easy to miss discrepancies in lists of dates and places if you are trying to talk to someone and read at the same time. Go through it and mark any areas that don't look right.

When you have both the person and the paperwork in front of you, explain that you want the candidate to talk you through the CV. This is a comfortable starting point – both sides have a structure and know where they are going. Control the talk-through, starting at the beginning and paying special attention to any potential problem areas you have marked in advance.

If you adopt a warm and interested manner you can get away with asking questions which might otherwise seem threatening or stupid. It's perfectly OK to ask: "Was this a full-time course? Which college was it? What sort of certificate did you get?" A two-hour-per-week typing class can appear in print as a one-year full-time secretarial course. The candidate could actually have been doing anything at all during the day, from having triplets to serving a prison sentence for embezzling funds from a previous employer. Neither the babies nor the fraud may necessarily disqualify them from the job you are offering, but you owe it to your company to know the facts.

Gaps in the CV are often very cleverly disguised. But once you start to question people directly you can easily spot the sticky areas, even if you don't actually get to the truth. If you suspect that "restaurant management" means washing up, ask the applicant to describe a typical working day. Challenge him or her to explain exactly what skills gained during those years on the mink farm could be put to use in running your customer service desk.

Smart Office | 11 Steps to a User-Friendly Office

DON'T LET YOUR PREJUDICES WORK AGAINST YOU

Be aware of any prejudices you may have yourself, in relation to race, religion, sex or disability. You will be giving yourself a better chance of finding exactly the right person for the job if you can clear any blind spots you may have – simply because you will have more choice.

Be sensitive to the possibility of accusations of prejudice. The policy of equal opportunities, while being an excellent principle, is occasionally exploited by job candidates who have more to hide from a potential employer than they have to offer.

Be fair to your business. If the firm doesn't get the right people to do the jobs, then, ultimately, it may not survive – and that doesn't help anyone. That may mean not being afraid to ask someone questions which they may feel are personal, but which do affect their ability to do the job. These may touch on sensitive areas such as childcare, pregnancy, the ability of a Muslim woman to work comfortably in an office full of men or the safety of a partially-sighted person in a particular office environment. Prepare well for interviews where this kind of issue may arise. Focus only on the facts which affect the job and avoid crossing the boundary into areas which are not your concern. If your potential bookkeeper chooses to spend his weekends trainspotting or lounging around an exclusive bar dressed as a rubber wasp, it's none of your business's business.

COMPULSORY QUESTIONS

- **Why did you leave?** *Always* press for reasons for leaving each job – if you are a good lie detector, this is the time to pay some attention to eye movements.
- **Do you have children?** They don't have to answer this, of course. But if they won't, you may want to ask yourself why. After all, many adults do have them, and most parents can't wait to talk about them. If the answer is yes, you are quite entitled to ask about ages and childcare arrangements – just as you would be justified in asking about travel time if your candidate was planning to commute to London from Leeds daily. Defensive or aggressive reactions to any reasonable questions in this area may well indicate problems.

22 CATCH QUESTIONS

Considering the number of good books on interview technique that are available, it's surprising that so many people still get stuck when you ask them "What aren't you good at?" All job candidates who are worth their salt will have worked out the answers to all of the standard questions. But you do still need to ask them, because it's a good way of eliminating the people who don't bother to prepare for an interview. People who do their homework before coming to see you are more likely to take a similarly conscientious approach to the job itself.

Change the pace of the interview at least once and don't save the usual questions until last. Dot them around your walk through the CV, so that they come when they're not expected. You're more likely to get real answers that way.

1. What are you not very good at?
2. What is your energy level like? Describe a typical day.
3. Where would you like to be in five years' time?
4. What was it that attracted you to apply for this particular position?
5. What is your USP, your unique selling point, as far as this job is concerned?
6. Describe a situation where you solved a tricky problem in the workplace.
7. Is there anything you don't like doing?
8. What do your colleagues say about you?
9. What did you dislike about your last job?
10. What did you like about your last job?
11. What sort of people do you like to work with?
12. Are you a team player?
13. How do you deal with people who let you down?
14. What do you think would be the most crucial aspects of this job?
15. Are you willing to be flexible about hours?
16. What is the job you have least enjoyed?
17. What is the job you enjoyed most?
18. Why did you leave it?
19. Is there anything you would change about this job, from what you know so far?
20. How long would you be staying with us?
21. What is your greatest professional achievement so far?
22. How do you react to working under pressure?

Always ask two or more questions which are similar (like numbers 1, 7 and 9 here, for example). It's useful to be able to check for consistency in the answers.

Print yourself a checklist of these questions (or draw up your own), with boxes for the candidate's answers, so that you can note them down during the interview. It's a useful exercise to go through them again after the candidate has left.

HEALTH

This is a whole subject on its own, because it's the one question you can't ask straight out with any hope of enlightenment. Nobody *ever* tells you whether they are mad or ill in an interview, just as nobody ever writes anything but "excellent health" on a CV.

It takes a skilled interviewer who is adept at relaxing candidates and getting them to open up to spot the person who feels entitled to several attacks of flu per winter, who gets "run down" and "overdoes it". It's actually more difficult to deal with the person who is normally well and highly motivated but suffers from something both real and acute. These people tend to be much better at concealing their heart attacks or their schizophrenic episodes.

Health isn't just about the candidate in front of you either. Some people seem to have a whole infrastructure of significant others whose health problems impinge on their working lives. And it's not just children. The kind of person whose children have every ailment known to Penelope Leach generally also has cats with rheumatism, parents with his and hers heart murmurs and a partner with ME.

Of course, these things aren't absolutes. It's a well known fact that self-employed people are rarely ill and that people who are too sick to make it into the office can sometimes drag themselves out the same evening to play for the darts team. We're back into the realms of motivation here, which means that, if you pick the *right* person for the job in the first place, there's less chance of time being lost through sickness.

But wait. Shouldn't the candidate be responsible for deciding whether he or she is applying for the right job or not?

Not in times of high unemployment and social instability. Desperation and lack of realism about their own capabilities can drive people to put themselves in positions they can't handle. On the other hand, you know exactly what the job entails, what the pressures are and what kind of person the team needs. In the end, it is down to your judgment to decide, for your sake and the candidate's, whether there would be a good, functional match between the person and the post.

USING PROFESSIONAL HELP

There's a lot to be said for psychometric testing – particularly if you have done your own homework well and have a clear profile of the person you are looking for (this should include the type of personality which would fit in best with the team, as well as the formal skill requirements of the job itself). Hiring professionals to do this testing can be expensive, however. If you interview often, it may be worth investing in some training that will qualify you to run psychometric tests yourself.

BE YOUR OWN INDUSTRIAL PSYCHOLOGIST

If you can't afford or don't have time to get professional help, here's a rough and ready type of personality matrix you can use for rule-of-thumb guidance. You will have to insert your own criteria and add some extra lines if you need to. Don't make it too long and

Step 8 | Trust Teams To Work

complicated or it will be cumbersome to score your impressions while you're talking to candidates.

1 scores low and 10 scores high.

Aggressive	1	2	3	4	5	6	7	8	9	10
Passive	1	2	3	4	5	6	7	8	9	10
Team player	1	2	3	4	5	6	7	8	9	10
Flexible	1	2	3	4	5	6	7	8	9	10
Staying power	1	2	3	4	5	6	7	8	9	10
Likely to get on with clients	1	2	3	4	5	6	7	8	9	10
Likely to get on with colleagues	1	2	3	4	5	6	7	8	9	10
Likely to get on with managers	1	2	3	4	5	6	7	8	9	10
Relevant experience	1	2	3	4	5	6	7	8	9	10
Skills in *****	1	2	3	4	5	6	7	8	9	10
Location	1	2	3	4	5	6	7	8	9	10
Paper qualifications	1	2	3	4	5	6	7	8	9	10

GOOD SIGNS TO WATCH OUT FOR

- Candidates who ask you questions about the job first and the pay and conditions last
- Anyone who *doesn't* say:
    "I don't suffer fools gladly"
    "I'm a bit of a perfectionist" (a total perfectionist is all right)
    "I don't like filing – but I don't mind doing it."

GETTING THE TRUTH IN REFERENCES

It's amazing how often people don't bother to take up references, and how many times they accept the photocopied standard letters which candidates produce at interviews. The reference is the only way you can check on whether someone is telling you the truth about themselves or not.

The rules about taking up references are:

- Go for three at least, including two professional ones and one from the last employer.
- Go for verbal references if the referees are willing. Referees may lie because:
    – they want to get rid of someone who is an impossible employee but who has not done anything definably wrong and who will create more problems if this

interview doesn't turn into a job
- they have a personal interest, which is not disclosed, as well as a professional one which is
- they feel embarrassed about having hired such a no-hoper themselves and do not want to admit it
- they think the candidate may react aggressively if he or she finds out about a bad reference

Even if one of these reasons is lurking in the background, the referee will be far more likely to tell you the truth than write it down, especially if you make it clear that your discussion is firmly "off the record".

Ask the referee some detailed questions. Don't just enquire whether Mr X was a satisfactory employee. Be specific.

Was he a good timekeeper?
Did he get on with both his managers and his customers?
Was he a team player?
Did he do the job intelligently?
Was he healthy and motivated?
Why did he leave?

This makes it much more likely that you will get at least one or two realistic answers, rather than just one superficial one. If the referee is actually being bribed or blackmailed by your candidate, nothing will tease out the truth. But most people do take this sort of enquiry fairly seriously, especially in larger companies. There may be a rule, in larger firms, though, that all references must be in written form and must be kept on file.

MANAGING AND MOTIVATING STAFF
PERFORMANCE MANAGEMENT

Once you have found and recruited the right staff, you have to tackle the two great challenges of modern management — motivating people to give you their ideas and energy, as well as their time, and keeping them for as long as your business needs them.

In an office environment, where people are often working very closely with each other day in and day out, social tensions and friction can build up. Routine, repetitive elements in the workload can drive your brightest employees wild with frustration and there may be little opportunity to offer people a radical change of scenery or task.

It is this kind of situation that poses the toughest problems for the motivational manager — far more than inspiring people to feats of endurance and derring-do in a struggle against

Step 8 | Trust Teams To Work

nature or opposing forces. It was once said of Field Marshal Montgomery that his genius as a general was proved by the fact that the Pay Corps began to believe it could turn the tide in the North African campaign.

The traditional tools used in classical performance management programmes are known, in the technical jargon, as carrots and sticks.

Carrots	Bonus or incentive schemes, commission-based pay and performance-related pay
Sticks	Disciplinary procedures of all kinds

The most common major disciplinary procedure is to fire the substandard employee, since corporal punishment was banned from the workplace long before it became illegal in schools. Demotion is also a possibility in large companies, although it tends to have a demoralising effect not only on the downgraded employee but on his or her colleagues as well.

Since computers have made a lot of the traditional donkey work in the office unnecessary, carrots and sticks are now supported by more sophisticated techniques. These are generally based on the principle that treating employees more like human beings will help persuade them to bring their human intelligence and creativity to the workplace, instead of leaving them behind at home.

Every organisation has a different name for these new techniques. But they all work in a similar way, by building in a kind of artificial "family" network of communication and support. Individuals are mentored and coached by their managers, formed into teams and paired off in buddy systems. They are encouraged to set up self-help groups to discuss their goals, their ambitions and their progress both inside and outside the company. Sometimes the company will provide a facilitator to get the groups off to a good start.

Sometimes and in some places, of course, this kind of thing happens naturally. In modern firms with high staff turnover, high stress and great insecurity, it often doesn't. But if there's a company rule which says that each manager must spend at least an hour with each member of staff every month or so, it builds in consistency of communication and opportunity.

TIME FOR TALKING AND TARGETING

But what do they actually talk about in that one hour per month? Guidelines are needed to help both sides through this initially stressful quality time. When people are first told that their professional development sessions are nothing to do with pay, promotion or discipline, they tend to lose interest. But after a few sessions even the most sceptical of managers usually sees an improvement in his relationship with even the most stroppy members of staff.

Frequently the areas covered are:

> Smart Office | 11 Steps to a User-Friendly Office

- competencies and employability
- personal problems which may impinge on performance
- upgrading of skills
- levels of performance

Often the discussions lead to SMART (specific, measurable, affordable, realistic and time-related) target setting for each individual, encouraging people to strive to improve their performance by setting themselves some higher standards or wider areas of development to stretch out for. A famous study of Harvard students interviewed in their college days and followed up 30 years later showed that the 5 per cent of youngsters in the original survey who had actually written down their personal and professional goals had achieved more in the intervening years than the other 95 per cent put together.

If people formulate and write down goals for themselves, they are more likely to achieve them. People who are aiming for the stars are usually energised and motivated in all areas of their lives, including work.

The key to helping people set goals against which they can measure their own performance is to ensure that these goals have a dual function – they must have real value for both the individual and the company.

Bonjour, mesdames et messieurs...

On the London Underground, for example, even the ticket collectors are now coached by their managers and encouraged to set SMART targets for themselves.

As one of the train drivers said recently:

"At first I thought this targets business was just a way of getting us to do more work without paying us any extra money. But then my crew manager told me I had to think of something that would benefit me, as well as the Tube. That really made me think about my future and I remembered I used to be pretty good at languages at school, though I couldn't be bothered to stay on for A-levels.

"The management agreed to pay for my French evening classes, provided I would make announcements in French whenever it seemed appropriate. At first, I got my teacher to help me write out some simple ones for stations like Victoria and now I'm more or less making them up as I go along. I've got my name down for an exchange with the Paris Metro next year and I feel I'm really making a contribution. My mates have stopped teasing me about it – in fact, one of them's doing German at the moment!"

One manager in another large organisation regards the effect of target setting as little short of magical. It seemed to tap into a power source in some employees that was normally capped off in the workplace and only used at home, he said.

Quality Office Products For Your Business Needs.

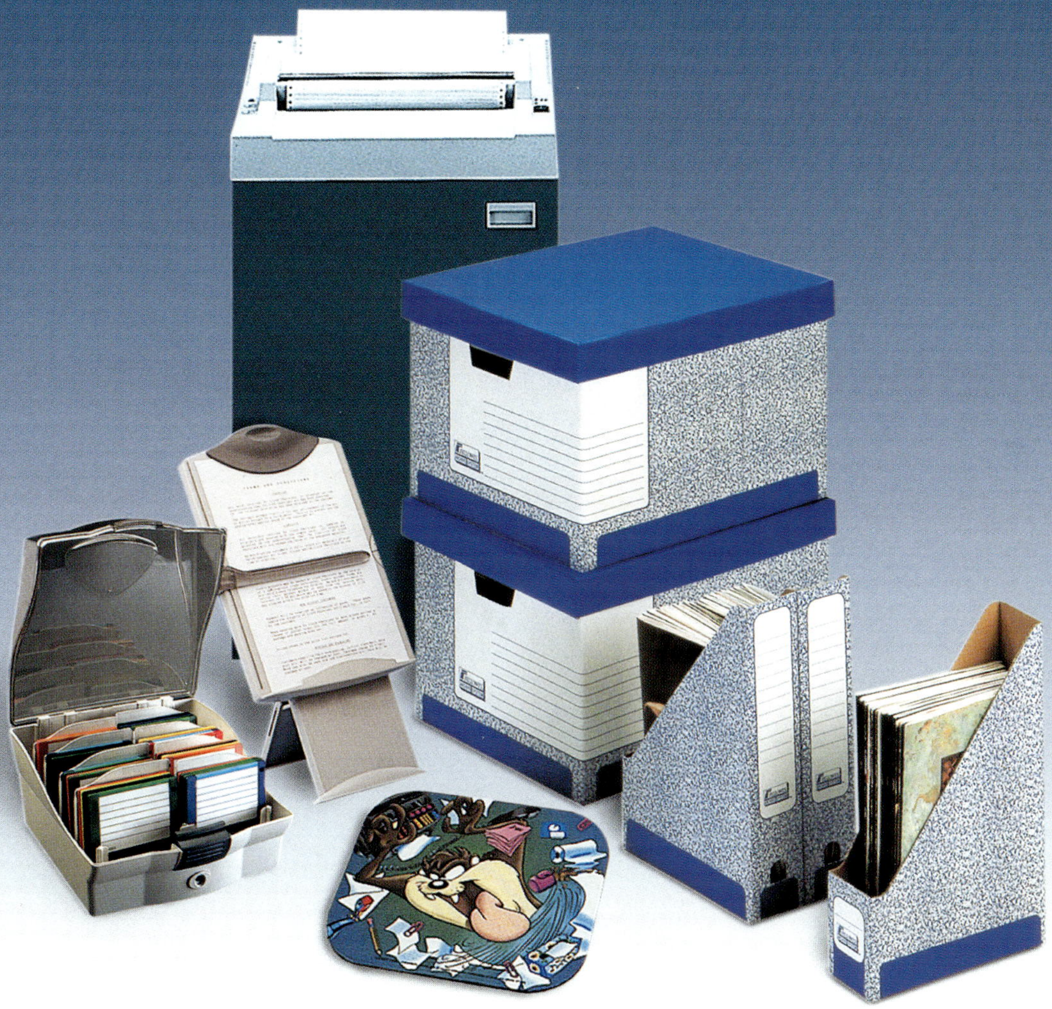

Archival Storage • Literature Organisation • Planning • Cleaning Products
• Diskette Storage • Printer Stands • Paper Shredders • Glare Filters • SoHo Products

DONCASTER ROAD, KIRK SANDALL DONCASTER, SOUTH YORKSHIRE DN3 1HT
TEL: 01302 885331 Fax: 01302 890003

...because appearance matters

Now 100gsm and Chlorine Free

When it comes to business correspondence, first impressions really do count. That's why many businesses have long been aware of the name Plus Fabric as synonymous with superior strength and guaranteed quality.

Now this name is even better.

For a start, we've increased the envelope to a bulky 100 and 112gsm.

What's more - on an environmental level - we now use elemental chlorine-free pulp.

Not only this, but you'll find new Plus Fabric envelopes as clean, crisp and white as ever. With some of the toughest sealing methods available.

Plus a wide range of sizes, and now the envelopes will run through laser printers.* In addition, there's also a range of matching cut sheet, watermarked papers in the same hi-white ECF finish.

Naturally, we are justifiably proud of new, improved Plus Fabric. That's why we're giving away a free sample pack of envelopes to everyone who returns the coupon, together with some super purchase-related offers.

Please photocopy this coupon and fax to
01223 835484
or send to the address below

```
Plus Fabric Offer, Spicers, FREEPOST, Sawston,
Cambridge CB2 1BR.
Name _____
Company _____
Address _____
_____
_____
Postcode _____
Telephone no. _____
Fax no. _____
Usual stationery supplier _____
_____
                                      OS/96
```

A **SPICERS** PRODUCT

*DL gummed + Securseal envelopes successfully tested on most laser printers

"It's like joining up two parts of the person, so that, instead of just the usual robot reporting in for work and doing the job, you suddenly have enthusiasm and energy and, best of all, some delighted customers."

What you have here is the virtuous circle again. Employees who act as if they enjoy being in the front line tend to get enthusiastic responses from customers they meet. And so it goes on.

THE SMART WAY TO RUN A BUSINESS

The well documented results of professional development programmes like this include such benefits as:

- lower absenteeism and sickness rates
- lower staff turnover
- early warning of industrial unrest and dissent and even personal unhappiness and distress
- self-motivating people who spur themselves and each other on to greater achievements

Recognition v competition

These methods, which involve people challenging themselves and running against their own best times, seem to work much better than competition between staff. One big travel firm has stopped offering glamorous holidays to its top-performing sales teams since it found that, besides high sales revenue, it was getting:

- disgruntled customers who had been pressured to buy holidays they didn't really want
- salesmen sabotaging each other and enlisting partisan support from admin staff, who were divided into factions, with resulting losses of data and sometimes even payments
- low morale among the losers

When the company switched to offering a less glitzy weekend break to everyone who achieved a certain percentage increase in sales, it found that both customer satisfaction and employee satisfaction increased enormously. And sales rose as well. Even McDonalds gives gold stars to everybody who earns them. The stars aren't rationed to one per restaurant. By and large, competition is best kept on the outside of companies – or saved for the annual karaoke contest at Christmas.

Celebrate together

You can't even afford to treat your staff to a weekend in Clacton if they do well? Well then, what about an event tailored to some specific interest within your little organisation? One small firm held a "company do" three times a year – each run on a theme suggested by a different member of staff.

In summer, the maintenance man, who liked fishing, organised an angling contest and picnic. In winter, the MD held a snowman-building competition at his farm in the country, with everyone treated to B&B at the local pub. Use the interests and talents that you have as a group to encourage sharing and the generation of ideas and energy.

If you can measure it, you can manage it

And what about the incentives that don't cost any money at all? Encourage people to race against themselves by posting wallcharts of performance near their desks. It doesn't matter much whether the charts measure the number of dustbins they sold, the amount of paper they recycled or how they performed according to their own SMART targets.

The important thing is to start up a culture of measuring, managing and multiplying success.

Getting the best from people

Apart from choosing the right staff in the first place, it is the job of the manager to ensure that, once the team is in place, people give their best and are repaid for their commitment with the greatest possible personal satisfaction. One of the most effective ways to measure whether you are succeeding is simply to track your staff turnover levels.

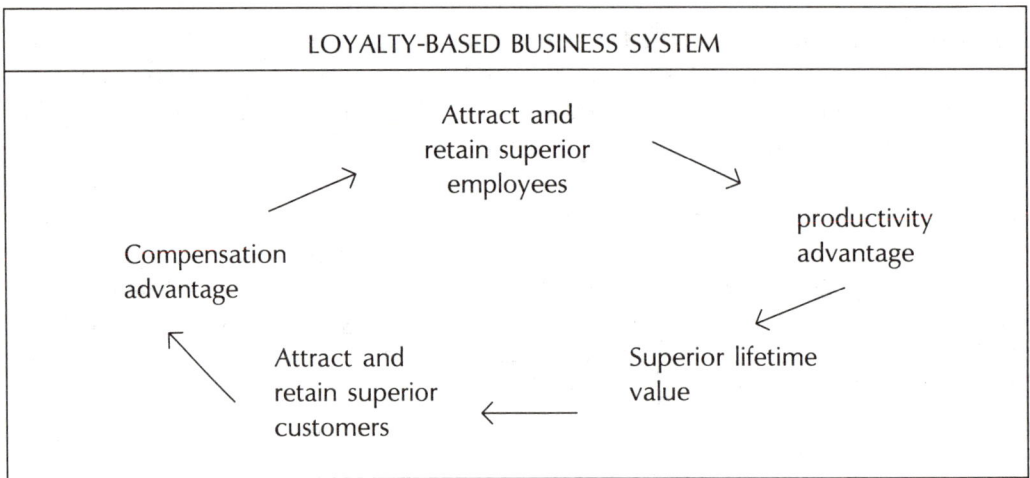

LOYALTY-BASED BUSINESS SYSTEM

Step 8 | Trust Teams To Work

Happy customers like happy staff

In most businesses there is a direct link between keeping customers happy and keeping happy employees. The value of low staff turnover is at last being realised and companies are looking for the magic formula they can build into their recruitment and personnel policies.

So far, it seems to boil down to:

1. Hire the people best suited for the job
2. Treat them well
3. Encourage them to understand the company's USP and how it makes its profits
4. Encourage them to identify with the company, using coaching, mentoring, team building, support groups and whatever else suits the firm's culture and environment
5. Train them continuously
6. Equip them with the best technology

If you are a small company, you may not be able to manage numbers 5 and 6 – at least, not in the formal sense. But even an office of 20 people or fewer should strive to achieve 1,2,3 and 4. And you don't actually need a huge training budget to adopt the culture of curiosity and continuous self-improvement. If you run the kind of organisation where people are encouraged to feel curious about what they do and how other people do it, they are likely to share their new ideas with you.

It pays to help your people grow

At the very least, if they do learn so much more that they want to move on to some bigger job, you can be sure that they will have been putting in their best efforts while they are actually with you. It's a false economy to teach people only what they need to know to do their particular job, especially if you've recruited intelligent, capable people in the first place.

Reining them in may stop them leaving for a while. But it may mean they spend their time with you feeling bored and frustrated. People who feel like this are not only low in energy and enthusiasm, they may also become corrupt. A high proportion of fiddling arises from boredom and a need to challenge the system, rather than the apparently obvious motive of a desire for goods or money. Even worse, the attitude of disillusionment is like a virus, capable of spreading quickly to other staff. Once a company is infected, it takes more than a few squirts of motivational rhetoric from the MD to clear the air.

STAFFING LEVELS FOR THE NEW OFFICE

When starting a new business, or even going through a phase of expansion, perhaps accompanied by an office move, always take on fewer people than you think you need.

Smart Office | **11 Steps to a User-Friendly Office**

When a business is in the throes of this kind of crucial change, the disadvantages of having too many people to manage are greater than those of not quite having enough. Being slightly short means you have to work harder. But when you do staff up, you will know just what the newcomers need to know. This makes it easier for you to pick the right people and manage them when you've got them.

Most businesses start with an MD doing everything, including sales, buying and accounts. But research commissioned by Barclays Bank shows that there is a clear pecking order when it comes to delegating tasks to other people.

As a small firm finds its feet, most owner-managers will shed day-to-day responsibility for customer liaison, buying and stock control and finance tasks first, in that order, followed by marketing. Control of staffing, salaries and business planning is only relinquished later as the business moves closer to the conventional corporate model. But it is a sign of the times that fewer and fewer firms are growing up to look like that conventional model. Business courses used to teach formulae which would help you work out exactly how many middle managers, salespeople, secretaries, clerks, typists, bookkeepers, gophers and tea ladies a company would need. This was calculated with the aid of an equation in which the variables were the type of business, the first year's turnover and the fixed overheads.

This is no longer relevant, because almost every kind of business is downsizing vigorously, regardless of whether its sales, or even its profits, are rising or falling. The general trend is to hang on to the professionals and cut back hard on middle managers and clerical staff.

The only way to arrive at a realistic projection of required staffing levels now is to look at your own annual turnover and the number of hours that everybody involved was working to achieve it. Ask yourself:

- Could we do that all over again next year?
- Did we make enough profit to be able to hire somebody else?

If the answer to the first is no and the second is yes, don't rush out and hire your best friend's brother. That's what most people do and that's one reason why so many small businesses fail. Stop again and ask yourself:

- What bits of the work did I like least or do least efficiently?
- What part of the work would it be cheapest to hire someone else to do?

It's surprising how many lively people who have invented new widgets and love talking to other engineers about them spend half of their time typing their own letters with two fingers, when they should be out selling their products and their enthusiasm to potential customers.

Step 8 | Trust Teams To Work

Don't hire full-time staff too soon

Before you take on a full-time member of staff, try answering the following questions:
- Could a part-timer do it?
- Could two part-timers take on two different parts of it more efficiently?
- Are you giving away something you like doing?
- Could a computer do it, instead of a person?

As a general rule, buy in computer programs, rather than people, for all functions which don't require a customer interface. It's easy to bin them if they don't work and you needn't spend time taking them out to lunch.

CHECK YOUR COMPANY'S PERFORMANCE

If you are opening a new office, you have the advantage of being able to adopt "best practice" from the word go. If not, you may find you're doing well by luck and instinct, rather than judgment. But, equally, you may have discovered, while reading this chapter, that there are some quite tangible reasons behind the mysterious, indefinable malaise in your office.

Try this checklist:

- What is your current absenteeism rate? Has it increased over the past five years?
- What do people do in their lunch breaks:
    - eat in and talk to each other?
    - eat out in groups?
    - go out in different directions and get back to their desks one minute before they're due to start work again?
- How often do your staff come up with good ideas for your business?
- Do you have a high incidence of flu and back problems?
- Do people make informal arrangements to cover for each other in the event of personal difficulties?
- How many people do you feel you could ask to cover for you if the need arose?
- How often do you have company functions out of hours?
- Who chooses the venue for the Christmas party?
- How many members of staff could quote the company mission statement without hesitation if asked?
- Do people talk to you if they have problems?
- How many of them could *you* talk to if you had problems?
- Do you have company jokes and a company shorthand language?
- Do staff ever meet outside office hours for recreational activities involving their families?
- Is there a key person in the office other than yourself?

Smart Office | 11 Steps to a User-Friendly Office

DO YOU TALK TO YOUR STAFF?

If you do have problems and you're stuck with the wrong staff, too few staff or, much worse, too many, you can't change the company culture overnight. But you can make a start.

The best way is always to begin as you mean to go on, with excellent communication. Call a meeting. Tell everybody what you think the problems are and ask them for their confirmation (or contradiction) and their suggestions. Then share with them what you intend to do – whether it's training, coaching, goal setting, job sharing or whatever appears to be most appropriate. Remember, nothing you can do will work reliably unless you have their buy-in from the start. If they are involved from the outset and feel that they own this new system, whatever it is, you are already off on the right foot.

Starting from now, you could make this meeting a monthly occasion. OK, so you see the staff every day anyway. But a formal, regular meeting conveys a completely different message. It tells people that they are important, that there's space in your diary set aside for them and that you want and value their input. For many people in offices around the world, a single convincing sign that their presence is valued is all the motivation that would be needed to work a transformation. It's an index of how dull much traditional management thinking has been that managers, who are driven by the same needs as their workers, have so rarely cottoned on to this simple fact.

IN A NUTSHELL

1. Manage projects, not people

2. Find the right people to manage the projects

- Using an employment agency or doing it yourself
    - cost in your time realistically
    - make sure you're not missing anything important

3. Doing it yourself

- Be aware of your blind spots
- Interviewing techniques
- Getting information from CVs and references
- Supplementing your own selection procedures with professional advice

Step 8 | **Trust Teams To Work**

4. Managing the staff you've selected
- Performance management techniques
    - sticks and carrots
    - communication
    - professional development
    - setting SMART targets

5. Telltale signs of a well-managed organisation
- Use of recognition rather than competition
- Business relationships extending into social support

6. The right staffing levels
- Keep numbers low:
    - lean and keen is currently fashionable and makes economic sense
    - people are less motivated with too little rather than too much to do
- Keep levels monitored: in a dynamic, growing organisation the skills and numbers shouldn't be static
- Points to watch:
    - absenteeism levels (tangible)
    - morale (harder to measure but not impossible)

7. Communication
- Good communication – the single most important success factor for any organisation

STEP 9: LEARNING TO LEAD AND LIGHT

Step 9 | Learning To Lead and Light

WILL YOU TAKE ON THE ROLE?

You could look through the formal job descriptions for a great many positions as facilities manager or office manager before you came across one with any direct reference to the idea of leadership.

Responsibilities are a different matter. Responsibilities are often piled up ten deep, until you know for certain that whoever drew up the job description had at least half an eye on the possibility of lining up a convenient scapegoat for future disasters. Yet to load someone with formal responsibility for matters that are outside his or her control is actually to admit that something has already gone badly wrong in the managerial structure of the company.

Leadership is seldom asked for, simply because there is rarely a clear understanding of the vital role it has to play in the running of almost any office. The work of a busy office is always likely to involve a wide variety of activities, including *ad hoc* on-the-job training, covering for absences and helping other people out, which will never be written down in anyone's job description.

Offices run on give and take. And you can't order people to muck in and dig each other out of the mire. All you can do is demonstrate your own willingness to go the extra mile when necessary and foster the kind of atmosphere that makes people feel supported by a genuine team spirit. This is real leadership in action – a notch or two short of King Henry V's big speech before the Battle of Agincourt, perhaps, but undeniably the real thing.

They'll take a lead from you

The point is that you set the tone. You let your people know how much you really want them to stretch themselves and try new ideas. You choose the right balance between caution and creativity. If you believe it's worth taking risks to succeed, it's up to you to make it clear that people should not be petrified by the fear of failure, as long as useful lessons are learned.

Smart Office | 11 Steps to a User-Friendly Office

Leaders get the followers they deserve. If you can stimulate an atmosphere of alert, flexible thinking and mutual support, you will be able to run a successful office in almost any industry sector, whether your people are a newly-recruited bunch of ambitious young hotshots or long-serving staff from the days before the computers came in.

INSPIRATION OR UNDERPINNING?

The two key roles in any office environment are traditionally defined as supporting ones. But they are so crucial that they can set the tone of the business, provide a focus and make the difference between a working environment and an environment that works. They are, of course, the Office Manager and the Receptionist. They may even be one and the same person. In some small organisations they may be the MD and Tea Maker as well. But however few (or however many) people it takes to fill these roles, they are the ones who set the tone.

STARTING WITH YOU

Just as your house, your car and your dog reflect your personality, the way you set up an office reveals a lot about your approach to work, your leadership qualities and your management style.

But how do you approach the design of a working environment? Perhaps design isn't quite the right word to use. You may have inherited someone else's mess. You may hold the title of office manager in the kind of small business where two or three directors like to make their presence felt by agonising over paper clip sizes, box file colours and chair designs at board level. Or you may be just setting up, with a clean slate, a lot of ideas and no budget for putting them into practice.

Wherever you are starting from, whatever the constraints, the chances are that you could be *at least* 50 per cent more effective than you are. The environment you create and the tools you install actually affect the way people work, the way business gets done and, most importantly, the control you have over the running of it all.

STARTING FROM WHERE YOU ARE

MANAGING YOURSELF

If you want to introduce change, begin with yourself and let the consequences ripple out from you. If you know who you are and know what you want to do, you can achieve tremendous leverage, even in a large office or a traditionally conservative corporation.

The fact is, work – and often life, too – is just a holding operation for many people. They

Step 9 | Learning To Lead and Light

aim to get by. That doesn't mean they are necessarily gloomy or negative individuals. But it does mean that they are very unlikely to initiate and inspire change, even when they can see it is beneficial. If you come powering through with simple, positive, clear-cut goals, you will be surprised at how many of your colleagues will be happy to go along with you.

That's not to say that every office manager should try to become a new Winston Churchill or Joan of Arc – an overdose of charisma has its own down side. But there is actually scope for a large element of leadership and team building in the setting up and running of an efficient office. Very few office managers usually see themselves in this light. And that's a shame, because a little inspiration, a dash of vision and a touch or two of applied psychology can often generate improvements in quality and productivity that no amount of new computing equipment or Total Quality Management training could guarantee.

Start by asking yourself a few questions about your approach and your internal resources.

- What is your personal style?
- Do you instinctively manage your situation, or are you mostly reactive?
- How much power could you really exert to create a more effective working environment, using the tools and budgets that are available to you?
- How much control could you exercise if you took a more dynamic, assertive approach?
- How are you going to achieve your goals in an office full of individuals with their own views of what is good for the organisation and for themselves?

The answers to these questions may seem obvious now. But they may well be changed or modified slightly as you go through this part of the book. Make a note of them, on paper or at least in your head, for comparison purposes later on.

MANAGING OTHER PEOPLE

People bring their own motivations to work with them. All the company can do is provide a good, healthy and encouraging environment and then stand back and hope for the best. On the grand scale, leadership is what top management does to earn its money. But real leadership is something that cannot be delegated, and the influence of the successful office manager should never be underestimated.

Your job is to bring out the best in people and influence them to make things happen. If you are organised yourself, you are in a much stronger position when it comes to organising other people and their projects.

You can make life easier for everybody by doing what you can to help people work smoothly together and get the most value out of the office supplies and equipment that represent the basic raw materials and tools of the trade.

Smart Office | 11 Steps to a User-Friendly Office

Executive managers – even assuming they are mainly office-based, and these days they may not be – are focused on getting the job done, rather than *how* they do it. This is a significant difference of emphasis. The determined office manager can achieve surprising results by concentrating on improvements in the process and the environment.

A well-organised manager who is able to plan ahead, communicate that plan convincingly, implement it speedily and follow it through tenaciously can be a major positive influence on any organisation. Don't underestimate the difference you can make if you:

- improve the way you organise your own resources
- fit everyone else into the plans you have made
- lead by example
- set high standards
- provide equipment that is consistent and easy to use
- create a motivating work environment, with the right tools and furniture
- facilitate communication at all levels
- incorporate as much positive input from everyone else as possible

ROLES AND TEAMWORK

First be clear about your own reasons for being here. Then take a little time to think about what everybody else is doing around you and how they all fit into a coherent team.

The working environment and the communication channels within it are a sadly neglected and underestimated element in teamwork.

Many companies spend thousands sending their staff away on team-building adventure weekends in the Lake District or on Dartmoor. But they often ignore the fact that the whole office environment and the systems within which these people are expected to work may be actively undermining the team spirit that emerged among the crags and tors. It's a sad mistake to think that durable teams can be built outside the office environment.

MANAGING TIME

The chances are that you are a fairly well-organised person anyway. If you weren't, you probably wouldn't be taking this opportunity to stand back and appraise the way your office is run.

So you won't be starting from scratch. You will already have systems, or failing that, lists, or failing that, mental priorities, or failing that, habits, that help you apportion and control your time.

Everyone has a way of relating to time, whether it does them any favours or not. The more complex and time-critical the various elements of your life and work are, the more formal and systematic your approach to time is likely to be, regardless of whether the organising is done on a computer, on a wallchart or in your head.

Step 9 | Learning To Lead and Light

The fact is, though, almost all of us, almost all of the time, do it very poorly. Most business skills trainers know that the easiest training to sell in to a new corporate customer is invariably some sort of time management course.

Every manager senses that he or she should be using time more productively. Every manager can do the sums that say gaining an extra couple of productive hours a week would soon pay for the training. And given a clear enough system to work to, almost every manager can make those gains, for at least long enough to cover the cost of the course.

How long a formal time management system persists after that usually depends on what else is going on in and around the office, though some useful ideas and good habits may stick around for years and become genuinely assimilated into the way the office runs.

An ideal time management system will give you the power to marshal your resources in five ways.
1. Enabling you to plan ahead
   – each day in detail
   – one month at a time
   – at least one year in advance

2. Accounting for other people
   – colleagues
   – clients
   – suppliers
   – family and friends
   – your network of useful contacts

3. Making macro prioritisation manageable
   – what is my ultimate personal aim?
   – what is my ultimate career plan?
   – how do these two mesh together?
   – are they possible, and what adjustments might I need to make?
   – where do I want to be in five years' time?

4. Making micro prioritisation possible
   – what are my work or business goals this month?
   – what do I need to do, week by week, to achieve them?
   – how do I prioritise my to-do list for tomorrow (in rank order)?

5. Helping you use time more effectively
   – avoiding "dead" time between meetings
   – saving time wasted putting off unwelcome chores

Smart Office | 11 Steps to a User-Friendly Office

How are you doing it now?

How many of these functions does your present system perform for you? What are the gaps? Do you need to replace your current system, add to it, upgrade it or adapt it?

- What planning and management tools do you use for yourself?
    - a diary
    - a to-do list
    - an electronic diary
    - a computer diary, networked or personal
    - a wall chart
    - your head
- How far ahead do you plan – a day? a week? a month? six months? a year?
    - for your business projects
    - for your personal business objectives
    - the delegation of projects to others
    - budget and purchasing requirements
    - personnel matters – holidays, shifts, hiring and firing, office parties
    - for your clients
    - for your supplies and suppliers
    - for your personal life

Your answers may vary from one area of your life to another.

- Do you ensure that you complete all your tasks for the day?
    - by prioritising your to-do list?
    - by allocating times to each task and making realistic allowances for slippage?
- What would happen if you lost all or part of your current time management system?
- Is the system you use co-ordinated with anyone or anything else?
    - schedules, shifts, holidays or responsibilities of bosses, colleagues or subordinates
    - schedules, movements, delivery dates and so on for suppliers and clients
    - your home and personal life and leisure interests
    - requirements to monitor and prioritise business projects
- How many people affect your planning? Who do you have to take into account?
- How many people would benefit by your planning intervention? Could you help people by introducing wall charts, responsibility rotas and similar planning aids?
- Do you keep separate systems running for all of these different parts of your life – a calendar at home, a personal diary *and* an office diary? Do you have an office day book, perhaps, and a networked diary and a wall chart for holidays and staff shifts?
    - Do you ever lose track of things by doing this?
    - Do you always have to write things down twice or more?

Step 9 | Learning To Lead and Light

- How many different places do you have to check for details of overdue deliveries, staff holiday dates or unpaid invoices?
- Is your time management system, or any part of it:
  - visible to anyone else?
  - accessible to anyone else to make entries (definite or provisional, firm or pencilled-in) on your behalf?
- Has anyone tried to standardise the way everybody tracks and organises their time in your organisation? Or is there sometimes duplication, slippage and lack of teamwork?

Plan the planning

Did a few gaps and problems show up as you went through the list? Maybe some new areas occurred to you. But what can you actually do about them?

It sounds like obvious good practice to make some attempt at benchmarking the ways things are organised and build the best into the system. But a lot of companies still run as collections of individuals, each regarding the organisation as a vehicle to further his or her own career. Computerisation has made this worse. Even in offices where e-mail and networked diary systems exist, individuals are usually left to use them or not as they wish.

Working on computers makes it hard to see what people are doing. It's possible to work away relatively inconspicuously in a large office — like Nick Leeson at Barings — while potentially changing the fate of the organisation and affecting the livelihood of the people whose desks are all around you.

The idea of a co-ordinated time management system may have to be sold to other employees. But the best way to do this is always to lead by example. Based on what you have just discovered through your answers to the questions in this chapter, why not see what practical improvements you could make straight away?

MANAGING THE OFFICE

Whatever time management system you use, make the part of it that relates to the office and everyone else openly visible and simple enough for people to understand what it's telling them.

At the moment, office management is going through a difficult transitional phase. Networked diary systems are a great idea, but we haven't yet worked out a foolproof way of using them. At the moment, a PA might set up a complex schedule for his boss, involving a series of meetings in London with important clients who are notoriously difficult to get hold of, only to find that the MD herself has typed in a lunch in Edinburgh on the same day. This kind of situation involves calling around again and possible friction and recriminations.

Most offices have several systems running at the same time. But you really can't beat the wall chart as a clear, publicly visible way of organising a group of people. In future, offices may have electronic wall screens where everyone can input and update data to show where they are and what they are doing. In the meantime, we have to compromise. As technology develops, it's a good idea to constantly re-assess the systems you use and accept that you may need to be prepared to change them, often.

SOME PRACTICAL WAYS AND MEANS
First things first

Prioritisation and monitoring are the keys to productivity, project management and people management. You need to know how you're doing or you won't know how much time and money you're wasting. You need to be able to measure every aspect of your organisation – and the office itself is a good place to start.

If you can't measure it, you can't manage it.
- *One senior manager in London's public transport system has a to-do list that usually runs to about 300 items. He keeps it on his computer in a relational database and everything on the list is flagged from four different points of view:*
  - *time sensitivity and deadlines*
  - *particular meeting dates*
  - *particular people*
  - *particular projects*

  At the beginning of each day, he runs a search based on whichever dates, projects or people seem to be most urgent and the system prioritises his list for him.

Priority management

Allocate a reasonable amount of time to your daily tasks and allow some extra time for slippage and Sod's Law. This may sound faintly obsessional and over-prescriptive. But merely writing down formal task allocations like this can revolutionise the way you approach your days and what you can plan into them.

- Always have clear objectives in mind for everything you do. Stop and think before you act. Drifting into decisions and projects wastes more time than any other single factor.
- Know what you want. Before you make a phone call or attend a meeting, have an outcome and an agenda in mind.
- Jot key points and figures down. Don't rely on keeping things in your head. Note down bare memory joggers about people's requests and conversations.

Step 9 | Learning To Lead and Light

- Track daily events, visitors and transactions of significance (if not in a day book, find another way). A chronological log of what happens from day to day can be invaluable for tracing problems back to the source.
- Keep your own personal filing system in order, whatever form it takes. Maintain an alphabetical log of people and projects to tell you where detailed information is stored.
- Use the 5-D system to organise your desk:
    - Deal with
    - Dispose
    - Delegate
    - Defer
    - Do difficult things first

  and make sure you only handle each piece of paper once!

- *Whatever you do, make sure it works for you. One sales executive in one of the major telecommunications companies hardly ever writes anything down. But she does ring herself up several times during the day, calling in to her voice mailbox and leaving herself messages. Back at the office, she can work through the list, deleting each item as she deals with it.*

THE OPTIONS FOR STAYING IN CHARGE

Two key factors need to be brought under control to make sure that the underlying style of the office tends towards managed chaos rather than the other sort. Whatever the official status rankings and pecking order, the office manager or facilities manager should always take absolute charge of both the wall chart system and the e-mail.

There is no substitute for Office Management By Walking About. But you should back up your OMBWA activities with whatever other systems the office uses.

The list of possible planning tools is almost endless. But that, in itself, means you have to plump for either chaos or customisation. How every individual organises his or her working life is ultimately a personal matter, except where the consequences of that organising style impinge on other people. At that point, it becomes a management issue.

In the list below, using or updating some of the planning tools can be made optional. But others must be insisted on and made mandatory. It is unforgivable to fail to enter an important event in the central Office Diary, because that is where everyone is used to looking for that kind of information. The seven planning tools you are most likely to base your system on are:

1 Office Diary on the reception desk
2 Series of office diaries, one for each manager or executive
3 Day book

Smart Office | 11 Steps to a User-Friendly Office

4 E-mail and networked diaries
5 Wall planners and whiteboards
6 Charts
7 Post-it notes

Whatever combination you adopt (and it is always likely to be more than one method), the key to success is to enforce and reward its consistent use. Above all, <u>make the system easy to use</u>.

You can't really stand over people day in and day out and force them to use the system the way you want them to. But if it is clear, sensible and easy enough to use, people will slip into doing things the way you want without any overt pressure.

Techniques

Introduce some personal motivational and planning ideas and see if you can get them accepted into the office culture:

- SMART target setting
  (as in Step 1: specific, measurable, affordable, realistic and time-related objectives)
- progress plotting
  (use of Gantt charts, for example, by people other than those officially labelled as project managers)

Leading by example

- Back up the diary for yourself or someone else. If you are responsible for co-ordinating meetings and the relevant information, have a mini filing system to ensure information is always ready when it's needed. Either tag necessary documents where they are in your own personal filing system, keep a section per person you look after, or just have a column in your own or the main diary.

If particular documents don't have a place in the overall filing system, allocate a drawer for them. When planning for future meetings, set up one section per month for six months ahead to act as pigeon holes and stacking points for papers that will be needed. Have the front section, for the current month, divided into days with each day's meeting papers in the appropriate pocket.

Step 9 | Learning To Lead and Light

BEHIND THE SCENES

Most of this organisation won't be visible to most of the people who pass by your desk every day. They will take for granted the fact that things are where they should be, messages get passed on and there's always coffee in the pot. Of course, if they do ever ask you how you do it, you will be ready to give an on-the-spot run-down on the principles of time management and office organisation. In fact, you might want to suggest some seminars on that topic for the rest of the staff in any case.

APPEARANCES MATTER

But there's one part of the business which has to present a transparently efficient front to the world at all times. It's almost as important to have a receptionist who *appears* friendly and efficient as to have one who *is*. And it's definitely counter-productive to employ a receptionist who makes everything run like clockwork but comes across as chaotic, stressed and grumpy.

LIVING ON THE FRONT LINE

There's plenty of scope for originality when it comes to being a receptionist. Styles range from the casually over-familiar to the daunting mask of icy professionalism which can make signing in at the front desk as intimidating as a meeting with the chairman.

What is actually needed is a human face and a human voice for the company. It sounds cruel, but receptionists are disposable. They could usually be replaced (in larger companies at least) by high-tech gimmicks like interactive computer terminals and entry phones, if that was what was wanted. The reason this has not happened is that most organisations realise the importance of having a real person up front. Whether they also understand the need to invest some thought in making the most of this asset is less clear.

The worst thing that can happen to a good receptionist is not having enough to do, because that leaves a bright person effectively trapped in a small space. When you employ a receptionist, think about it carefully. What kind of person do you really need? What is the right balance between appearance and capability? Do you have a high staff turnover in this particular role? And is that a coincidence?

Give people scope

It may mean a lot to an organisation to have one or two receptionists who are prepared to stick with the job, get to know customers, suppliers and courier companies and start to become useful problem solvers. But the fact of the matter is that the more critical the receptionist's image is to the business, the more likely they are to be dissatisfied and not stay long in the job. That is almost inevitable, because even companies that really depend on alert and efficient receptionists don't think carefully enough about how to provide them with job satisfaction. Frankly, a charming, intelligent, capable person is unlikely to be happy typing name badges and telling people to sign the book for six or seven hours a day. Try to find ways of increasing the interest and buy-in to the job and you will get better value out of your receptionists, just as they will get more out of doing this key job.

People in small companies generally end up doing more than one job, whatever it says on their job descriptions (if any). This is actually good for morale, because human beings are problem solvers with a very deep psychological drive towards variety and complex interpersonal contact. One way of solving the problem, for companies that have the resources, is to take on at least two people to man the reception desk, so that one of them will almost always be able to do something else at the same time. The other responsibilities could include:

- operating the switchboard
- acting as the post room
- dealing with outbound couriers and deliveries, as well as incoming packages
- ordering the stationery and other supplies
- providing a back-up typing service
- organising the petty cash and keeping the office day book
- making arrangements for travel and office functions

In very small offices, the receptionist may also be the office manager, the bookkeeper and the typing pool, too. It's a role that can mean a lot. But even when it's pared down to the absolute minimum – greeting visitors, establishing why they have come and directing them appropriately – it is a job that involves giving many people their first impressions of the company. The personality and attitude of the receptionist will probably stick in people's memories at least as clearly as the reception area itself. So if image and customer relations are important to your business, think carefully about who you employ.

The receptionist should be fully trained in emergency procedures and should know what to do and who to call in the event of fire, illness, injury or terrorist activity.

Threatening phone calls

Switchboard operators should have a written prompt sheet, within easy reach at all times, explaining what to do and say if they are faced with a threatening telephone call. Specialist companies can provide useful information and advice and train operators to keep a caller on the line long enough for a recording to be made or a number check to be set up.

Step 9 | **Learning To Lead and Light**

Since the recent introduction of the 1471 Call Return service on BT lines, casual or careless bomb hoaxers and troublemakers often leave the most damning of calling cards — the automatic recording of the number the call was made from. It hardly needs saying that some types of business are far more likely to suffer from threatening calls than others. Where this kind of emergency is likely to arise, key staff should be given special training. It could save lives.

Friendliness and responsiveness

Responsiveness shouldn't be confused with friendliness and it doesn't mean wasting time. In fact, the receptionist who is also a good communicator will save time by getting to the heart of the matter and passing it on faster than the person who is more interested in the crossword under the desk. Nevertheless, it's a tough world and there are some strange people about, even in business circles, so a bit of formal training in assertiveness and recognising and defusing problem situations is often a good investment.

Taking messages

Taking messages needs an office policy to make it work. All incoming messages which can't go straight to the right person should be recorded. The duplicate message pad, kept on the reception desk or by the switchboard, used to be the only way of doing this. Now, even though there are far more options, the one factor that does not seem to have changed at all is the capacity for human error.

The modern office can use:

- Voice messaging. This needs a sophisticated telephone system. Only larger offices or small ones which rely on an answering machine are likely to record spoken messages.
- Electronic mail. Some operators type messages straight into the e-mail system. But it only works if the office has a networked computer system which people use as a matter of routine.
- Post-it notes. This is the modern low-tech favourite, and the source of many of the worst office horror stories of the past few years. Post-it notes stick to anything, but don't often get as far as the desk of the person for whom they are intended. They are, however, better than the backs of envelopes and sandwich bags, which are more likely to slip off the reception desk and into the bin.
- The good old-fashioned duplicate telephone message pad. These still work, and work well. The format prompts you to write the date and phone number of the caller as well as the name. They also cost almost nothing, which makes them the ideal stopgap until you can afford to move on up to a computer network with ten flavours of voice mail services.

| Smart Office | 11 Steps to a User-Friendly Office |

IN A NUTSHELL

1. Office managers can inspire as well as support
- Shape the environment you know will work best
- Set the tone and make things happen

2. Lead by example
- Manage yourself and be aware of your own role in the team
- Manage others to make them more effective
- Manage time so that more gets done and everybody sees how it's done
    - set up effective systems
    - set up visible systems

3. Leading an effective team
- Stay in control so that you can give real support
- Make sure everyone else knows their roles

4. Managing the front line
- The role of the receptionist
    - getting the image absolutely right
    - supporting the reality behind the image
    - training, systems and back-up

STEP 10
FROM NETWORKING TO INTERNET-WORKING

Step 10 | From Networking to Internetworking

NETWORKING

Networking is a pretty simple idea really. It is just a question of how you handle links between your business and the world – customers, suppliers, dealers and distributors, employees, pensioners, competitors, unions, banks, shareholders, MPs, journalists, neighbours, trade associations, civil servants and local authority bodies. The links are formed by the exchange of various more or less meaningful types of information, which can range from the trivial exchanges known as passing the time of day to the exchange of contracts, catalogues, complaints or writs.

In modern business jargon, of course, the words "network" and "networking" are used to describe complex systems of physical links, like a computer or telephone network. But they also refer to the social or commercial networks of contacts that people and businesses build and maintain. Since all your personal and commercial networking, other than face-to-face meetings, has to be done over some kind of communications network, it does make some sort of realistic sense to group them both together.

We will be looking at the most exciting developments in the world of physical networks, the Internet and the World Wide Web, later in this section. But first, it's important to focus on how the principle of person-to-person networking can help any business use its information and contacts to make itself more efficient and more profitable. There's no doubt now that we're heading for a one-to-one future, with a lot less emphasis on mass production, mass communications and mass marketing. The ability to exploit networks ingeniously and tirelessly to sustain useful relationships with individual people and firms is becoming a key business skill.

YOUR WORLD IS WHAT YOU MAKE IT

Networking is the buzzword of the nineties, but Successful Business Persons have always been brilliant at it. They are the kind of people who never pop into the supermarket without checking out whether each person ahead of them at the checkout might be:

- a potential customer
- a potential competitor
- a potential supplier
- a potential source of new ideas
- a potential employee.

And, if all else fails, they resign themselves to using the queue around them as a ready-made, randomly selected focus group and do a quick bit of market research. SBPs don't hang about reading *Family Circle* – they get a conversation going.

This is rather exhausting if you do it all the time. But the Richard Bransons of this world don't stop networking outside the hours of nine to five. Even if *you* only extend your hours a little bit, there's no doubt that you'll increase your effectiveness a lot.

MAKE MONEY OUT OF YOUR RELATIONSHIPS

That may sound a trifle cynical. But, actually, it should be the other way round. Because there's a great deal of mileage in making your business contacts into real relationships. There's nothing new in this. Great salesmen have always known that sales are built on rapport. That's why they keep slots in their databases to file notes about their clients' hobbies, obsessions, families and affairs. What you end up saying to the customer may sound spontaneous. But unless you have the kind of brain that breaks casino banks, your best hope of achieving that easy, well-informed spontaneity is to write all these potentially relevant details down. Asking someone about her holiday in Florida is a great rapport builder. But if your memory played tricks and she actually went to Bridlington, you might lose a sale. Especially if Florida was where she really wanted to go.

Management By Walking About works on the same principle. It's an idea that went out of favour when a lot of old-style managers tried walking the shop floor, surrounded by their retinues, and then wondered why productivity didn't suddenly shoot up. You can only sell your deal to people (whether its efficiency or dishwashers) if you can make them feel they matter. The successful MBWA exponents are the ones who not only remember the name of the third typist from the left, but also enquire kindly about her cat and her migraines.

It's easier to work with people you know. Your calls are more likely to get straight through to them, if nothing else. So why aren't you getting to know the people you work with?

Who are they?

Who do you select to belong to your network? Is it the supermarket queue? Your family and friends and the traditional old boy network? Your colleagues? Your fellow Round Table members? Is there anyone you don't want to include?

Your network should certainly take in people from the following categories:

Step 10 From Networking to Internetworking

- clients
- colleagues
- competitors
- suppliers

If there is anyone around who doesn't currently fit into any of these groups, you must, of course, be prepared to slot them in as well. It is a prime mistake of amateur networkers to decide far too early who is and who isn't likely to be useful – and to act in ways that let people know which category they have been placed in.

Where are they?

The short, hopeful, answer is "On your database of course." If you're going to take this spontaneity business seriously, it's worth planning ahead and investing in one of the cheap and easy-to-use relational databases currently on the market. You can stick to the card index, but that won't automatically pull out a list of everybody who needs calling on Friday 13th or everybody who ever bought your ginseng-flavoured pens and might need another one.

You can buy ready-made databases for every one of hundreds of different business categories from retailing baby clothes to running an airline. But most smaller businesses do better designing their own. Take advice from outside experts by all means, but don't let anybody tell you what you might or might not want to know. A typical database might look like this:

Field 1   Name
Field 2   Title
Field 3   Company
Field 4   Address
Field 5   Postcode
Field 6   Phone
Field 7   Fax
Field 8   Type – i.e. Supplier, Client, General Contact, Employee
Field 9   Personal details
Field 10   Other eventualities field
Field 11   Summary of contacts to date
Field 12   Last contact date
Field 13   Next contact date

There is probably no realistic way of defining in advance what kind of information should go into Fields 9 and 10. It will just have to be salient points that might be useful to remember at some future date. But it is a good idea to make every field mandatory. In other words, the system is set up so that it won't accept a file record that doesn't have *something* in every field – however dull, however facetious even, in the first instance.

Making fields mandatory forces you beyond "What's interesting about him?" to the fallback position of "What is true about him?"

If "went to a middlebrow south London grammar school" hardly seems enough to stir the blood, that might change when you find out, later, that the school was Rutlish and your contact was an exact contemporary of John Major. Now that is interesting information – and it will certainly give you something to talk about next time you meet.

GROWING YOUR OWN ORGANIC NETWORKS

It may sound brutal to talk of farming your contacts and consciously setting out to expand and profit from your networks. But isn't that simply close-quarters marketing? It's just what you are trying to do in more conventional marketing – creating the positive pre-conditions for a sale through targeted communication with potential customers. Only this time you're in a position to target clearly identified individuals and firms. And you can develop a more long-term strategy that does not depend on capturing sales immediately. To make all this work, though, you must nurture and tend your network with care and a clear sense of how you want it to work for you.

1. **Encourage your network to breed.** Customers have colleagues and clients and suppliers of their own. You don't have to be a poacher to take advantage of this. Fill the gaps, but don't filch the profit.
2. **Inject new blood**. Don't neglect your gene pool. Healthy databases grow. To stay fit and active, to adapt and survive, you need new buyers and new suppliers. You also need the flow of new ideas that comes with new contacts, to keep you at the forefront of whatever business you're in. If the network doesn't seem to be expanding the way it should, try stepping back and looking at the whole picture. Where could you get some new sources of useful contacts? The answers might be surprising. OK, start with trade directories, Yellow Pages and specialist publications. But don't rule out your squash club, the Chamber of Commerce, your NCT childbirth classes or your doctor's surgery. There's no need to take up hang-gliding just because it attracts fearless entrepreneurial types, but don't turn down invitations to boring cocktail parties either. You don't have to stay right to the end.
3. **Cull as required.** Don't let out-of-date addresses, details of defunct businesses, people you feel guilty about and no-hopers sit there for ever, using up hard drive space and slowing down your reactions. You should be updating and pruning at least every six months to remove the people you just don't want. But you don't want any unnecessary symmetry here – new business cards and notices from the receiver

about companies falling over should be logged in weekly, so that you are using the best possible information about current prospects and customers.

PUTTING THE NETWORK TO WORK

Once you've got them, don't just let all those contacts sit there in the system. Call them – whenever your built-in diary bleeper reminds you to. Visit them. Have lunch, play golf or do whatever works for your business. Just make sure you keep in touch.

RELATIONSHIPS WITH SUPPLIERS

Does life with your suppliers always have to be a battle? And if it isn't, does it always degenerate into the cosy corruption that supposedly characterised some local government departments in the 1980s – a world of deals and backhanders where individuals had dinner and cash was exchanged but the goals of the organisation were short-changed? If you get on well with your suppliers are they bound to exploit you?

This is a particularly poignant question for office managers, who may find themselves having more to do with their company's suppliers than with their company's clients.

Surprisingly, perhaps, the same rules apply to suppliers as to clients and general network contacts:

1. **Establish a good, friendly relationship.** That way you'll always get that extra bit of service, that extra effort to get your stationery there on time or your photocopier fixed before the deadline.
2. **Always be on the lookout for a better deal.** You need comparisons so that you'll know if your current contractor is overcharging or underperforming. If things are going wrong, you can either find yourself a better deal somewhere else or give your original supplier the opportunity to come up with more competitive terms.
3. **Cost in your own time and effort.** How much are you worth per hour? How many hours per month are you prepared to spend on the phone trying to save 10p a ream on 40 boxes of A4?

Sometimes a balance has to be struck between becoming over-reliant on one source of supply and spreading your custom around so thinly that you never get any discounts, special deals or extra special service.

Businesses usually get what they deserve, both in terms of customers and suppliers. If morale is low and staff turnover is high, you are more likely to be paying double the normal price for paper clips because the latest temp has accepted the offer of a shopping voucher (or worse still, the fluffy seal) as a personal incentive from a telesales person.

Smart Office | 11 Steps to a User-Friendly Office

THE CASE OF THE BEMUSED TEMP

To be fair to the temp, this is often not straightforward corruption. The telesales staff who work for disreputable stationery firms like this deserve better jobs, because they have such a finely tuned instinct for the weak link. The script (and it's worthy of a larger audience, for its real-world understanding of the way offices tick) goes like this:

Telesales
Person: "Hello. This is Bloggs Stationery — who am I speaking to?"
Jane: "This is Jane."
TP: "Oh, I was expecting Mike. He's usually on reception, isn't he?"
Jane: "I don't know. I'm just temping."
TP: "Well look, Jane, perhaps you can help me. Mike put in your usual order for paper towels last week and the supplier has been messing us around. I just called to say we're sorry they're a bit late, but we'll definitely deliver tomorrow. Will you be on the desk?"
Jane: "Yes, I'm here all week."
TP: "All right then, Jane. I'm sorry for all the trouble we've caused, but there will be a little something for you, just as an apology from us, when you sign the delivery note — you've been so helpful."
Jane: "Oh, it's OK. Its really no trouble."

The chances are that this little exchange will happen so fast, so casually and so amiably that Jane won't even think about it again until she gets a ton of paper clips, some paper towels, a delivery note to sign and a little envelope with her name on it the following morning.

Even then, she may not tell anyone, because it really won't seem that important. It won't be until the bookkeeper is going through the invoices three weeks later that anyone notices anything unusual — and by that time Jane will be working somewhere else and Bloggs Stationery will be able, if challenged, to produce proper documentary proof of delivery and acceptance.

THE BOUNDARIES OF ETHICS

Clearly, this is just as bad as having such a cosy relationship with your supplier that you will pay a bit over the odds for your paper clips just so that you can have your monthly chat with the saleslady about American football.

The shading off between perfectly normal business (own up, don't the nicer sales people always notch up more revenue?) and petty corruption is blurred at the best of times. The

office solutions

Avery... leading the way in IT business solutions

Avery label and card products are pre-formatted in most popular desktop software packages for easy printing. Avery are also leading suppliers of office, mailing, filing, communication and presentation products for enhanced image and improved office efficiency.

For free label samples and advice call

**Helpline
0800 80 50 20**

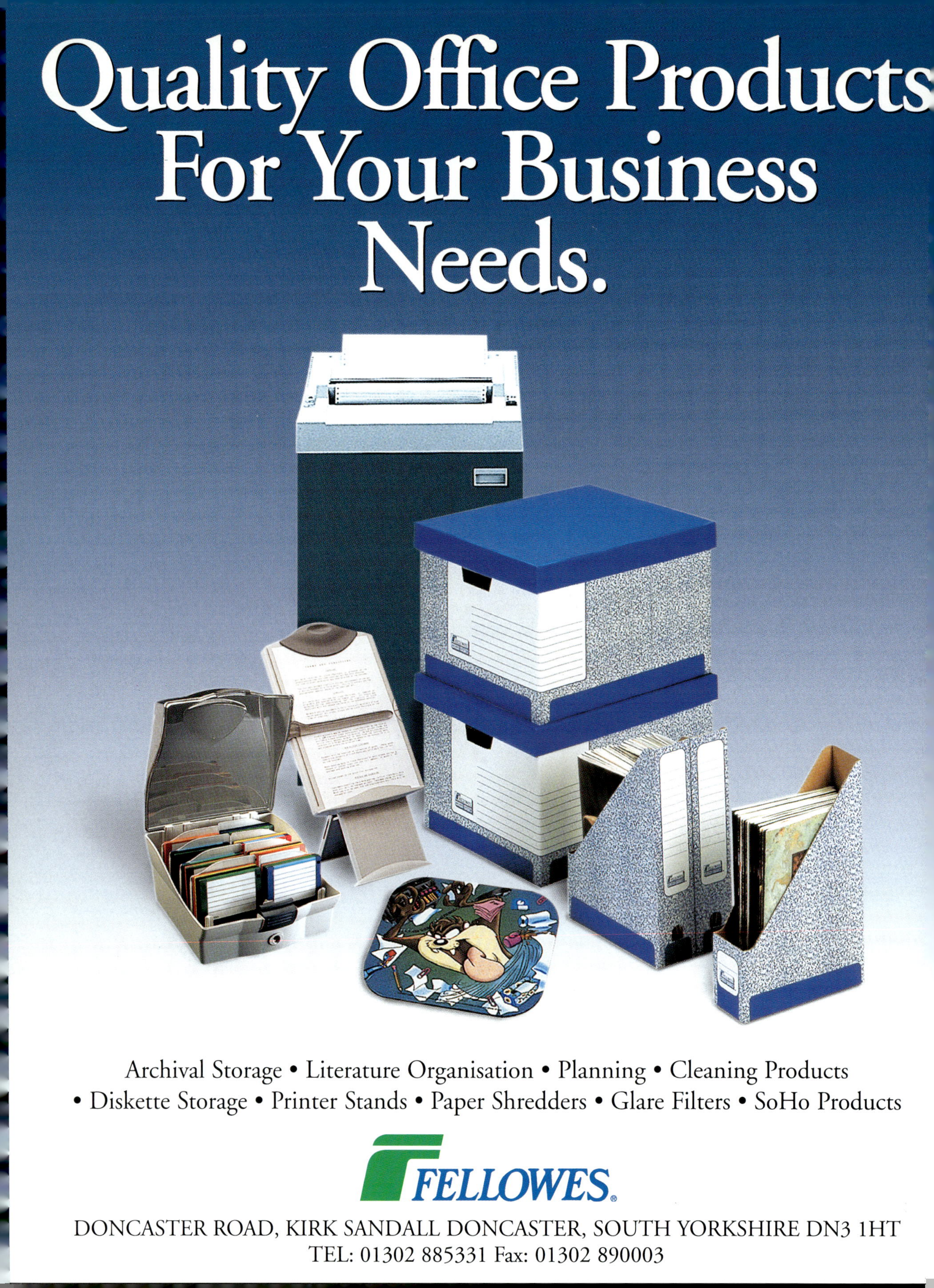

Quality Office Products For Your Business Needs.

Archival Storage • Literature Organisation • Planning • Cleaning Products
• Diskette Storage • Printer Stands • Paper Shredders • Glare Filters • SoHo Products

DONCASTER ROAD, KIRK SANDALL DONCASTER, SOUTH YORKSHIRE DN3 1HT
TEL: 01302 885331 Fax: 01302 890003

Step 10 | From Networking to Internetworking

people who are most certain and sanctimonious about these issues have frequently failed to think clearly enough about aspects of their own purchasing patterns.

Is being seduced by an individual's personal charm more or less blameworthy than accepting a bottle of wine or a shopping voucher? And if the bottle makes no difference to the destination of a £30 order, but the smile affects where £1,000 is spent, does that change matters? The bottle and the voucher are certainly more tangible and easier to prove. But the smile can also be used on those who pride themselves on being incorruptible.

Petrol station stamps give drivers and sales people undeclared perks, while Air Miles and frequent flyer schemes would not be commercially viable if they did not influence managers' travel habits. It's hard to know where on the spectrum of vouchers, promotions, incentives, commissions, kickbacks, bungs and bribes one should start tut-tutting.

HOW DO YOU KNOW IF YOU ARE BEING GIVEN THE BEST DEAL?

The only way to be really certain that neither you nor any of your staff can be accused of succumbing to undue influence is to be sure that you are getting good, competitive deals from all your suppliers. Here is a rough and ready checklist that will help you judge that.

- Do you always get competitive quotes for any major item? When was the last time you did insist on competitive tendering?
- How often do you negotiate price (particularly on service contracts) for items valued at more than £100?
- List your major suppliers (equipment, stationery, janitorial, cleaning, agencies, professional services). How long have you been working with each of them?
- Do you use the same suppliers as any other companies in your building? If so, have you discussed with them the possibility of joint negotiations on price and service?
- Have you thought of running a quick check with other similar businesses as to what suppliers they use and what they pay?
- Have any of your suppliers asked you for a reference recently?
- When did you last talk to your suppliers about anything other than what they supply?

GETTING MORE THAN SUPPLIES FROM YOUR SUPPLIER

Suppliers can be a great source of information, about your business and other people's, about market trends and about new technology.

Smart Office | **11 Steps to a User-Friendly Office**

When they feel like talking, make sure you listen and give them time.

Sometimes suppliers will talk to you more realistically than your own clients will. Always take a while to check out which way the market is going. Sound them out for hints and information about how well your competitors are doing (the chances are you're not the only fish food company or design group they supply) and take the trouble to ask what other people in the business are buying. Never mind the "This is very popular at the moment" line – it's probably either old stock they need to clear or just the line that carries their highest profit margin. You want to know everything they're prepared to tell you about who does what and why.

Because of their position in the marketplace, office supplies companies are particularly useful intelligence sources. They are often the first to pick up indications of economic trends and to learn about experiments in new ways of working and revolutionary ideas like teleworking and hot desking. You can learn a lot from talking to them – as opposed to just haggling over prices or chatting about golf.

Backscratching's not illegal

As long as it's based on good, honest service, backscratching is one of the biggest feel-good factors in networking.

A firm of builders and partitioners in Surrey installed a new office layout that was needed for a block of serviced offices. The serviced offices, because of the nature of their business, nursed the start-up of many promising new companies.

When these seedling businesses grew big enough to transplant into offices of their own, they would often ask the office manager for advice on how to set up and survive. The OM would give the name of the partitioning company and, in return, was able to ask for re-vamps of his own office layout at a much reduced rate, whenever they were required. The partitioners insisted on having little signs on the partitions with the name and number of their company, but nobody minded that. It worked. But it only worked because *both sides benefited and both gave quality service.*

Be warm, be wary, be successful

At the end of the day, your best guarantee of a good deal is the success of your own business. Just like the rats leave the sinking ship and the fleas leave the dying cat, your opportunities for extended credit, bigger discounts, faster deliveries and flexible, personal attention will diminish rapidly at the first sign of any decline in your company's health.

Step 10 | From Networking to Internetworking

TAP YOUR CUSTOMERS FOR INFORMATION

How many people really listen to their customers?

Sometimes it's as if all those Total Quality Management books had never been written at all. There are still plenty of firms approaching business as if the customer was their enemy. There are still plenty of companies training their salesforces to learn a script and talk at their customers, rather than listen to them. Even the reps who know they have to sell the benefit, rather than the product, are often far too keen to list their ideas of what the benefits are, without giving the customer room and time to decide how they match up to his needs. It's worth remembering that once they start to talk, customers quite often convince themselves they should be buying – and, at the same time, drop invaluable hints as to what triggers may be useful in other sales situations.

WHO TALKS?

It's not just salesmen who talk to customers. When customers call, they don't usually get right through to their personal contacts straight away. If things have already gone wrong, they may want to be put on to the complaints or customer support department immediately. Does your office present a warm, efficient, consistent, professional image from the moment of the first hello at the switchboard to the time the Help Desk staff spend talking the customer through a software failure? Are there weak links in the chain? Where are they? Whose business is it to find out? And what is being done to strengthen them?

WHO LISTENS?

Even if you have managed to train everyone in the company to present the best possible face to the clients, it's unlikely that you will have specifically trained them all to listen.

Not all complaints are voiced at the complaints desk (even if you have one). Often there are early warning signs of problems to come, or even potential customer defections, which can be picked up by observant and friendly receptionists or delivery staff. The trouble is that, even if they notice these signals, they often don't report them. Their job is seen as being to answer the phone, make the tea or get the delivery note, not to pass back information about customer satisfaction levels.

It doesn't have to be that way. If you can train people to think that this kind of intelligence gathering is their job, you will open up an invaluable channel for unofficial information. What's more, you will be increasing their job satisfaction and involvement and reinforcing their loyalty to your company. It's a classic win/win scenario, so you are unlikely to come up against much resistance. People like to be made to feel important. When it's true that they do have an important role to fill, they will often respond magnificently.

Smart Office | 11 Steps to a User-Friendly Office

> ## According to Dr Johnson
> If you think talking about the ins and outs of networking brings out the worst in people today, you may enjoy the definition included in Samuel Johnson's *Dictionary* (1755).
>
> *"NETWORK – Anything reticulated or decussated, at equal distances, with interstices between the intersections."*
>
> Compared with that, today's niggling little twentieth-century pomposities hardly seem worth worrying about.

THE BIGGEST NETWORKING TOOL OF THEM ALL

There are around 500 million telephone lines in the world. That means, give or take a bit of duplication caused by people in rich countries having a phone at home and one in the office, that roughly one human being in ten has access to a private phone.

No one knows exactly how many people and firms are connected to the Internet now, but it's a comparatively small figure – roughly 35 million, according to some of the more cautious recent guesses. So why all the fuss? The answer is simply that the potential, especially for business, is virtually unlimited.

People can send messages and computer files around the world for the cost of a local phone call, because distance doesn't matter. People can search for information electronically and download it from over 2 million files and documents. People can tap into over 14,000 discussion forums (known as newsgroups). And the present rate of expansion is so fast that every one of these statistics is likely to double within a couple of years, making the Internet a gigantic, worldwide resource pool. For the impoverished peoples of the Third World, the spin-offs will come indirectly. But every business that can afford a computer can now afford to link into this global network. And that opens up commercial possibilities that can only be guessed at.

DO I WANT TO KNOW ABOUT THE INTERNET?

Just because everyone is busy name-dropping and jargonising (and isn't it amazing that that word is 200 years old?) about the wonders of the Internet, you mustn't assume there's nothing in it for you. Being cool is OK, but not if your determined ignorance is actually going to do you and your company a disservice. There has been a lot of hype and claptrap about the Net, but there really is something solid, interesting and useful at the heart of it all.

Step 10 | **From Networking to Internetworking**

In Amsterdam in the sixties, groups of well-meaning hippies and anarchists persuaded thousands of people to give them their old bicycles, which were then sploshed with white paint and put out on the streets for anyone to use, free of charge, at any time. If you wanted to go somewhere in the city, you just walked up to the nearest white bicycle, got on and toddled off to your destination, without having to ask anyone or pay anything. Eventually, of course, the bicycles disappeared, stolen by less communally minded souls or pushed into the canals by vandals (or, possibly, by mixed gangs of bicycle shop owners and taxi drivers). The system, if that's the right word, was chaotic, inefficient, liberating, rather awe-inspiring and ultimately, probably, doomed.

And you could certainly say the same about the Internet. Nobody owns it. Nobody profits from it directly. Nobody manages it, in any real sense. It's all a bit Heath Robinson. Yet even very small companies are finding it can open up surprising new opportunities for them.

A world of potential

The Internet is really nothing more nor less than a worldwide network of computer networks. But because of the things that are kept on those computers around the world and the power of those linked processors, it has become:

- a global electronic library, with astounding information search capabilities
- a dirt-cheap international electronic mail (e-mail) system
- a conference and discussion forum
- a way of giving people access to distant computing resources
- an uncensorable worldwide news service
- a new medium for electronic publishing

The Net now stretches out to more than 200 countries and territories and links over 40,000 computer networks. But what may be even more significant than the sheer numbers is the way it has moved on from its academic and research roots, so that the business sector already represents over half of the Internet and is now developing very rapidly. Simple e-mail applications are growing at breakneck speed, as businesses latch on to the down-to-earth benefits of a system that lets them upload a message by modem and route it automatically to any other computer anywhere on the Internet, in any country, for the price of a local telephone call.

What's really in it for my firm?

There is seldom any danger of Internet enthusiasts underselling the Net's virtues. But amid all the gushing talk about what it could do, it's worth looking at what it actually does usefully do, day in and day out, for ordinary small and medium companies.

| Smart Office | 11 Steps to a User-Friendly Office |

Apart from the ability to pull in almost limitless amounts of information for competitor analysis and market research purposes, it is usually the e-mail connection that makes the most immediate difference for the smaller business. Closely linked to this is the potential for remote working. If AdHoc Computing rides its corporate bicycle to Heathrow and flies to Scotland for a couple of days' consultancy work, it can operate through a modem, down any phone line in Edinburgh, just as if it were back at base in Surrey. Most important of all, any e-mail messages can be picked up just as they would be at the office. For one-man bands, small partnerships and any organisation that is not big enough to have its own communications infrastructure, this ability to work and be in touch, regardless of location, is a major asset.

The principle of remote working can be extended further. A firm that regularly does business in the USA can set up an account with an Internet service provider in America and arrange for its British service provider to forward all e-mail automatically to the American system. So if your people are on a sales drive that will take them from Los Angeles to Chicago and on to New York, they can be in contact all the time, by e-mail, for a total cost that usually works out at about £200 a year.

Plugging into the Net

What do you need to plug into the Internet? In theory, almost any computer, a cheap modem and a connection to an Internet service provider will do the trick. In practice, to avoid hours of frustration, you will want a certain amount of processing power and memory at your disposal.

A 486 PC with at least 4Mb of RAM and a substantial hard drive, the modem (14.4bps or better) and a subscription to any one of 50 or so on-line service providers should add up to a reliable basis for setting out across cyberspace.

Service providers offer different tariff formats (pay-as-you-go or flat fee) and different levels of service and response time, depending on factors such as whether they are based in Britain or the other side of the Atlantic. Among the most popular are:

- CIX (Compulink)   0181 296 9666
- CompuServe   0800 289458
- Demon Internet   0181 349 0063
- BBC Networking Club   0181 752 4159
- Delphi Internet   0171 757 7080
- Pipex   01223 250120

You will need a suite of communications software, which will often come free on a set of disks from your service provider. This will include a communications program (known as a Winsock – Windows socket – for Windows users) which will manage links between the Internet and the rest of the suite, programs for sending and receiving e-mail and an offline mail reader. There will also be a Web browser, a Usenet reader for connecting to newsgroups (again with an offline reader or OLR) and an FTP (file transfer protocol) program which you will use for downloading all sorts of files that are not in mail format, from pictures and music to software.

The offline reader functions are especially important because this is the software that will keep your Internet costs down. After all, the stream of text you are downloading flies down the line far too fast to read.

You could slow it up, but that would mean staying on-line for ever and running up huge bills. OLR support lets you download information from discussion groups and newsgroups and disconnect quickly. You will then be able to read the downloaded text at your own pace, without feeling that the meter is ticking in your ear all the time. Instead of standing in the library to read the whole book, you can take it home with you.

> ## Regs on the Web
> For office managers and others who risk drowning in a sea of paper in an effort to keep up with health and safety rules and procedures, the Web can provide useful help.
>
> The Health & Safety Executive has just recently got its act together and added its two-penn'orth to the government's big World Wide Web site. Contact numbers at the HSE, plus a great deal of regulatory information can now be found at:
> http://www.open.gov.uk/hse/hsehome.htm.

There's a lot of mileage in the World Wide Web

The World Wide Web (WWW) was originally developed to facilitate information sharing among high-energy physicists in different countries. It is the fastest-growing area of the Internet and the part that is most likely to offer something to your firm. The Web links together an almost undreamed-of range of information resources, in text, graphics, sound and even video form. Using clever stuff known as hypermedia technology, it allows users to flip between these resources at the click of a mouse, without needing to know anything about how it happens.

The user has a Web browser program, usually Netscape or Mosaic, which helps find a way round this electronic world and handles the task of displaying Web pages as they were meant to be shown. The browser calls up the information from a Web server, the computer

Smart Office | 11 Steps to a User-Friendly Office

on which that particular set of Web pages is stored. Each Web page or site has a unique address, known, poetically, as its URL, or uniform resource locator – Tesco's, for example, is: http://www.tesco.co.uk, while the UK Government's new information service is at: http://www.open.gov.uk.

There are bits of highlighted text linking separate information resources – known as hyperlinks – embedded in each document and these are the only aids to navigation that the curious seeker after truth needs to use. If you are familiar with the way Windows offers "help" when you click on a highlighted word, you will recognise the technique – it's just about as close to intuitive computer use as you'll ever see. You just look for the words or images highlighted (usually picked out in blue) and choose the direction you wish to explore. Then it's simply click and go.

Surfing with Cantona or troubleshooting with Sir John

Following these links through, the user can gain access to electronic magazines and newspapers (including the internetted versions of the *Sunday Times* and the *Daily Telegraph*) and brochures, advertisements, armchair shopping malls and a host of support services for all kinds of computing and consumer goods, as well as a mass of information about hobbies, environmental concerns and other non-commercial matters.

Click on "Cantona" in today's Electronic Telegraph story about the explosive Frenchman and you'll go back to an earlier story about him. Following a chain of such links back, you would come to details of his kung fu kick at a football supporter, his triumphs on the pitch and eventually right back to his basic biographical details. Change tack halfway through and you might find that clicking on "kung fu" could take you off towards details of Bruce Lee's film career. Start with "Harvey-Jones" and you could find yourself going via ICI to information about work study methods in the 1950s, when Sir John left the navy and began toting a stopwatch and clipboard.

You can wander, following your nose or "surfing", in the jargon. You can search by keywords for the subjects you are looking for, using powerful search engines that you can access directly through a hyperlink. Or you can drop down through the layers of menus in a more traditional directory structure that will take you, say, from a heading called "business", through "engineering" and a couple of sub-menus to "rapid prototyping" or "drives and motors" or your own firm's area of specialist interest, arriving at very detailed information within a few minutes of logging on.

Credibility is at a premium

Glimpsing all this may well start you thinking of ways your firm might exploit the new technology. But you do have to be realistic. One problem with the Web, and the Internet generally, is that it is difficult to know how certain you can be about the accuracy of the

Step 10 From Networking to Internetworking

information you find. There is a lot of rock-solid, factual information. But there is also a lot of opinion masquerading as fact.

There is already a growing tendency for business people to ignore information that does not come from a trusted and reliable source. But the other side of that coin offers you an important opportunity. If your company speaks with unimpeachable authority in its own highly specialised area, the sight of your name and logo on your Web pages will be a guarantee of reliability. However strong the content of your pages, you still need the people who matter to you to want to visit your Web site often. Authority and reliability in your field can make that happen.

To persuade potential customers and others who don't already know your company to visit your Web pages, it is essential to get your URLs (addresses) listed in as many of the directories or search engines as possible. An unvisited Web site is as efficient a way as any of pouring cash down the drain. Luckily, arranging this presence in the directories' listings is mainly a matter of persistence. You fill in an electronic form at the search sites for Yahoo, Global On-Line Directory and others (there's even a Submit-It site which specialises in holding forms for many different directories: http//www.cen.uiuc.edu/~banister/submit-it).

You can also contact other companies that run Web sites covering related areas and ask them if they would incorporate a hypertext link to your site, in return for the same thing in reverse. Combined with conventional publicity activity, such as letting relevant trade magazines know of your new site, this should make people aware that you have something worth visiting.

How would we set up a pilot?

You could set up any number of WWW pages advertising and giving information about your company and its products, stored on your own Web server. But it would be an expensive business, making a start this way, at a time when a more experimental, toe-in-the-water approach might be more sensible. You would want a dedicated Pentium-powered PC with a big, fast hard disk and plenty of RAM, a leased line connection to the Internet, to ensure that people could get through to your pages at any time, and a suitable software package. Since the leased line alone is likely to cost £10,000 or more in the first year, you would be making a major commitment right from the off.

Luckily, smaller firms can afford to try things out on the Web at a far less ambitious level, gearing up bit by bit if they find they have hit on successful ideas. The key to this is renting space on an existing World Wide Web server.

If you want to create a WWW site of more than just one or two pages, you will need to rent several megabytes of space on the server. There is no such thing as a typical size for a site, but a small, simple presentation, with straightforward information and very few graphics, might need as little as five megabytes. At the other extreme, a large and lavish

Smart Office | 11 Steps to a User-Friendly Office

Web site, stuffed with graphics, audio and video, could take up 1,000 megabytes – a good quality half-minute sound clip alone might need 1MB. If you are interested, find friends with access to the Web and look over their shoulders at sites run by firms like AT&T, Federal Express, Virgin Music, Apple, Time-Warner and, inevitably, Microsoft, to see what the big players are doing. (You can find almost any company that's on the World Wide Web by pointing your Web browser to http://www.yahoo.com/business/corporations/.)

Renting a basic five or ten megabytes will cost you anything from £25 to £80 a month, plus a small set-up fee, from service providers such as Pipex or Demon Internet – which boasts one of the biggest Web sites in Europe and numbers huge corporations like Rank Xerox and at least one police force among its customers – or smaller operators like Frontier Internet (0171 242 3383) or the Scottish-based Almac (01324 666336).

Just keep it simple

Although WWW pages are written in what appears to be a daunting code called HTML, or hypertext mark-up language, creating a straightforward Web page is not as difficult as most people fear. And it can be made surprisingly easy by using Microsoft's Internet Assistant, which effectively turns Word for Windows into a basic HTML editor.

If you are going to put a few pages together for a trial run, the trick is to keep it simple. As long as you write clear, emphatic headlines and text, stick to a maximum of two graphics or logos per page and build in a link back to the starting point (known as the home page) every couple of pages, you will end up with something people can understand and use.

Simplicity also makes it easier when you need to update an existing page, which will happen often if you experiment with some of the more commercially interesting applications, such as on-line sales, where prices and product details must be right all the time. Again, the procedure is not difficult. Updates are generally carried out by modifying your HTML files, uploading them to the server's holding area and merely informing the server's operators that the update is waiting there to be implemented.

If you find it hard going, try asking your designers

As you would expect, there is no shortage of computer consultancies wheeling in the sky and waiting to assist firms anxious to explore the World Wide Web. But there is also another, less obvious, source of advice and expertise that might be appropriate, particularly for the smaller firm.

If you have a good working relationship with the design group your company uses for brochures or pack designs, talk to the designers. Many of them have quickly built up a good working knowledge of the Internet and the World Wide Web. And because they tend to come at it from a less computer-dominated point of view, you may understand a lot more of what they are saying the first time round.

Step 10 | From Networking to Internetworking

IN A NUTSHELL

1. Expand the network

- Don't draw the lines too rigidly between your work and the rest of your life
    - the whole world consists of potential customers and market research material
    - try to think beyond nine to five
- Networking is about building good lines of communication between yourself and as many people and organisations as possible
    - it helps you to sell your product
    - it helps you manage your staff

2. Look after your network with a relational database

- Customise it to suit your requirements
- Start by recording as much data about clients as possible. You can be more selective later
- Once your database is set up the way you want it, there's no limit to the size of your network, so keep it growing!
- Keep it tidy, take out the dead wood, update as businesses grow

3. Build good working relationships

- Rules for suppliers and clients
    - treat them very well – you will get back the treatment you give
    - go for win/win whenever possible
    - cost in your time and effort
    - try to promote a two-way information exchange

4. Learn to listen

- The greatest network management tool isn't the computer database – it's the ability to listen
- Encourage a culture of information gathering and feedback among employees

5. Networking without frontiers

- How the World Wide Web gives you unlimited networking capabilities
- How to get in, how to get out and what to do while you're there

STEP 11: LASTING IMPRESSIONS

Step 11 | Lasting Impressions

SMART PRESENTATIONS WORK

WHAT COUNTS IS WHAT'S BEHIND THE PRESENTATION

Once you've succeeded in making some significant progress towards creating the smart office, it's time to look at how you project that new approach in your dealings with the outside world.

If you don't market, you don't make it, they say. But some companies manage to market themselves and their attitudes as the brand, quite apart from any individual products. Marks & Spencer has done it brilliantly for years, the Body Shop, more idiosyncratically, for a decade or so. Sony pulls it off around the world. All three are utterly convincing. Scratch the surface at M&S and what do you find underneath? More M&S. It's consistent, it's credible and you just know there are going to be no ugly surprises.

What's more, the most important of all the marketing media for Marks is not above-the-line advertising but word of mouth. You can't buy that, but you can encourage it. The main marketing activity of M&S is the maintenance of the quality of experience each customer enjoys on each visit to the store.

But it is not just retailing chains and Japanese multinationals that can benefit from projecting values such as consistency, integrity and inventiveness. Even tiny firms operating in specialised or local markets can gain by letting the world know they work on smart office principles, rather than dragging unwilling and demotivated staff in to do boring jobs in unhelpful conditions five days a week.

It can be as crude – and as crucial – as getting the overdraft facilities you need because the bank manager was impressed when he visited the office. Or it can be winning a giant order because the customer believes your people have the ingenuity to gear up for it without taking their eyes off the ball.

> Smart Office | 11 Steps to a User-Friendly Office

How you put the message across is largely beyond the scope of this book. Major advertising budgets are likely to be placed in the hands of specialists, though the facilities manager will often be left to sort out the unglamorous, detailed stuff, such as exhibition stands for the smaller shows, entries in Yellow Pages and trade directories, customer open days and presentations and lining up promotional gifts and company Christmas cards.

Face-to-face work moves mountains

These are all worth taking seriously. You may not be talking to millions, but the people you are talking to – customers, potential customers and suppliers – will all have some interest in what you do and how you go about doing it. The hit rate for converting customer contacts into done deals is very high in this kind of close-up, non-mass media promotional activity, so you can make a real difference to the bottom line if you do it well.

The face-to-face situations are particularly important. Exhibitions and presentations give your people the opportunity to make a big impact, through their positive attitudes, their enthusiasm and their alert professionalism, in a very short time. People remember people, long after they've forgotten the details of what was said. Every face-to-face contact is a chance to roll out the smart office concept and extend it into your dealings with the wider world. Take those chances and make the most of them and you'll be making a huge contribution to the marketing of your company and your products or services.

ABOVE ALL, KNOW YOUR AUDIENCE

Organising presentations is yet another of those jobs that doesn't logically fall within the responsibilities of an office or facilities manager. It's a specialised business and should really be left to dedicated and highly trained professionals from the marketing communications unit or the press and PR department, backed by enormous technical resources and infinitely flexible budgets. However, back in the real world, that's not what happens, except in a few very large organisations.

The sorts of presentations you are likely to be volunteered into handling will probably come into a few fairly clear-cut categories. There are internal presentations, sales conferences, inspirational rallies and so on, which are basically in-house affairs, with a supposedly tame audience, and may well be conducted on company premises. There is another breed of presentation where some or all of those attending have a common interest in the success of the meeting and your product. This would include the launch of a new product or catalogue to your dealers or distributors or even to customers.

The third – and potentially most expensive and disappointing – category is the press conference. Because it is the toughest nut to crack and because most of the things that can go wrong with the less public presentations can do it even worse at a press conference, that is probably the most interesting place to start.

Step 11 | Lasting Impressions

If you know the people you are trying to communicate with, presentations are easy to manage. If you don't know them personally, but know a lot about them and what they care about, you can build on that common ground. When you are dealing with journalists, though, it is planning and attention to detail that will see you through.

MEET THE PRESS – AND COME OUT SMILING

Never hold a full-blown press conference if you can help it. You can always draw up lists of dozens of journals that might be interested. But unless your situation is very unusual, the bald fact is that there will be just two or three that really count, that really matter in your world.

If that's the case, it may not be a good use of resources to go through all the hassles and expense of setting up a press conference for 20 or 30 reporters. If there's one key opinion former you must get, bear in mind that for the cost of even a small-scale press conference you could afford to fly him or her anywhere on the planet for a face-to-face chat with your chairman or an on-site demonstration of your American partner's new technology. Focused attention and focused resources swing the odds in your favour.

But it may not be up to you to decide whether the press conference happens. You may simply be lumbered with making it a roaring success.

Realism is going to be the key, so you start by accepting, despite what's been said above, that your bosses will want to see journalists there in numbers. Send out 100 invitations three weeks in advance (have cards printed, with a map on the back, rather than sending letters) and you might get provisional yeses from half those journals, though you'll have to get someone chasing them up on the phone to reach a 50 per cent acceptance rate.

If 50 journalists say they'll come, plan for 30 and set out the room with 25 chairs.

Assuming 30 people do turn up, the last few laggards can act like Cecil B De Milles' armies of extras and stand at the sides and back to make the place look packed and busy. It's a common and costly error to imagine you need to cater for a big crowd of journalists, unless you're launching Windows 95, announcing the reunion of the three surviving Beatles or awarding Nobel or National Lottery prizes.

THE RIGHT VENUE

Where and when you choose to hold a public presentation or press conference can often make all the difference between success or failure. There are classic mistakes, for example, like trying to get the press to come to an event on any sort of moving boat or ship. (They won't turn up, because they know they will be unable to go when deadlines or boredom prompt them to make their excuses and leave.)

Smart Office | **11 Steps to a User-Friendly Office**

But generally – unless you have privileged access to the Tower of London, the Lloyds building, HMS Victory, Brands Hatch, the Channel Tunnel or a suitable palace or stately home – the location you choose will be no more than a neutral background to the main event. Picking a place the journalists who matter can get to easily is often the most important factor and it is possible to be quite specific about some of the London venues that will help you get it right.

For example, a hotel such as The Savoy or The Ritz has status and style. Both are attractive and accessible. Neither, of course, is cheap. If your press conference is linked to a trade show at Earls Court or Olympia and the relevant journalists will be around that area, pick one of the Kensington hotels within easy reach of the exhibition halls.

And it needn't cost an arm and a leg

On the other hand, if you need to reach the women's magazines or sport and leisure journals, there is one less exalted, but highly practical, venue that often trumps the lot. Some 30 leading women's magazines and countless specialist, leisure and sport titles (from *Melody Maker* to *Amateur Gardening*, *New Scientist* and *Yachting World*) are published by IPC from the twin peaks of King's Reach Towers, on the South Bank. IPC has a press conference room there that can be hired by outsiders, virtually guaranteeing the presence of at least some of the editors working in the twin towers, particularly round about lunchtime. Being able to go to a press conference by lift, rather than taxi, has definite attractions for the working journalist. You can find out more from IPC's Presentations Department on 0171-261 5000.

If your budget has to be kept realistically small, don't trim costs by going for a cheap hotel – apply a bit of lateral thinking instead. For example, it is worth investigating the headquarters buildings of some of the many institutes and professional bodies based in London. Glasgow and Edinburgh, Cardiff and cities like Birmingham, Manchester, Liverpool, Leeds and Sheffield offer similar opportunities, though it is a simple matter of fact that the greatest concentration of journals and journalists is in and around London. The principle of taking the show to the press can be well worth pursuing to its logical conclusion, though, which is why the area around Sutton and Croydon, where there is an enticing cluster of trade and technical magazines, gets more than its fair share of press conferences.

In the provinces, as well as in the capital, there are grand and imposing rooms available for hire at many museums, art galleries and universities. And the Institute of Contemporary Arts, in the Mall, just down the road from the Queen, is one attractive Central London venue that offers an element of artistic cachet, combined with down-to-earth value for money.

THE RIGHT TIME

Exactly when you decide to hold your customer presentation, your sales team briefing or

Step 11 | **Lasting Impressions**

your dealers' get-together is up to you. When you hold a press conference, though, it's a different kettle of fish. It will pay you to stick tightly to the accepted, conventional wisdom of the PR trade. Timing is a simple matter and the golden rule is "be early".

For maximum impact, hold your press conference early in the day, early in the week and early in the month.

The underlying reasons are many and complex. National dailies have to have their stories lined up by lunchtime, trade monthlies are always tied up with production matters later on in the month and experience shows it's easier to get reporters out of their offices on Mondays, Tuesdays and Wednesdays. If the journals that matter most to you happen to be evening papers, there's even more of a premium attached to an early start. In fact, you might even scale the event down and make it a breakfast briefing with a handful of key journalists, because reporters on the evenings will want their stories by about 10a.m., at the latest.

GIVE THE PRESS SOME RED MEAT

Organising a presentation for the press is a different matter from laying on a conference for your sales force or arranging a get-together for a couple of dozen of your favourite customers.

Many journalists, particularly outside Fleet Street, are warm, sympathetic human beings with happy families, well-tended gardens and no particular cannibalistic tendencies. Some of the trade press editors in your area may well be long-standing friends of yours. But it is worth remembering, right from the start, that every journalist you meet will have some agenda of his or her own — and whatever's on it, it won't be what you would ideally wish to see there.

Reporters, feature writers, technical correspondents and editors will all be looking to get something out of your presentation that they can take away with them. And though they may be happy to accept any samples or freebies you feel inclined to offer them, it is a big mistake to think that's what they want. What they want is stories.

Cynical as some may seem, they are all, without exception, closet romantics. They get their kicks from the applause that rings in the air when they unearth a good story. But, unlike most other performers, they carry their own audiences around with them, in the back of their heads. If you have an interesting, surprising story to impart to a journalist, watch his or her reaction as the penny drops. You can spot the adrenalin rush at a distance of ten paces as the hunter picks out the outline of a good story.

So Rule 1 in dealing with the press is:
Never pretend you've got something to offer if you haven't.

Smart Office | 11 Steps to a User-Friendly Office

Rule 2 is equally simple:
Don't lie. You're under no obligation to blurt out the whole warts-and-all truth about anything, but what you do say must be true.

Rule 3 completes the set:
Be organised – that means planning a long way ahead, inviting the right people, chasing up the invitations, lining up good speakers, preparing press kits and sticking to schedule.

Tell people what's going to happen

When you send the original invitation, don't just announce the start time – state a finishing time, too.

Short is good. If you can keep the main presentation to 20 minutes, with five to ten minutes for questions, it will feel like an event, rather than a meeting. Part of the invitation pack should be an outline of the programme. If this says "10a.m. start, 10.30a.m. finish", journalists will be able to plan their morning and will know that you are not going to keep them hanging around for hours waiting for a punch line that's not worth the trouble.

The press kits you give out on the day (before, rather than after, the presentation) can be simple and cheap to produce. Full text of any speeches, names and titles of key executives (to avoid mis-spellings and mistakes in print) and a single sheet of product and company background information (with some relevant facts and figures) should do the trick. Pin photographs that are available up on a display board, clearly numbered, and let journalists place orders for the shots they want.

In the aftermath of a press conference, there is one more thing you must do before you collapse in a corner. Courier a press pack round to those journalists of any importance to you who promised they would come and then let you down. Couriers cost money, but your investment can pay off handsomely. If the reporter or editor in question is a decent sort, the guilt that's triggered by the arrival of the press pack may actually lead to more coverage than you'd have had if things had gone as originally planned.

GO EASY ON THE FOOD

Very short press conferences and brief internal presentations will not usually require you to become involved in the niceties of catering strategies. All-day salesforce conventions will mean providing some sort of lunch, plus two coffee and tea breaks, while any event you lay on for customers, dealers, distributors or wholesalers must offer them a buffet and bar.

The common-sense rule is to avoid food and drink wherever you decently can – it costs a lot and can lead to unpredictable behaviour.

Step 11 | Lasting Impressions

If you are offering food, go for quality rather than volume, but make sure there are some items with a bit of substance. People who have skipped a meal to get to your presentation will have to wolf down an awful lot of those delicate little canapes to stave off the pangs of hunger and might be more appreciative of a hunk of bread and pate or a slice of quiche.

When briefing caterers, always order less food than you expect to need. This is a safe bet and will obviously save you money. However definite people seem the day before, some of your "certainties" will not turn up. Other people will be in a hurry and leave as soon as the main business is over. Some will just not feel like eating, while very few will actually require double portions.

BAR BEHAVIOUR

The reactions of journalists when faced with a free drink are the subject of a lot of ill-informed humour. As a general rule, they will have to go back and face the baleful glare of either a monitor or an editor afterwards. But there are some — and some customers and dealers at trade presentations — who find the magnetism of a cashless bar hard to resist. You need to maintain some control.

The simplest way, at both press conferences and trade receptions, is to arrange that the bartender will shut down at a specific time and start to serve coffee. This will wind the proceedings up neatly enough and, since many guests will already have drifted away, you need only order half as many coffees as the number of people attending.

PRESENTING YOUR BUSINESS PROFESSIONALLY

Whether the audience consists of journalists, shareholders, employees or customers, make sure you get your message across as clearly and powerfully as you can by preparing properly for the occasion.

MAKING THE PRESENTATION

It is often the job of the office manager to organise presentations, rather than give them. But when you do find, occasionally, that it's going to be you up there on the platform, remember you don't have to be a natural to be a success. Any reasonably warm, intelligent human being can act the part of a successful speaker.

You are already an expert on presentations. You know all you need to know. You have been a critical member of audiences since you first went to school, so all you have to do is recall the good ones and the bad ones you have seen over the years and figure out the differences.

But, of course, one reason why people dread giving presentations is that they don't do it often enough. And there's a simple remedy for that.

START SMALL AND PRACTISE

Quite apart from your need to practise your skills, a brief presentation from the office manager, weekly or fortnightly, is an excellent way of binding a team together and soon becomes the kind of habit everybody takes for granted. Start scheduling this as part of the office routine.

If it works well, you may find that, even without your sending the e-mail round, people will start to gather at the usual time and doughnuts will appear. It's a great way to scotch rumours (or spread them), float new ideas and congratulate people who've brought in a new client or had babies. It's good for morale and good for team working. You might like to send a standard memory jogger round two days before and invite people to send you agenda items.

Always make sure you keep it short and sharp. Half an hour should be the maximum – and 20 minutes is better.

There should be plenty of positive spin-offs. But, if it does nothing else, a scheduled slot like this will give you the chance to polish up your own presentation skills for when you really need them. In sales-oriented offices, it can also be used to let new recruits practise sales presentation technique, with the rest of the staff offering constructive criticism and support.

SETTING YOURSELF UP

Most occasional speakers, if pinned to the wall, would admit that their aims are simple:

1. Not to make a fool of myself
2. To put my message across

Experienced presenters are more likely to have a different way of looking at it. The aims would be seen as:

1. To entertain my audience
2. To let the messages come across, as they will if the audience is alert and interested

Group Two has a lot more chance of success than Group One. Messages travel without being pushed, if the situation is right. But the Group Two people still run some risk of downgrading both the message and themselves. The real successes on stage are the ones who put a third factor first – the audience. If you can tune in to an audience and speak the language that's right for this particular gathering of people, the chances are that they will love you and listen enthusiastically to what you have to say.

Let's take a look at the three important parts of every presentation.

Step 11 | Lasting Impressions

1. The Message

This is what needs saying. Since most things can be presented in many different ways (the half-full, half-empty glass, for example), don't assume there's only one way to tell it.

- **Summarise your message inside your head.** Before you put anything on paper, spend *five minutes only* defining, for your own benefit, the points you need to put across to this particular audience.
- **Gather your sources.** This is the time to collect the information you need, including data, quotations and anecdotes. Have it all to hand and read it through. Double check the accuracy of all your facts, as one wrong number will devalue all the accurate and trustworthy things you say. Don't quote too many statistics – it's usually best to put them on the OHP or handout and simply refer to them.
- **Write out what you're going to say.** Put it all in – every point, every detail, every joke and every spontaneous throwaway line. Then mould it into shape and prune it, making sure you have a beginning, a middle and an end.
- **Read it.** Amend until it fits the time allocated to you. Always include a couple of optional anecdotes in case you over- or underrun. An underrun is less important because you can normally extend the question and answer session to cover this. Bluntly, no one in the world has ever complained that any monologue of more than ten minutes or so was too short.
- **Re-read it.** Do it in front of a mirror. Include gestures and pauses and time the whole thing. Choreograph your performance.

2. The Medium

This is you, whether you like the idea or not. Success depends on preparing yourself properly.

- **Assemble your props**
    - Postcards are the classic way to keep yourself on track. Stick to less than ten and number the cards in red – this makes it much easier to get them back in order when you drop them. You can also Treasury-tag them loosely together.
    - OHPs can double up as working notes, so that you will be looking at the same points as your audience. Don't overload each slide. Acetates are cheap. If necessary, use two, rather than cramming too much onto one. The visuals should be both clear and entertaining and there is no harm in letting your audience see the numbering of your points. It gives them some idea of timing and pace.
    - Multimedia back-up to your talk is great, as long as it doesn't either break down or

overshadow you. In the age of TV, audience expectations are high, but many presenters still end up with graphics on a par with a Victorian magic lantern show. Even if you can't afford state-of-the-art material, whatever you do use must be perfect – not necessarily high-tech, but well laid out, in the correct order, technically accurate and with no spelling errors. Get other people to double check everything for you. They will spot errors you have got used to seeing.

- **Run a dress rehearsal**. Wear whatever you plan to wear on the day. If this is not your strong point, emulate Mrs Thatcher and take advice. Simple styles and strong colours work best – a striking tie or piece of jewellery can distract from what you are saying. Looking good is important, as it shows you are taking both the subject and the audience seriously. If you can manage without them, always remove your glasses before speaking. If possible, check out the actual place where you will be performing. Know how many steps there are up to the platform and how the equipment works.
- **Check with your supporting cast**. If you are organising the event yourself, it goes without saying that you have to know what each speaker intends to cover, when and for how long they will talk and what equipment they need. But even if you are just one of the speakers on the list, take the trouble to talk to the others in advance, so that what you say complements, and doesn't overlap or contradict, points made by other speakers.
- **Be a star**
  - Make an impressive entrance. Head for the lectern in a purposeful, enthusiastic manner and stand with your feet firmly on the platform. Pause for a few seconds before you speak. Start with a joke or a humorous remark if possible.
  - Use humour, even if you are giving out bad news. People switch off if they see an entirely black, or even grey, picture. You don't have to be a stand-up comedian, but even a few good-humoured remarks can make the difference between keeping and losing an audience. Go for the nod, not the nodding off.
  - Ad lib (just once at the beginning, if you can't manage more than that). Refer to something an earlier speaker said, a news item or even the weather. It sends a signal that says: "I'm a real person – I'm talking to you and I'm not tied to a script." This places you and the audience in the same world and creates empathy. Then go back to your script.

When you have your message engraved on your heart and feel sure you could deliver it in your sleep, give some thought to:

3. The Audience

This is a bunch of people who, whatever their formal and official reasons for being there, are hoping to be informed, stimulated and entertained. Few will have been sent at gunpoint.

Most will be hoping you succeed in giving them something of value. So if you have something worth saying, remember the audience will be predisposed to be interested in it.

- **Tailor both message and medium to the audience.** Don't use jargon and acronyms to the uninitiated, though if you are talking to a group of experts on a technical subject they will be irritated if you spell everything out. Be appropriate.
- **Talk to the audience beforehand.** If possible, be seen by and speak to at least some of the people you will be addressing during the coffee session or lunch prior to your talk. This is a great way of getting them on your side before you start.
- **Speak in your normal style – but project your voice.** This is one technique that does need practice if you are to make yourself heard without sounding artificial. If possible, record your rehearsal and listen to the playback.
- **Make eye contact with individual members of the audience.** Avoid blankly scanning the audience with your eyes. Don't fix on any one person for too long and don't be thrown by body language – if you are noticing someone looking away from you or shaking their head, you are probably focusing on them too much.
- **Have 50 heart-to-heart conversations at the same time.** It's difficult, but essential if you want to put your message across. And it does become easier with practice. Like all conversations, a presentation is two-way communication. That means you should be aware of noise and movement levels and, in smaller groups, body language as well, while you're actually speaking. It also means giving some value, as well as just some time, to the question and answer sessions at the end. Don't be afraid of these. They are usually easier to handle than the talk itself and, from the speaker's point of view, they are bound to be the most interesting and useful part of the whole affair.
    - Feedback can be a powerful management tool. Some people will give out information and insights in a group which they would never do in a one-to-one. In any case, the group will have a dynamic of its own which you, as the speaker and the person in control of the situation, can influence to your advantage.
    - To get the most useful feedback, you need to stay in control. If you lose it, you do both yourself and your listeners a disservice. If the situation begins to feel anarchic, the audience will feel uncomfortable and stop learning and contributing. You are responsible for creating a safe but stimulating environment, in which ideas can usefully be aired and exchanged.
    - Restate the question when giving your answer. It buys you time and helps other people to think as well.
    - Do try to answer at least one question with a one-word response. This dramatic technique makes you look authoritative. But don't overdo it.
    - Don't acknowledge any questioner by name, unless you can do it for everyone present. You risk alienating the ones you don't recognise.

- Don't say "Good question." If you say it every time, it sounds tedious and can be taken as patronising. And if you don't, you may upset the people you fail to say it to.
- Don't make eye contact with the questioner – that's too personal. But do be sure to make eye contact with someone else while you answer.
- Don't ask whether they got the answer they wanted. This gives away too much control.
- Don't fudge an answer you don't know. Turn it into an advantage by inviting someone else to contribute an answer. There will always be someone who can. If the questioner remains dissatisfied, he or she will usually seek you out afterwards.

SETTING UP SOMEONE ELSE'S PRESENTATION

Organising a presentation for someone else may not be as nerve-racking as actually delivering it yourself. But if you've been told to take charge, you still have a responsibility to organise it comprehensively. Many presentations are a shambles, simply because the organiser thinks that his or her duties come to an end as soon as the date has been set and the flipcharts have been ordered.

- **Check out the performer.** You may not have any choice about this if it's your company chairman or some vastly expensive celebrity. But if you do have a choice, you might subtly try to ensure that the person who does this sort of thing best in your organisation (as opposed to the person who thinks he does) takes centre stage.

    If you are working with outsiders, always double check that the speaker knows where he or she is meant to be, and when. You can actually improve the performance by ensuring a smooth passage from the speaker's own office to the rostrum, finding out what he or she may need and making sure it's provided. It can only do harm to your organisation if speakers are not met, shown the restrooms, given tea or whatever else is appropriate and made to feel comfortable. The more famous or expensive the speaker, the more likely he or she is to have a well-drilled roadshow routine that more or less takes care of itself. Check, though, and don't assume that this will always be the case.
- **Make sure the performer is briefed.** Does she know how long she has to deliver her talk? Has he been given any vital updates about your organisation that might affect what he says? If your chairman dropped dead in the lift at lunchtime, don't leave it until the last minute to tell the speaker, especially if they were golfing partners.
- **Set up the set.** Any presentation, however small, is theatre. Whether you are organising it or giving it, go for maximum impact That means ensuring that there are enough flipcharts, the whiteboard markers haven't run out and the projector has both a working bulb and a ready-checked reserve.

Step 11 | Lasting Impressions

HOW HIGH TECH SHOULD YOU GET?
Keep it simple and keep it safe

Every year, the range of presentation equipment available to ordinary businesses increases. And so does the potential for finding yourself very publicly tangled up in a high tech nightmare.

The temptation to go for the gasp of admiration from your awestruck audience as your new LCD projector throws a brilliant PC-generated colour video image onto the screen behind you is always going to be strong. The lure of the videoconferencing link-up and the electronic whiteboard is hard to resist. If you have access to this kind of advanced presentation equipment, this is where you need to demonstrate a will of iron.

It is an absolute rule that anything that can go wrong will do it in a press conference, if you give it half a chance.

So there is every reason to play safe. If you want to show people what amazing tricks your sophisticated toys can perform, do it in a presentation to your own sales staff and not in the public spotlight.

Keep the revolution indoors for now

Some of these new machines are very slick indeed. Polaroid's top-of-the-range Polaview 105 LCD projector, for example, is an extraordinarily flexible multimedia presentation tool, even if it does cost nearly £7,000. It is aimed at letting you project onto a big screen exactly what you see on your PC, matching still or video images with fully integrated stereo sound. 3M is also working towards the same goal of PC-driven interactive multimedia presentations, with a series of mono and colour LCD projection panels that are used with an ordinary 400W overhead projector and range in price from about £1,100 to over £4,000. Used in conjunction with a graphics program such as PowerPoint, these LCD panels can make for strikingly effective presentations, without demanding a great deal of skill.

Other innovations, such as the Rapesco True Image Projector (about £1,000, and possibly the eventual successor to the OHP), better and cheaper videoconferencing units and Casio's board copier (point it at a whiteboard, blackboard or flipchart and you can print out A4 paper copies for everyone in the meeting) are also beginning to change the face of live presentations.

But there are two possible disadvantages if you use any of these newfangled devices in public. One is the flummox factor if anything does start to go wrong. The other is the fact that unfamiliar and eye-catching bits of technology may well distract your listeners from the message you want them to hear.

Smart Office | 11 Steps to a User-Friendly Office

For the time being, the more public the occasion, the more conservative your choice of equipment should be.

Ring the changes with slides, video, OHPs and flipcharts

Use 35mm slides for their unsurpassed brightness and clarity. Use film or video clips that you have seen and checked through before. Use OHP transparencies for their simplicity and flexibility. Use a flipchart with pre-written pages for dramatic "reveals" or ad libbed diagrams for an impression of action and spontaneity. Switch from one to the other and back, to change the focus of the audience's attention and vary the pace of the presentation. But do keep to the tried and tested methods. This is no time to be sticking your neck out.

Show and tell whenever you can

It's not always possible to find an excuse. But, generally speaking, when in doubt, do something.

People lose concentration fast if they are just sitting watching men in suits talk, even if the subject matter is genuinely interesting. So do something. Pass out samples of your company's new heat sensors, jelly babies or spring washers. Introduce the weightlifter who claims your new keyboard is the only one he can get his fingers round. Use a giant model to show how your new suspension system cushions shocks. Prove your cardboard packaging is ten times as strong by jumping on it.

Do something. In the end, it hardly matters what you do, as long as it has some marginal relevance to your products or services.

A clear, decisive, highly visual demonstration of exactly what makes your product superior to the worldwide brand leader would obviously be ideal. But we're not all going to have that kind of opportunity.

What you can be sure of, though, is that journalists, buyers, distributors and ordinary mortals will always remember any presentation where something happens far more clearly than another event where people just stand up, say their piece and sit down again. The visual memory of movement and action provides a mnemonic for your whole presentation, making it stick in the mind when it would otherwise be forgotten and making it more vivid whenever something – such as, perhaps, your advertising – prompts people to recall it.

Step 11 Lasting Impressions

OPEN DAYS

If you work in the kind of company that holds its own open days or sends you out to represent it when invitations come in from suppliers, customers and competitors, you'll be very familiar with the limited range of standard formats. The name badge always comes first, but it can be followed in any order by the other ingredients: information (visual displays, lectures and presentations), refreshments and relationship building. Information-gathering on the part of the host company is an optional extra.

The acknowledged purpose behind these functions is simply to expand business. Whether you are Capital Radio in London, an organic farm in Northumbria or a prestigious management training college, the aim is the same — to impress your clients and anyone else whose goodwill and understanding you need to stay alive.

KNOW WHY YOU'RE DOING IT

The problem with open days is that they tend to be a company tradition (or not). How they're run or whether they're held at all tends to be accepted and taken for granted after the first time. "We've always had an annual open day, we're doing well and our customers seem to like it. Why would we stop now?"

But is it really cost effective? And could you do it better? Usually, all that an office manager asks of an open day is that nothing goes disastrously wrong. As long as the brochures are printed on time, the sandwiches are delivered and there are as many visitors as there were last year, it's considered a success. But you wouldn't plan any other expensive promotional activity as casually as this, would you?

Before you decide whether to go ahead, what to spend and who should be invited, be very clear about what you want to achieve.

To impress your clients	– Show them that besides having an impressive product range, your firm is also modern, efficient and caring, with friendly and knowledgeable staff
	– Make them aware of any new developments they may not know about and of any new products you might want to sell them
	– Thank them for their business
To sweeten relationships with suppliers	– Show them that you are an impressive, solid, reliable company to do business with (this should improve both your credit facilities and the service you get)
	– Make them feel that they are a valued part of your business environment and that it's a dynamic place to be
	– Thank them for the service they've given you

Smart Office | 11 Steps to a User-Friendly Office

To facilitate networking and put your company at the centre of the web	— It's useful to run a printout from your database and take an overview from time to time. It can be even more enlightening to run a three-dimensional check on the people and organisations that sustain your livelihood. Virtual reality may make real cocktail parties unnecessary in the future, but right now there's no substitute for sending out the invitations, buying in the drinks and hiring the extra cleaners to sort the place out afterwards
	— Helping companies make informal contacts, with your own business as the focus, can have useful spin-offs. Two clients of Acme Designs who ran complementary engineering businesses came up with the idea of a joint brochure. Since their joint budget was so much larger than the two separate ones, the result was far more eye-catching and adventurous — good for them and good for Acme
To enable your people to meet your clients and your clients to get to know your staff	— Long-standing communication problems have been solved in five minutes over a glass of wine or a cup of tea. When real people talk it can add a new dimension to every telephone conversation between them for the next year
	— Having a chat without a deadline on the agenda sometimes makes it possible to talk around a problem and see new angles that can make all the difference
To make sure you know what's going on	— Observing your clients and suppliers as they wander around your open day may show you connections you never suspected and make it possible to communicate in ways that never happen in hurried one-to-one meetings
To raise awareness of your company and what it does in the wider community	— Even if you don't happen to be the local hospital or radio station, there are benefits from having a good community profile: • Talented local people may come looking for jobs before you even put the advertisement in the newspaper • Any proposed expansion or change of use on your premises is likely to be considered more sympathetically • You are more likely to get free PR from positive comments in the local press

Step 11 | **Lasting Impressions**

To raise staff morale	– There's something about the team effort involved in getting an office ready for an open day that can really bond a group of colleagues together. The need to put on a bold front is the best of all antidotes to petty in-fighting. Once a year at least, everyone is united in the common cause. The wise office manager taps into this surge of positive energy by:

- following the open day with a staff social evening
- noting any alliances and unexpected talents which emerge in the flurry of preparation and trying to capitalise on them in the rest of the working year

To find out what you could do better	– You can learn a lot from the casual comments people make when they are drifting around your factory or office, with no pressure to buy or sell. Make sure that your staff are briefed before the event to be aware of and feed back to you any suggestions or criticisms they may hear during the course of the day. This isn't just about impressing your contacts, it's an information-gathering exercise as well

GOLDEN RULES FOR OPEN DAYS

The only golden rule about style is that there are no golden rules.

But when it comes to organisation and efficiency you really do have to walk your talk. Running an event like this well takes time and skill. Like so many other occasional activities, it often falls naturally into the lap of the office manager to organise, even though it may be quite detrimental to whatever else she or he is trying to do. If this is the case, either keep it very low-key and simple, so that the minimum of work is required, **or** consider outsourcing the job. There are companies who do this for a living and if their initial quote sounds high, it probably wouldn't if you actually costed everything in at its full value, including:

- the hours/days your own staff would spend setting it up
- the cost of hiring extra equipment
- the catering costs

If you do decide to do it in house, remember that you are, voluntarily, putting yourselves on display. The effectiveness of your business will be judged by the effectiveness of your open day.

- Check and double check the guest list. Make sure names are right and everyone is included

> Smart Office | 11 Steps to a User-Friendly Office

- Send invitations out well in advance and ask for replies. Making invitation cards look impressive adds weight to the occasion and makes it more likely that you will have a high attendance rate. Send reminders a few days before the event, with the excuse of adding a new piece of information – a guest celebrity, a champagne raffle or whatever suits your audience
- Match the style of catering to the style of your business. Don't give the wrong message by looking too lavish or too penny-pinching
- Brief staff thoroughly in advance and make it clear to them that they have key roles in the operation
- Be prepared to have your premises spring-cleaned (or decorated, if it's time for a new coat of paint)
- Try to capitalise on the event to get free (or even paid-for) local and national publicity. And take photos for the noticeboard which include all members of staff

ONCE UPON AN OPEN DAY

Acme Designs, a prestigious but well established graphic design company in Fulham, had a tradition of holding two open evenings per year. One was for clients and one for suppliers and other contacts. The second group even included a few firms like Acme, only smaller, because it was sometimes convenient to farm out work. In order to save having to put up displays and hire the glasses twice, the clients' party was held the day before the suppliers were invited. But there were two interesting differences between these parties. The clients were entertained with smoked salmon and champagne, served to them by the company's partners, while the following night's guests were handed coffee and sandwiches by the office manager and her support staff.

As Acme continued slowly expanding, it was noticed, with some surprise, that the firm was being overtaken by some of the smaller businesses that had formerly been subcontractors. Although Acme was selling creativity, the partners were not applying it to the way they ran their own business. Then disaster struck and change caught up with them. The senior partner had a heart attack while pouring champagne at one of the parties and opted for early retirement. They replaced him with a bright young graduate from one of the little local design groups they used for overload work.

The new graduate's combination of technical skill and willingness to try new ideas made her an inspired designer. But her lack of respect for tradition also extended to the office itself. Even the normally imperturbable office manager was upset. She'd been there since the beginning and, while she knew she wasn't as important as the designers, she had her own domain and ruled it efficiently. It wasn't that she didn't like the new girl, but she did like people to stick to what they knew.

The older partners liked it that way too. They were aware that their firm probably had a filing system somewhere, but they didn't want to waste creative brainpower on it. As long as

New! Post-it® Meeting Charts

Little Notes

Big Ideas

(Actual size 25 x 30 inches)

Post-it® Meeting Charts can be used with or without an easel stand and are easy to carry and store. Now any room can be a meeting room.

Post-it® Meeting Charts have paper specially coated to avoid marker bleedthrough on walls or the next page. No more wasted paper, marked walls or need for special markers.

Post-it® Meeting Charts are a guarantee of a more professional meeting. You can easily peel off the sheets. No more ripping, tearing or uneven pages.

Post-it® Meeting Charts have a special adhesive that will stick to most surfaces. No marks are left behind from adhesive residue, pins or tape.

Call your regular office supply dealer now, or 3M on 01234 268868. . . *and capture those big ideas.*

Are you *really* happy with your training or conference facility?

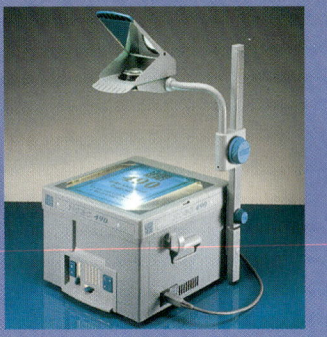

We have the solution!

Call now for details of your local OfficeSMART branch
Tel: 0181 893 4488

ELECTRONIC NOBOBOARD

- a real breakthrough in technology, the Electronic Noboboard gives instant copies of anything written on the board surface, ideal for meeting action notes

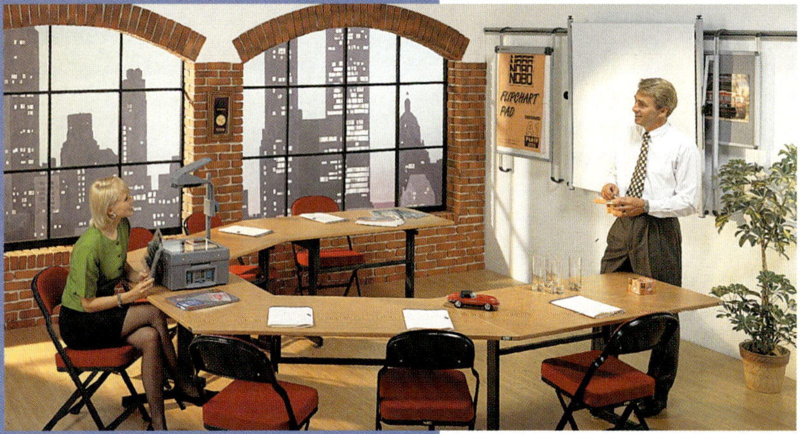

NOBORAIL II

- double-rail system with a full range of hanging units

CONFERENCE FURNITURE

- stylish folding tables which link together to suit any meeting

LCD PANELS

- offer the facility to share information from a PC with a wider audience

PROJECTORS

whatever your budget, you can be sure there's an overhead projector to suit your need - rugged, light-weight or portable!

Step 11 | **Lasting Impressions**

there were orchids in reception and real coffee in the kitchen, all was right with the world.

Matters came to a head when the office manager presented the two guest lists for the annual parties. "I used to be invited to those parties," said the new girl. "I always wondered why I never met anyone but suppliers and other designers — why don't we have one big party this year and invite everybody?"

"We can't do that," said everybody else. "It wouldn't work."

Why not? Because (said the OM)

- we'd have to buy champagne for everybody (too expensive) or give everybody beer, which would make the customers think we'd gone down market
- there isn't enough room
- the suppliers would lower the tone of the event by trying to sell things to the clients

On the other hand (said the new partner)

- Nobody minds decent sparkling wine and, anyway, we're supposed to be creative and innovative. Why don't we go for something completely different each year? Maybe a Mexican evening this time, and then try something different for the next one. People won't know what to expect. It'll be much more interesting and less expensive all round.
- And it's time those guest lists were revised. I happen to know that several of the clients on that list have either gone out of business or taken their custom somewhere else. Anyway, when did you ever get a full turnout? It was half empty last time I was invited.
- What's wrong with everybody trying to sell something to everybody else? If they're having a good time, they won't be too serious about it anyway. If our work and our wine are good enough we shouldn't be paranoid about competition. It's what business is all about. I don't know what your client evenings are like, but we suppliers always felt we were just being patronised.
- And you weren't the only company that invited me to open evenings. I used to go to one where they invited everybody in their network, regardless of which side of the fence they were on. It worked well because everybody felt valued and the whole business ecosystem was there — it was like seeing a whole anthill in full working order.

The moral of the story

The recurring theme of this book is not to take anything for granted. Always question your own organisational assumptions.

Before you embark on anything, whether it's buying a new spider plant or changing a computer program, there's a very practical checklist you might want to run through:

1. Define exactly what you are trying to achieve

2. Assess the physical and budgetary limitations
3. Decide how you will know whether you have succeeded
4. Select two or more ways of achieving your objective (including the way you've always done it) and run a checklist of "fors" and "againsts" on each

The Acme Designs open day story illustrates the kind of routinely repetitive habits firms of every size slip into without even noticing. Shaking up the ingredients and stirring up new ideas is important in every part of your business and it is often the office manager – particularly the person who is new in the job and untrammelled by previous assumptions – who is best placed to introduce new thinking.

The smart office is smart business too

The whole point about presenting and marketing your business to the outside world is to convince others that you are bright, capable, flexible and just the right sort of people to be doing business with. But if you've taken to heart the themes covered in Steps 1 to 11 of this book, your business contacts shouldn't take too much persuading.

Of course, if there's no substance to what you're offering, no amount of marketing flair or window dressing can disguise the truth for long. But if you have managed to create a genuinely user-friendly office, a place and an ethos where people can thrive and give their best both as individuals and as part of the team, that is the greatest guarantee of real quality and the most powerful marketing tool of all.

There's nothing more humane, more stimulating, more fun, more productive or more profitable than the smart office. It's everything business should be. Even if perfection is hard to reach, it's a target that's worth aiming for. And the spin-offs that come your way as you move step by step towards the goal are certain to make the journey well worthwhile.

IN A NUTSHELL

1. Let them see the smart approach coming through

2. Tuning the presentation to the audience

3. Getting the coverage you deserve

- How to run successful press conferences
    - venues
    - timing
    - entertainment

Step 11 | Lasting Impressions

4. The right message at the right time

- Presentations to groups and larger audiences
    - techniques
    - technical support
    - matching the performer, the performance and the audience
- Open days
    - PR value
    - staff benefits
    - two-way communication
    - cost effectiveness

APPENDICES

DOING IT RIGHT: BACK TO BASICS

CHOOSING THE RIGHT OFFICE AND EQUIPMENT EVERY TIME

- A decision-making structure for everyday use
- Outline your plan
- Get down to the details
- On location
- Selecting a new office
- Chart your progress

TAKING GOOD CARE OF WHAT YOU'VE GOT – SECURITY

Smart Office | 11 Steps to a User-Friendly Office

CHOOSING THE RIGHT OFFICE AND EQUIPMENT EVERY TIME

A decision-making structure for everyday use

Setting up an office for the first time, or even thinking about how you could rationalise the one you already have, is a daunting task. Take the heat out of it by applying your time management and logistics skills.

Approach these large tasks in the same methodical way that you approach your in-tray or tackle your weekly work schedule. Remember, you can do anything – anything at all – if you can only see how to go about breaking it right down into small enough chunks.

Outline your plan

The first thing to do, and you may as well do it now, is make a list of key questions.

1. What do you need?
2. What do you have to do?
3. What do you have to get rid of?
4. What do you want to change (if your office is already up and running)?
5. How many people are involved and how will it affect them?
6. How much will it cost?
7. What time frame have you got to work in?

The best way to start is by using the section headings in this book as a checklist. With luck, not all of them will be relevant for you. But if you run through everything that's been covered in the 11 Steps to the Smart Office, you won't miss anything important. When you make your list, have three columns on the right-hand side for your priority rankings, cost and time frames.

For example:

	The New Office Design		
Item	**Priority**	**Time**	**Cost**
Replace partitioning to accommodate new staff members			
Expand telephone system			
Buy coffee machine			

When you have made your list, it will just be a skeleton plan. But at least you will have some idea of what you are up against and, most importantly, what your deadlines and budget constraints are.

Get down to the details

Your outline plan is just the beginning. Now you need to break it down into its smallest components and go through exactly the same process with each one. Plan the time and cost of each. For example, if the first item on the first list is to acquire new premises, it should be broken down into logical steps.

Choosing a new office

There are six basic stages to bear in mind as you set out to find the right office for your business.

1. Define the right geographical area, according to the factors that are most important to your business, including:
    - access to relevant facilities
    - key employees' locations
    - public transport and car parking facilities
    - cost of properties in the area
    - other considerations (prestige, ambience and so on)
2. Decide whether to rent or buy – and define the budget that's available.
3. Determine the size and facilities required. Draw your ideal floorplan, as well as making a written list of "wants" and "essentials". Score each building you see according to how many of the criteria it meets. *Don't rely on feel or intuition.*
4. Decide how much of the building management you want to take direct responsibility for. The answer to this may well dictate your choice of location in the first place. Serviced office buildings are becoming increasingly popular with small companies. If you are a one- or two-man band, it doesn't necessarily make sense to try to cope with everything yourself. Having the cleaning, security and hygiene supplies taken care of may be cost effective – and you may be attracted by the idea of sharing the costs of major items of hardware such as copiers and phone systems.

    Bigger firms may prefer to deal with some or all of these functions directly. There are certainly advantages in terms of status and PR value available to those who can afford to run their own premises. There may even be windfall capital gains, if the property market ever gets up a head of steam again.

    You have four main accommodation options:

Smart Office | 11 Steps to a User-Friendly Office

- business centre (many services and some equipment provided)
- serviced office (cleaning and security included)
- own building (PR and prestige value)
- shared building (choose complementary companies to share with)

5. Register with business property agents. Try to tell them clearly what you want. But tell them you also want to know if any oddball buildings come up, within your budget limits, that might be interesting. The old fire station or school or the tollkeeper's cottage on the bridge might be just as suitable for you as a purpose-built box.
6. Start to view properties. Be prepared to visit several unlikely candidates to get a feel for what is on offer in your chosen areas and budget range. Shop around.

Get into the habit of going through this kind of procedure every time you have a major decision to make regarding the office set-up. Nothing is ever foolproof. But if you do make a proper list of the details, time, cost and steps involved and then share the information with a colleague, you are far less likely to make an expensive mistake.

Chart your progress

Even better, plot out what is required and when it has got to happen and stick a project timetable up on the wall. If you're familiar and comfortable with Gantt charts, make it a formal structure, just as you would for any other major project. The important thing is to make the process visible and hard to ignore. That way, even if you miss some vital point, somebody else is bound to think of it – and you'll still get the credit in the end.

SECURITY

If your premises are your own, it's obvious that you have to take full responsibility for your own security precautions and procedures. If you rent a floor of a serviced building, you have less to worry about. But you still have to do your share of checking and protecting.

- Data — Taped back-ups from your hard disk drives can, and should, be regularly taken home by designated members of staff. They should not be left at the office. Papers should never be left lying around. They should be locked in desks and filing cabinets at night. Even filing trays should be locked in cupboards. It is unlikely that files would be stolen, except by someone looking for specialised information, but if a break-in occurred they would very probably be disturbed. You will have enough to worry about if your equipment is taken, without having to think about what has happened to the invoice file.

- Equipment — Computer equipment is relatively light, valuable and easy to move and has become a fashionable target for thieves. Apple Macs and large (17-inch plus) monitors are particularly sought after and it is very clear that many of today's office break-ins are aimed at specific hardware items. Some thieves will even leave the box and just remove the chips.

    You are less likely to lose desks and photocopiers, although it has been known for "removals vans" to clear entire offices over weekend or bank holiday breaks, even down to removing the light fittings and taking up the carpets.

- What can you do? — The first precaution is to security check all your staff when they join the firm. This may sound like overkill. But if we assume you have good personnel management and don't experience a high staff turnover rate, it won't be difficult to keep up. We have to be realistic, though, and this is one of the aspects of downsizing and outsourcing that doesn't get much of a hearing from the high-level management gurus. Never before has so much relatively casual labour been employed to work in the midst of so much expensive equipment. When you look at it in those terms, it's surprising the number of thefts isn't higher.

    — Have a burglar alarm system (if the building doesn't provide this) which will give each member of staff a unique pass number and log the times people come in and out. There must be a master pass holder on duty at all times, in case the alarm goes off accidentally, and the names and numbers of these pass holders should be posted on the alarm itself. Arrangements must be made for cover over weekends and holiday periods. This kind of cover is particularly important if you have the kind of business where certain members of staff are on flexitime and come in to work in the evenings and at weekends.

DOING IT RIGHT: PAPER TRAILS AND FINDING SYSTEMS

SETTING UP A PAPER TRAIL YOU CAN FOLLOW
    4 STEPS TO SANITY
        Step 1 Requisition
        Step 2 Logging in
        Step 3 Payment
        Step 4 Filing

FROM FILING SYSTEM TO "FINDING" SYSTEM
    SHAPING A SYSTEM TO SUIT YOUR NEEDS
        Centralised or departmental filing systems?
        File categories
        Don't discard your index cards
        Get those files tagged properly

Smart Office | 11 Steps to a User-Friendly Office

SETTING UP A PAPER TRAIL YOU CAN FOLLOW

How do you set up an office system that really works, for everybody? It should ensure that all the information which is relevant to the functioning and survival of the business (particularly the bits that are related to accounts) should be quick and easy to find. In particular, it needs to eliminate the black holes that faxes, invoices and urgent messages often seem to pass through on the way to their destination.

Four steps to sanity

This four-step system is simple and practical and should make sure that nothing slips through the net. Compare this framework with what actually happens in your office. The steps can be implemented equally well on a computer system or on paper. But bear in mind that even when a wholly computerised system is used, there will still have to be a physical file to hold delivery notes and invoices from your suppliers.

Step 1 Requisition

The paper trail begins and the first step is recorded when goods are ordered or requisitioned. There may well be a standard form for this which has to be approved by more than one member of staff for amounts larger than, say, £50. A copy of the order must be physically filed or kept on the computer.

Step 2 Logging in

When goods are received, there may well be a section on the requisition form for checking them in and confirming that they are satisfactory. This requisition paperwork should be filed, physically or by entering the details into the computer (or both – even if you are fully computerised, you may need to keep the signature on the original document).

Stock levels should be checked and amended on the computer, card index or ledger.

Step 3 Payment

If the trail has been kept on the computer up to now, your accounts software package will usually trigger payment prompts. If not, your outstanding invoices should be checked weekly. Most invoices will be paid in monthly batches, but there will always be exceptions. Checks need to be run every week to confirm whether or not all orders have actually been received.

This is where some small firms may suddenly become aware of the weaknesses that can be caused by having a bookkeeper who comes in only once a month.

Even if all invoicing, out and in, is dealt with on a strict monthly basis, any system that lacks the order and discipline imposed by regular weekly monitoring does tend to break down more often. Mistakes are expensive. They can cost you money, prove frustratingly hard to pin down and put right and, worst of all, cause friction between you and your customers.

Step 4 Filing
Only when final payment has been made for an order that has been received in full and accepted can the residual paperwork be filed.

For the good of the business, this kind of filing needs to be kept up to date and meticulously correct at all times. Even if every detail has been entered into the computer-based accounting system, the annual audit will probably require the auditors to make a physical check on some, if not all, of the actual paperwork. Accountants often charge an hourly rate, so the easier it is for them to find what they need, the less you will have to pay.

FROM FILING SYSTEM TO "FINDING" SYSTEM

Tailoring a system to suit your needs

1. Design a system that applies to every bit of data your business needs to store
2. Make sure that everyone knows what the system is
3. Ensure that everyone is regularly reminded of what it is and how it works
4. Build checks into your routine so you know things are done in a consistent fashion

Whatever system you use for the next ten years is bound to end up being a combination of paper and bytes. Start with the paper and look on the bright side. You no longer have to store a copy of every single letter that is sent out, for example. If you do a mailshot, you only need a printout of the primary file, plus a photocopy of the labels. This saves time and space. And the whole point of filing, from the beginning of time, was to save time and space.

The exact details seem to have gone astray, but recent research claims that we all spend 5 per cent of our lives looking for things we've lost. Why not set yourself the target of cutting back that percentage in your working life, even if you can't do much about losing things at home?

Start by deciding what kind of filing system you need. There are plenty to choose from and a number of worthy paperbacks on how to select the right one are available in most public libraries. In fact, it is still possible to while away several weeks of your life writing up your NVQ module on filing, if you happen to be doing the Office Management course. In reality, though, most of the decisions are matters of straightforward common sense.

Smart Office | 11 Steps to a User-Friendly Office

Centralised or departmental filing systems?

Departmental filing is only an issue for larger companies. Small to medium-sized organisations usually keep all their paper filing in one central system (although it doesn't physically have to be all in the same cabinet).

File categories

These are usually divided into three:

Administrative files   This is the housekeeping area, and the least likely to overlap with a computer system. It is subdivided into subjects such as supplies, stock, equipment, invoices and bookkeeping and general housekeeping issues. Payroll and personnel come under administration filing, but are often kept physically separate for security reasons.

Project files   These record the *raison d'être* of the organisation and keep track of its progress and profitability. Part, at least, of this material is often kept on the computer system, so that it can be updated quickly and efficiently.

Information files   What this category consists of and how it is kept depends on the nature of the business. A major oil company, for example, would keep a huge database on world geological developments, political situations and rival companies, which would need constant maintenance. Smaller oil companies might well pay a fee to log into someone else's database rather than keeping their own. A small retail grocery business, on the other hand, might not need this third filing category at all.

Your method of storing all this information when it is not in a computer could be as follows:

Horizontal   This basically means keeping it in piles. Not recommended for anything but large charts and drawings. To be able to find anything, you need to keep these in very expensive cabinets, or plan chests, with wide, shallow drawers. It is not normally practical to computerise this kind of filing yet.

Lateral   This is mainly for use in the larger office, but is efficient and convenient. Expensive to set up, but economical in terms of floorspace – some manufacturers claim space savings of more than 50 per cent, which could translate into real money in high rent city-centre premises. Files are housed in large "wardrobes", usually of a roll-fronted or "tambour" design, so you can see at a glance what is there, without having to open and close drawers.

Vertical   Typical, traditional filing cabinet method, with everything in its slot. This system has been around for years. Many families even have an old filing cabinet at home for their bank statements and electricity bills.

The choice between vertical and lateral filing will depend on the space that's available and your furniture budget.

Within these systems, there are different ways of keeping your bits of paper together. Only you can decide which is most convenient, but most people use a combination of several methods:

Envelope, ring binder, string binder, wire binder, box files, treasury tags, clear plastic folders, bulldog clips, staples, paper clips ...

Your choice should be made according to:
- how much information each file is going to hold
- how easily you need to find bits in the middle and get them out again to photocopy
- how often they are going to be handled

You can make your life easier by using
- a colour coding system for folders and dividers, making them easier and quicker to find
- clear plastic, wherever possible

The one basic rule to remember about putting bits of paper into the files is that they should normally be arranged in chronological order, with the latest information at the front.

Having selected cabinets and folders, all that remains is to decide how you are going to categorise the contents:

Numerically   As with the Dewey library classification system, every topic or name is given a number and subdivisions are made numerically. For example, if Safety is number 1, then the system may look like this:
      1. Safety   1.01 Fire Drill
                    1.02 First Aid   1.02.01 Unconscious patients
                                        1.02.02 Bleeding

Geographically   Many companies divide their sales areas and their filing this way. It all depends on what you do, where you do it and how often location is likely to be relevant.

> Smart Office | 11 Steps to a User-Friendly Office

By subject   The subject might be your customer, your product or whatever else seems most relevant to your business. Within the list of subjects, subdivisions are usually alphabetical.

Alphabetically   This is the traditional way of doing it and does have the real virtue of complete predictability – as long as you're looking under the right keyword.

Of course, you can simplify everything by putting your file index onto a relational database, as mentioned above, so that you can sort according to any criteria you (or some other member of staff) may choose. Remember to design the key tag into the database which will contain the physical file reference. This is important because it will be your link between the paperless electronic office of the future and the everyday, hands-on reality of the next few years.

Don't discard your index cards

There are also some primitive little tools you can use to make your life as the maintainer of order a little easier. One of them is the familiar card index, standard or rotary, on your desk. Most managers keep a purely alphabetical list of contact names and numbers on it, although it may be divided into clients and suppliers. It is also a good idea to have this tagged or coded for problem areas (and people). The reason the card index has survived, when computers have swept so much away, is its sheer low-tech practicality. That comes down to two pragmatic reasons:

1. Your computer set-up and your version of Windows may not give you the ability to use one corner of your screen to sort for information in a database while continuing with the application you're already using.
2. The old-fashioned card index is a user-friendly resource for everyone. People don't need to know your password, disrupt your work, or even interrupt your telephone conversation if they need to call the sandwich shop. It offers no privacy, but it sets up no barriers either, even on the day a stand-in or a temp is trying to cover for you.

The big mistake many office managers make is thinking of the filing system as a static thing. Even if the files themselves aren't carved in stone, they think that, once they have defined a new system, ordered the cabinets and sent around the memo, that's it! Always and for ever!

Well, it's not. People forget. People go for the quickest option. They don't think about filing systems at all till they lose track of something important. To make any system work, constant reminders are needed – and a physical, manual, desk-to-desk collection system often helps as well.

The situation can only get worse, because it is suffering constant erosion as each individual discovers or buys some new little bit of software to put ideas and notes into. Paper filing systems will exist for some years to come, but they will constantly be whittled away as computer capacity and usability improve. What you have to do is track the changes and know what is where.

Get those files tagged properly

Even more important, though, is to bite the bullet and risk short-term unpopularity to institute a consistent, office-wide system for filing computer data. This is harder to introduce and police, but absolutely vital. For example, here is one straightforward idea that can make your life noticeably easier, but which may take six months to convince an office of six people to accept. Simply set up every word processing system to tag each file automatically with a footer including the hard drive path, as well as the date, the name of the file and the author.

The time and frustration this will spare your colleagues will probably make you a local hero — or would, if anyone ever noticed. In fact, of course, it is the accumulation of small ideas and improvements introduced by someone taking a positive approach to the facilities manager's role that leads whole companies to believe that their offices "almost run themselves". Make this whole business look too hard and they'll think you're not up to it. Make it look too effortless and you could work yourself right out of a job.

DOING IT RIGHT: IN TIME, EVERY TIME

IT'S A MATTER OF PRIORITIES
DOWN-TO-EARTH RULES FOR INTERNATIONAL DELIVERIES
WILL THE SKY FALL ON US IF IT DOESN'T GET THERE FAST?
SPEED, SECURITY OR NUISANCE VALUE?

GETTING THE MOST FROM THE ORDINARY POST
UNPRIVATISED AND UNDERPRICED
"IN LEICESTER BY WHEN . . .?"
PEDALS, POWER AND PODS
The good, the bad and the uncompromising

PREPARING FOR THE PAPERLESS POST ROOM
I DON'T LIKE MONDAYS
MAKING THE LEAST OF YOUR MAIL

Smart Office | 11 Steps to a User-Friendly Office

IT'S A MATTER OF PRIORITIES

The problem with priorities is that they are always in the eye of the beholder. Even a small business can quickly run up spectacular bills if it makes a lot of use of international courier companies and local despatch and delivery firms.

But when you sift through the invoices and try to pinpoint which individual deliveries were not as urgent as they seemed at the time, you are already applying a quite unfair filter of hindsight. On the day, in the heat of the moment, the risk of missing a deadline, delaying vital negotiations or holding up production always makes it seem irresponsible not to spend a few pounds on a courier.

It is probably this simple twitch of universal human psychology that accounts for the unstoppable worldwide growth and success of the big-league courier firms. Three of the four – Federal Express, DHL and United Parcel Service (UPS) – have their own major, and highly profitable, freight and mail airlines. All four, including TNT, have computerised parcel tracking systems of Pentagon-like complexity. They have made huge investments in the systems and people to do a good job and earn ever-increasing revenues. But part of your job is to make sure they don't recoup too much of that investment at your expense.

So how do you set priorities that make sense?

Down-to-earth rules for international deliveries

When it comes to sending urgently needed information, documents and small packages to overseas destinations, the choices are usually clear cut.

- Anything that can be faxed should be – it costs almost nothing and people can be reading your message in Moscow, Bombay or Rio within a minute or two.
- Anything that can be sent airmail should be, though it's usually worth thinking about paying £2.70 over the top for the express Swiftair service, which guarantees your letter or package priority handling and cuts one or two days off the standard airmail delivery times. Normal airmail timing is three to four days for cities in Europe and four to seven days for destinations elsewhere. With the Swiftair supplement, you get a pretty brisk service for an all-in cost of, say, £3.48 for a 100g letter to Europe or £7.43 to send a 500g packet to the ends of the earth, including the French Antarctic Territories, Mongolia or Australia. International Registered is also available. For a £4 supplement on top of the airmail price, you get proof of posting, barcode tracking as far as the airport, a signature on delivery and compensation of up to £1,000.
- Anything that really must be couriered to a destination that's unusual for you should go

with one of the big boys – people like DHL, Federal Express, TNT or UPS. If it turns out that you are going to be sending packages regularly to one particular country, you should move on to investigate a specialist service. The London South West Yellow Pages is a useful source of information here, as it covers the Heathrow area. You'll find listings for specialist couriers to Africa, Spain, Italy, the Channel Islands, Japan and the Far East, among many others. All these firms are likely to have built up local knowledge which may be useful to you and their prices will always be lower than those quoted by the worldwide companies.

Will the sky fall on us if it doesn't get there fast?

Half the times you are given a bundle and told it has to be in Cairo or Washington or Basingstoke by a certain deadline, the apparent urgency will be an illusion. Indeed, the best way of cutting your firm's expenditure on courier services at a stroke is simply to get everyone, including directors and senior management, to recognise that it is not impertinent to ask the key question, as a matter of routine: "What will happen if it doesn't get there by the set time?"

If the consequences really would be serious, then it's right to spend whatever it takes. Every day, dozens of courier vans fan out from Heathrow towards Honda's Swindon plant, Jaguar's factory at Coventry and Nissan's Washington site. They are carrying small but vital parts – switches, brackets and so on – without which production lines will stop and hundreds of car workers will have to be paid to twiddle their thumbs. The car makers have all moved to just-in-time production, so cash is no longer locked up in parts stockpiled on site. But "just in time" inevitably means "sometimes very nearly too late". If JIT ever gets to stand for "due in tomorrow", the cost implications are enormous. In this sort of context, courier charges pale into insignificance.

But if the answer to the key question is "Er...nothing much", you really shouldn't be using a courier at all. And if the expense of a courier cannot be fully justified, there's a useful rule of thumb that says you should always look at Royal Mail as your next option.

Many small business people are disenchanted and avoid using Royal Mail for anything except the ordinary First and Second Class post. But it can offer so many different postal and delivery services that it is a resource that's well worth bearing in mind. Once you go looking for a service to meet a particular need, you will often be able to find one that suits your requirements, perhaps in an unexpected way.

Speed, security or nuisance value?

For example, people sometimes use couriers merely for emphasis, to make it absolutely clear to an individual or a business that this letter or bill or contract is to be taken seriously. But for just 55p more than the ordinary First or Second Class postage rate, you can send any small package Recorded. That means that the postman has to get a signature on delivery.

At the reception desk, that draws attention to its importance just as much as arriving by courier would. And if the person whose attention you want to get is being written to at home, Recorded can be even more effective, as the postman may well be standing on the doorstep, ringing the bell insistently, as early as 7.00 in the morning. Recorded may appear to be all about security of delivery, but, for you, it could be the nuisance value that comes in handy.

Special Delivery, ensuring that your letter or package will arrive before lunchtime the next day, costs just £2.70 more than the First Class postage. By contrast, a recent survey of office equipment firms who were regular users of overnight delivery services revealed they paid an average of £12.17 per item. Special Delivery offers a double-your-money-back guarantee of delivery on time – not a huge compensation for the customer, but a useful discipline on Royal Mail, since frequent failures would quickly make the service a disastrous loss-maker.

Registered and Registered Plus are there to provide guaranteed next day service, with barcode item tracking through the whole Royal Mail system, and compensation up to £500 and £2,200 respectively. But what is virtually unpublicised and makes them a great deal more realistically useful is the fact that you can bolt on consequential loss insurance up to a value of £10,000 for an extra fee of only £1.35. Being able to claim compensation for the actual replacement value of disks, tapes, artwork or contract documents that have gone astray will not do you any good at all. But the ability to make a realistic claim for consequential loss of business, sales or profits constitutes a real insurance against disaster, at a bargain price.

GETTING THE MOST FROM THE ORDINARY POST

Unfortunately, Royal Mail's talent for letting smaller businesses know what it can do for them is negligible. As a result, many firms have very little idea how to make the most of the ordinary bread-and-butter postal service.

They send staff down to post letters when they could have a postman call at the office to make a collection, at a fixed time late every afternoon, for £400 a year. If the collection time is before 3pm, the charge is halved to £200. If they send a lot of mail, they will get this service free. And if you suddenly find you have a large volume to go, or you are short of staff and don't want to spare someone to go out to the post, Royal Mail only charges £2.50 to arrange a one-off collection.

Every office manager should also know the whereabouts of the nearest postbox with an unusually late collection. This may be a question of driving to the nearest sorting office. But there are going to be evenings when being able to put one or 100 First Class letters in the post at 6.30 or even 7.00 will be very useful and well worth a few miles' drive.

Despite people's grumbles about the basic postal service, it is actually very consistent these days. If you post early in the day, more than nine First Class items out of ten will arrive the following morning. And if you do rush to get 100 letters, invoices or brochures in that last-chance collection at the sorting office, you can still bank on most of them hitting their destinations the next morning, which is not bad going for a service that costs 25p a time.

Your leeches are in the post

If you asked most business people whether it is OK to send poisons, or explosives, or raw asbestos, through the post, they'd tell you, correctly, that items like that are banned by the Royal Mail.

So the fact that leeches, live bees, Christmas crackers, paints, fish, meat and fruit can all be posted may come as a bit of a surprise. Firms dealing in these or other out-of-the-ordinary goods need to check with a local Royal Mail Customer Service Centre, as they may have to comply with specific packaging and labelling requirements.

Detailed information on what can and can't go through the mail is given in two useful booklets, *Wrapping Up Well* and *Prohibited and Restricted Goods*, both available free from your Post Office.

Unprivatised and underpriced

Depending on your own business sector, you may need to make use of all sorts of other Royal Mail services, such as PO Box numbers, redirection when you change premises, Freepost or Business Reply, Mailsort discounts for large mailings (over 4,000 pieces nationally or 2,000 in one postcode area) or Household Delivery for reliable leaflet drops.

Generally speaking, Royal Mail services are underpriced compared with any direct commercial equivalent – and in many cases, of course, there is no equivalent at all.

At the time of writing, prices have been frozen on almost every service for the last two years, though this is likely to change some time in 1996. The best practical guide to what's on offer and what it costs is a free booklet called *Mini Mailguide*, published in January 1994 but still valid, thanks to the price freeze. You can pick up a copy at the Post Office or phone 0345 740 740 and speak to your local Customer Service Centre. Royal Mail will probably try to sell you this booklet's £25 big brother, which is called *Mailguide*. Unless you do a lot of mail order business or send out frequent mailshots, you can probably do without it.

Parcelforce's portfolio offers two fast Datapost deliveries (by 10a.m. and by noon), a 24-hour service and a 48-hour one, as well as the standard, non-guaranteed parcel service. Basic prices for a parcel weighing up to 10kg are £19.95 (10a.m. guaranteed), £14.95 (12 noon guaranteed),

Smart Office | **11 Steps to a User-Friendly Office**

£11.95 (24 hours guaranteed) and £9.25 (48 hours guaranteed). The standard service starts at £2.70 for up to 1kg. Reduced rates are available for some regular and volume customers (call free on 0800 22 44 66 for details).

"IN LEICESTER BY WHEN ...?"

Despite the arrival of fax machines in almost every office, "sending it by bike" has become part of the British way of doing business, though the bike itself may be anything from a pedal cycle to a Harley Davidson or a Luton Transit van. There are still plenty of notices around saying things like "Reception Second Floor: Couriers Please Dismount", but an uneasy working relationship has evolved between the bikers and the business people.

Transparencies, disks, cheques, X-rays, samples, material swatches and colour proofs can't be fed down the fax. Yet these are exactly the sort of things that are often needed in the right place in a hurry.

More and more work is project-based and deadline-driven, rather than a matter of daily or weekly routine. And if people are breaking their necks to meet tight deadlines, they do not want to entrust their work to a large, inflexible and impersonal postal service that they believe may not keep its delivery promises. Whatever its management might like to think, too many people see Royal Mail's staff as surly, demotivated and unwilling to make the effort when something starts to go wrong. As one courier company director said recently, "If they were any good, there wouldn't be room for hundreds of despatch companies and hundreds of international couriers. It's as simple as that."

If you are new to the job, or new to the area, how do you decide which of a dozen courier, despatch or delivery companies you should entrust your packages to? You could pick up the phone and ring TNT, UPS or one of the other heavily branded international firms. They are generally very well organised and offer a variety of different service levels (same day, next morning or next day, motorbike, car or van and so on) with prices scaled accordingly. It has to be said, though, that your occasional tiny one-off order may not be too important to these large concerns. You will certainly not qualify for any substantial discounts unless you are sending packages in some volume. Another option is Royal Mail's new Sameday service, currently available in and between a dozen or so major cities. Big organisations learn slowly, though, so Sameday may never get beyond being an ambitious pilot scheme.

At the other extreme, there are the small fry — Necessary Evil Couriers down the road, Third Endorsement round the block and Bikerama within a couple of minutes' wheelie. Are these little local firms likely to be any good to you? And how can you begin to choose between them?

Pedals, power and PODs

Most large cities now offer the ecologically satisfying alternative of youngsters tearing around on mountain bikes, rather than superbikes. In cities where large areas have been pedestrianised or circuitous one-way routes have been imposed, they can be the fastest delivery service of all, though their rates are seldom much lower than those of the Kawasaki cowboys.

For longer runs – and if ecological virtue isn't your main consideration – the choice of vehicle will be between motorbike and van. Bikes can be faster, a little cheaper and less likely to become snarled up in traffic jams. Riders usually have fibreglass boxes or panniers or large, waterproof pouches to protect your envelopes and packages, but the fact remains that items do get damp and artwork, for example, is safer tucked inside a van.

The other great advantage of vans is being able to deal with large, awkward, fragile or heavy packages. Many office managers fail to realise that most established van-based courier companies do not vary their charges according to the weight and size of the item. They will usually take your sack of packages to Newcastle or Plymouth for the same mileage-based price as they'd quote for a 2kg parcel of disks or machine tool parts. And since the Escort, Astra and Fiat vans that are used most are quite roomy and powerful, your package may even be of a size that needs to be loaded by forklift – though there will probably be some small surcharge to cover the delays and hassles of loading and unloading.

A good courier service will be sensible and imaginative about trying to solve your problems when the inevitable happens and packages are sent to incorrect addresses or deserted offices and will always offer you the option of a POD (proof of delivery). PODs can take the form of a mobile phone call to your office to confirm that your package has been delivered at a certain time or they can be the more usual written chit, signed by the person accepting the package.

The good, the bad and the uncompromising

Your first strategy in trying to find a reliable courier service should be to ask other businesses in your neighbourhood about their experiences. People like to grumble about couriers and delivery companies, so if someone you trust comes out with a ringing endorsement of one local firm's punctuality, politeness and flexibility, that is certainly worth following up. If you need to begin entirely from scratch, though, you can usually arrive at a reasonable decision working purely from first principles.

Nearness is a great virtue. It means people get to you fast. It also means that any problems can be dealt with quickly and, if need be, in person. Customers are often surprised to find that all despatch or courier companies have more or less fixed prices, so you can usually obtain a tariff sheet on request.

Ring up, gauge the helpfulness of the person who answers while you chat for a minute or so and ask to be sent a price list. Ask the unpopular question about how many staff they have, but bear in mind that this is almost meaningless except in context. If the answer is that there are just three of them, you may find that truly caring attention to your company's

Smart Office | 11 Steps to a User-Friendly Office

needs outweighs the lack of resources. If there are 20 couriers, it is statistically likely that they are a mixed bunch and the level of personal commitment may be regrettably low. Nevertheless, once you have made contact you will start to build an idea of which firms might be suitable.

The next step is to watch out for the firm's vans or riders on the roads. How clean are the vehicles? Most serious operators make a big effort to keep their vans spick and span. Do the riders care at all what impression they make on the people they pick up from and deliver to?

It sounds absurd to think of placing your business on the basis of an informal beauty parade of either vehicles or personnel. But if there's little other evidence to go on, it's neither dumb nor unfair.

These people are in a highly competitive service industry. A company that employs couriers or despatch riders whose appearance and manner is threatening or rude is placing limits on the kind of delivery you can use it for, almost as if you had no choice in the marketplace. But you have, wherever you are in the country. That's one thing in your favour. Use it and you should be able to find a company that will really make the effort to get you out of tight corners when you're nudging your deadlines.

PREPARING FOR THE PAPERLESS POST ROOM

In the office of the future, most mail will probably be opened at a central point, scanned and stored in an electronic document management system and distributed in ghostly form, as computerised images only, to the appropriate departments. That, at least, is the theory in many planners' minds – and the practice already in a handful of large and mail-intensive corporations.

Whether this futuristic mail handling approach is ever going to be a good idea for the general run of businesses is open to question. If many of the originals still need to be held and archived for legal reasons, electronic document imaging does not do away with ranks of filing cabinets, as its enthusiasts would have you believe.

It may mean that the paperwork can be handled and stored in Corby or Middlesbrough, rather than Central London, allowing savings to be made in wages and office rents. But companies with this kind of operation have generally decamped to cheaper parts of the country already over the past 20 years.

I don't like Mondays

A much more familiar situation is the morning headache that greets many office managers as they survey the bundles and sacks of mail that have arrived on the doorstep, especially after the weekend and during direct mail activity or a big advertising push.

The problem is that incoming mail can never be handled fast enough. It needs to be sorted, opened and delivered around the building, the site or the company before anyone can act on it. And it is not as if these envelopes only contain information. Some will bring cheques, which need to be matched against order documentation, checked and paid in as quickly as possible.

In some large firms, the frenetic half-hour bash to get the mail opened is the cue for a dozen or more people from other departments to come in early just to help out and earn a handy bit of overtime money. This is certainly one way of ensuring that the rest of the business is not kicking its heels waiting for important mail that's stuck in the front office or postroom.

The other way is to automate parts of the process, if the size of your mailbag justifies the investment. Modern mail opening machines are smaller, quieter and much cheaper than many office managers expect. The best desktop machines will cut envelopes on three sides and unfold them, so that the operator can see that nothing is left inside, and can automatically handle items of assorted sizes. Price is obviously a factor for small firms, but it is estimated that the saving on labour costs, with a workload of 500 incoming items a day, should give a payback period of about three years.

Making the least of your mail

For many smaller companies, the idea of a separate mail room is a joke. But it only takes a sudden upturn in the amount of business you do by mail order or the number of mailshots and catalogues you send out to make everyone long for a separate area where mail can be handled.

Mail room sorting, racking and automation systems can be very sophisticated and expensive, but most of us are not running direct mail catalogues or brochure enquiry fulfilment houses. We are unlikely to be investing in multi-station computerised equipment for collating, folding, inserting and sealing thousands of pieces per day. But we may well have enough postal traffic to justify something more than an old set of scales and a damp sponge pad for wetting stamps.

Franking machines, like everything else, have become smaller, lighter, cheaper and easier to use in recent years. Many can now be re-credited remotely, over the phone. They save time, both in buying and applying stamps, provide useful and specific information about your postal costs and avoid pilferage. Some can now be linked up to electronic scales, so that the weight and destination of a package automatically generate the correct charge. And clearly, the more the weights and overseas destinations of your postal traffic vary, the more time and effort is saved by getting the machines to come up with the right answers.

The late afternoon rush to catch the post is an unproductive, labour-intensive bottleneck in almost every office in the country. Partial automation, at the right level for your firm, is well worth considering, even in the crudest cost-benefit terms.

Because of the security aspects of franking, the Royal Mail insists that all franking machines have to be bought or leased from an approved source. The six approved suppliers are:

Smart Office | 11 Steps to a User-Friendly Office

- Addressing Systems International 0181 948 0241
- Ascom Hasler Ltd 0181 680 6050
- Francotyp Postalia Ltd 01322 287299
- Frama (UK) Ltd 01992 451125
- Neopost Ltd 01708 746000
- Pitney Bowes plc 01279 426731.

Whether or not you approve of such near-monopoly situations on philosophical grounds, there's not much you can do about it. But this Royal Mail-supervised regime does mean that all six suppliers really do have a wealth of knowledge and experience about every aspect of post room planning. And they are all surprisingly eager to talk to office managers in companies with modest mailing needs.

DOING IT RIGHT: MONEY MATTERS

CONTROLLING A BUDGET FOR STATIONERY AND SUPPLIES

HOW DO YOU BUY?
Don't be mesmerised by price
Today there's a better way

A CHECKLIST FOR FOOLPROOF PURCHASING
Getting the right information in the right order

CONTROLLING A BUDGET FOR STATIONERY AND SUPPLIES

Controlling your budget often takes more time and causes more anguish than it should. It's really simple, as long as you do everything in the right order.

1. Establish the overall budget limits, with clearly stated figures and business objectives.
2. Find out what is actually needed to run the business, as opposed to what people think you need or would like (don't forget to take computer stationery and toner supplies into account). This is easier in an established business, because you can use some simple arithmetic to work out what you ordered last year, compared with what you actually used. Don't forget to check for those items which were ordered in small quantities but reordered often because demand always outstripped supply. It's probably worth ordering them in larger volume and trying to negotiate a better price.
3. Establish a stationery supplies order book or computer program. Log what you order and when. Enter what you receive and when. Note what you pay and when. If you are regularly ordering large quantities of the same thing, you may need a simple stock control program like those used in retail and manufacturing businesses. You can develop a simplified version to ensure that you never run out of toner or Tipp-Ex by entering your level of supplies on stock cards or the PC. A basic stock card, like this, need be no more complicated than your bank statement:

Copier Paper		**Suppliers:**	
Max level	50 reams	Acme Paper Co	0171 494 2111
Min level	5 reams	Contact: Jane	A/C no 02020/B

Date	**Stock in**	**Stock out**	**Balance**
21/6/96			25 reams
26/6/96		15 reams to Accounts	10 reams
28/6/96	40 reams		50 reams

Of course, this can be done much more efficiently on a computer, which can even be made to bleep a warning at you if supplies run low. In smaller firms, however, people tend to rely on the office manager making notes in the stationery book and sticking a notice on the photocopier warning the person who opens the last full box to report it.

4. Even if you think you are being given good prices by your suppliers, ask for quotes from a few different sources. You have nothing to lose, so you are negotiating from strength.

You'll be surprised at the offers people will make. On the other hand, if your present supplier is flexible, fairly aggressive on price and gets your orders right, don't change for the sake of a few pence. Keep a sense of proportion. Box files for £2 each may sound like a bargain. But just how many will you buy this year? If that is your new supplier's loss leader offer, watch carefully to see where he is trying to make up his margins.

5. Don't underestimate the impact of interpersonal skills. Once you have chosen a company that will give you reasonable price and delivery, you can often squeeze something extra out of the relationship – perhaps having your order delivered early in the day – by cultivating a bit of rapport with the people you talk to regularly. Even if it doesn't get your envelopes delivered faster, it does make life more pleasant for both you and them. And the cheerfulness of the staff is not a bad index of the kind of supplier you are dealing with. A firm that has happy, friendly salespeople on the phone is more likely to stick around and provide the quality service you want than one where staff are edgy and tense.

6. Once you have established the minimum number and type of envelopes required to keep the company in business, you can go some way towards acknowledging people's personal preferences. Bear in mind that it's the people who determine the success or failure of any business. It's not a good idea to place a big order purely on the basis that every single member of staff has expressed an immediate *need* for the latest 166MHz Pentium processor PC with Windows 95. But it is truly surprising how happy you can make the people around you by checking whether they like yellow, blue or multi-coloured Post-it notes.

Sometimes it's the little touches that make the difference. If you can brighten the sales executive's life by spending an extra couple of pounds on Day-glo pink folders, instead of the cheapest sludge green, it's well worth it. Coloured files are bound to improve productivity, by making important things easier to find – but that's another story. It's certainly a nice touch in terms of relationship-building to check for personal preferences before you put in your regular order.

All too often, people feel pretty anonymous in their workspace. When the system is in danger of seeming more important than the individual, little concessions to personal taste cost little, but mean a lot. It's often just as effective and much cheaper to give in over this kind of small item than to have to back down in an argument over something expensive and strategically critical, such as the choice of new computer equipment.

HOW DO YOU BUY?

Ordering office supplies can be an irritating, time-consuming job. But it's a great deal more time-consuming and potentially costly if you keep putting it off and end up buying your coffee and batteries from the corner shop and your copy paper in small packets from

Smart Office | **11 Steps to a User-Friendly Office**

Ryman's. It's worth investing a chunk of time up front, while you're about the business of re-thinking your office layout and system design. Ordering folders and paper clips may seem trivial, but an office runs on consumables and having the right ones at the best price arriving regularly can save you time in the future.

It's always worth shopping around, but be careful of bargains. A company on a cost-saving binge recently discovered a brand of padded postage bags that were 5p cheaper per bag than the brand it normally used, as long as they were bought in bulk. As these people were getting through 1,000 per month, the apparent saving of £600 a year seemed well worth having. It was a few days before they noticed that the type of padding used in the cheaper bags made them heavier and 13p more expensive to post – giving them an annualised net loss on their "bargain" of £960.

Don't be mesmerised by price

If you discover a reliable supplier whose prices are generally competitive and whose staff have a helpful attitude, you may find it worthwhile ordering most of your supplies from the one source. It makes life a lot simpler and, if you are a good customer and they are a good company, they will always be prepared to talk to you about any items that you come across being sold much cheaper somewhere else.

One trap for the unwary is the unsolicited telephone call selling cut price bin liners, toilet rolls or, more recently, toner cartridges. The callers often offer some kind of "present", such as a shopping voucher, for the person who agrees to buy from them, and are unusually keen to take orders by telephone without written confirmation. Goods from these traders can be of disgracefully poor quality – and in one case recently the bin liners turned out to cost more than the equivalent at Sainsbury's.

Today there's a better way

A company you intend to use as your regular supplier may be able to offer you more than good prices, reliability and consistent quality. It should, for example, be able to suggest several different ways of placing your order, including phone, fax and possibly EDI (electronic data interchange). Ten years ago, of course, there was no such choice, because fax and EDI were simply not around.

For complicated, bitty orders, a clear pre-printed order form, where you need only enter numbers, colours and sizes, is extremely useful. It can be filled in and faxed off quickly, saving time and avoiding mistakes. But that is only the beginning. Some office supplies companies now produce customised versions of these forms for all their regulars, tailored to their most frequent purchases, updated on a rolling basis and possibly even broken down by branch or department.

Some can issue customers with electronic catalogues, for use with EDI electronic ordering

TOO BUSY
Working Hard,
to take a *HARD* look

at the *Real Cost*
of Office Supplies?

Don't Work Harder - Work Smarter with

The *Personal* Office Supplies Specialists
to Growing Companies
Tel: 0181 893 4488   Fax 0181 893 4466

**PEOPLE
LOVE
WORKING
WITH**

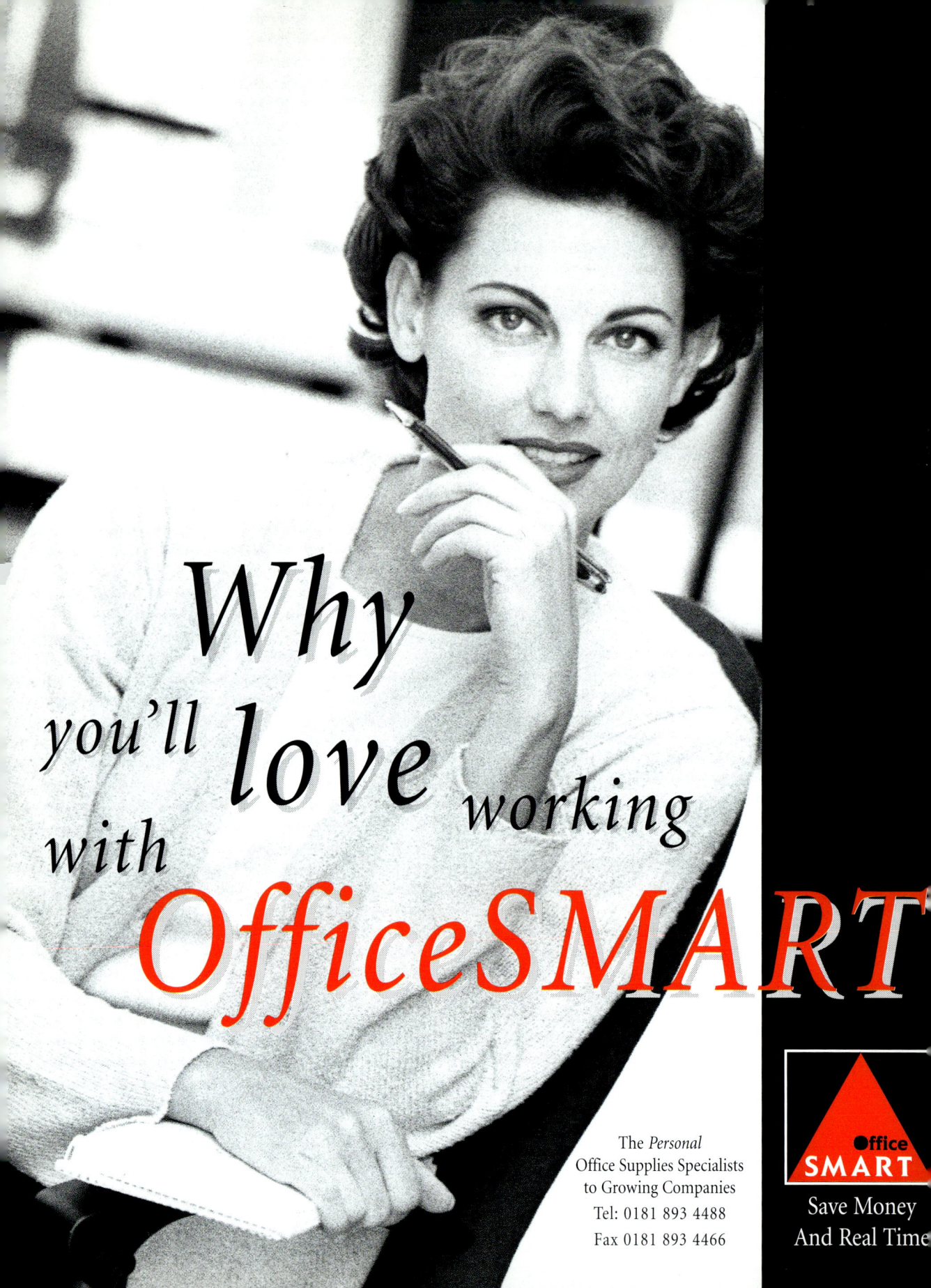

systems. The catalogue comes on a floppy, or sometimes a CD-ROM, and customers call up the relevant items on a PC screen, selecting their own lists and shaping their own electronic requisition forms, which can develop into powerful reminders and project planning guides.

Preparations for a sales conference, for example, might begin with typing in a code word (say "conf" for conference), which will automatically bring up a list of the items that might need to be ordered. Because it has grown out of previous experience, the list will probably include flipcharts, OHP film, pens, pads and pencils, but also items such as tea, coffee, badges and tissues. And it need not just be a list – sometimes it can show full colour pictures of every item. The buyer taps in the quantities required, presses a button and the whole order is transmitted electronically, down the telephone line, to the supplier's computer.

A CHECKLIST FOR FOOLPROOF PURCHASING

When you're about to buy a major item, having a system to protect yourself from expensive mistakes is as important as having a finder-friendly filing system.

Getting the right information in the right order

This is an important and underrated activity. But next time you settle down with a cup of tea and the phone off the hook to decide on your next telephone system, be sure to begin at the beginning, rather than in the middle of the process.

1. Make a detailed list of functions, specifications, features and price ranges for whatever it is that you need. If possible, use a PC to run off a table with several tick boxes, so that you can compare specific strengths and weaknesses of different systems (like the *Which?* consumer testing reports).

   Make three your minimum number of different brands for comparison.

   Equipment comparison checklist (rate 1–5 or *–***)

	Brand A	Brand B	Brand X
Outright purchase price			
Special features you need			
Special features you don't need			
Ease of obtaining supplies and maintenance			
Reputation of manufacturer			
Other			

   You can adapt this to a format that suits you best, set it up on your computer and use it for just about everything. Make sure that anyone else in the office who's contemplating a major purchase gets at least this much information for you before presenting the business case.

Smart Office | 11 Steps to a User-Friendly Office

2. Make sure you have several different manufacturers or sources to compare and that the literature is up to date. This is where your well-organised filing system pays off.
3. Check whether there have been recent consumer reports on what you want to buy. Compare their findings with your own survey, but don't regard them as conclusive. Magazine reports are no substitute for doing your own research. They won't be asking all the specific questions you need answers to.
4. Finally, call in the reps.
    - Ask them the uncomfortable questions the brochures avoided
    - Find out if there are any new developments in pricing or technology
    - Ask for the most realistic, practical demonstration you can dream up
    - Probe to find out how negotiable the final price will be

Don't forget to compare the terms of one company's contracts with those of another, particularly when leasing or maintenance commitments are involved. You will find some startling differences. Compulsory questions in this category are:
 - credit terms (should be a minimum of 60 days)
 - is a personal guarantee required? (don't do it)
 - is it a lease hire or lease purchase (if not outright purchase)?
 - how long is the lease?
 - is there a separate finance company behind the arrangement?
 - who, exactly, would you be making a contract with, what other parties are involved and what responsibilities and rights do they have?
 - who is liable if the equipment does not work properly?
 - what, if anything, can be renegotiated during the course of the contract, and what would the criteria be?

This may all sound rather daunting and complicated. But if you come across a rep who can't easily and comfortably answer any of the questions and back them up with appropriate documentation, move on to another supplier immediately.

The most common mistake is to approach this process hurriedly and in the wrong order and start with Step 4. Ultimately you should be selling to yourself, with the rep merely facilitating the sale. If you let the sales pitch get to you too early, you will risk being distracted from your own fundamental criteria.

DOING IT RIGHT: PEOPLE PRACTICES

EMPLOYMENT REGULATIONS

SWALLOW THE SPIDER

RULES AND REGULATIONS
    Contracts and conditions
    Part-timers
    Homeworkers
    Equal opportunities
    Handling grievances
    Absence and sickness
    Statutory Sick Pay
    Redundancy
    Dismissal

Smart Office | 11 Steps to a User-Friendly Office

EMPLOYMENT REGULATIONS

There are only two possible approaches to the question of keeping up with the employment laws and other legal and tax requirements placed on companies today. You can either devote most of your waking life to the study of these issues and the almost constant updating that makes them so elusive. Or you can teach yourself the basics, keep an eye on the press for news of any changes that will affect you and make up your mind to wheel in professional help and advice whenever it is going to be appropriate.

There's no shortage of guidance on these subjects, including whole libraries of government publications, many of which, these days, are surprisingly clear, helpful and well-written. We have a lot to thank the Plain English campaigners for. But if the quality is good, the quantity is overpowering. You may find you haven't quite got the time to read them all — unless you plan to pass the running of the business over into the hands of your new employees while you concentrate on the intricacies of VAT, SSP and PAYE.

A lot of small businesses break the law by not making the right tax and insurance payments, simply because they don't understand the regulations. Some of them are tempted to cut corners because they have found that it takes almost as long to do the paperwork for a part-timer in a menial job as it would take to do the job themselves.

At the back of this section, you will find a comprehensive list of all the sources of detailed information you are ever likely to need. But you won't go far wrong, when you're taking on a new employee, if you stick to the four-point sequence set out in the government's own documentation:

1. Tell your PAYE Tax Office
2. Work out the tax and NIC (National Insurance Contribution) due each payday
3. Pay it in to the Accounts Office monthly (or quarterly, if average monthly payments are below £600)
4. Tell your PAYE Tax Office at the end of each tax year (5th April) how much each employee has earned and how much tax and NIC you have deducted

SWALLOW THE SPIDER

If you have enough employees in your company to cause you worries over tax and insurance, but you're still not big enough to have your own human resources and accounts departments, one solution is to take on a part-time bookkeeper to digest all the information for you and take care of your VAT and Corporation Tax at the same time.

And if that idea is easy enough to swallow but still doesn't solve the problem, how about hiring an accountant (full- or part-time) to gobble up the bookkeeper's data and produce your year-end accounts for you as well? Why not go for a hat trick and install one of the many user-friendly computer programs for small businesses? They have the rules built into them, if you update regularly, and you only have to add your own payroll information.

You can adopt all three of these solutions, or just one, or any combination that suits you. You can still go it alone, if you really like to be in control. But, before you decide, ask yourself a few questions.

- Do you have expertise in the area of payroll management and bookkeeping?
- Are you computer literate?
- Can you work on the accounts and payroll without neglecting some of your other responsibilities?
- Is there someone else who can manage the office while you are trying to work out the Christmas bonuses and Statutory Sick Pay claims?
- Do you have fewer than six employees?

If you are scoring less than three yeses here, you should definitely get some help in. Luckily there seems to be an inexhaustible supply, all over the country, of honest and experienced freelance bookkeepers — often retired from full-time work — who can take the small firm's traditional shoebox full of receipts and transform it into a correct and orderly set of ledgers.

Part-time bookkeepers often work from home, charge remarkably little and can be very good value for money.

Choose someone who is well qualified and take up at least three references. You do not want to be the first employer of a beginner who has been made redundant and taken a short course in The Essentials of Bookkeeping (perhaps egged on by the leaflets dropped through the letter box promising "Government grant available"). Let these people gain their early work experience somewhere else. And do bear in mind that a corrupt, rather than incompetent, individual is in the ideal position to siphon off small amounts of cash over a long period or to go for the big one and ruin your firm in a fortnight. You must check and you must supervise, even though you may not have the expertise to follow every detail. Make sure any bookkeeper you bring in has experience with your kind of business and is happy to use the same accounting software package as you.

RULES AND REGULATIONS

There are a number of Acts of Parliament which employers (and office managers) need to be aware of and there are excellent summaries of all of them available from the Department of Employment and various local business organisations. If your company has fewer than 20 employees, you can probably survive on goodwill and common sense if you write down problems, as they happen, to provide yourself with a record. But it's still a good idea to spend half a day getting an overview of the legal basics. The Health and Safety at Work Act 1974 and the Factories Act 1961 are the most important and it's worth having a working grasp of their provisions, regardless of the size of your organisation.

Contracts and conditions

The Trade Union Reforms and Employment Rights Act 1993 (TURER) aims to create a fair balance between protecting the rights of individual employees and avoiding excessive costs and burdens to businesses. Employees now have the right to explicit written details of hours, pay and other conditions as well as 14 weeks' maternity leave and better protection against dismissal. There is also better protection than there used to be against dismissal for exercising statutory employment rights and against victimisation for action taken for health and safety reasons (sometimes known as "whistle blowing"). The best rule for any employer is to enlist professional help in drawing up a basic contract of employment. Read it yourself and make sure that you can understand it, too. You should also notify employees of all contractual amendments before attempting to implement the changes.

Part-timers

Anyone who works less than the standard 35-hour week may be called a part-timer. The most important thing to do is to define exactly what the hours are – there are plenty of resentful workers on part-time salaries whose hours creep up weekly. Some unscrupulous companies still take on part-timers in the belief that they have less protection than "real" workers who do five extra hours per week. This is a rash assumption, because part-timers are now entitled to many of the basics, including 14 weeks' maternity leave, an itemised pay statement and the right to complain to industrial tribunals.

Homeworkers

Homeworkers are defined by the Employment Department as people who "work in or from the home for an employer or contractor who supplies work and is responsible for marketing and selling the results".

It is the employer's responsibility to ensure that the jobs are suitable and to supply the main items of equipment, with manuals for their use. Homeworkers are covered by the Factories Acts, but the details of who is responsible for what can vary a great deal. It all depends on the actual contract between the homeworker and the employer.

Some of the regulations which cover homeworkers may also apply to teleworkers, although teleworkers are more likely to be self-employed or working on a commission basis and are more likely to be engaged in high-tech service or communication work, rather than manufacturing or assembly work.

Equal opportunities

Four major pieces of law cover this area, so it's no wonder it's such a minefield. The Race Relations Act 1976, the Sex Discrimination Acts 1975 & 1986, the Equal Pay Act 1970 and the Disabled Persons Acts 1944 and 1958 all operate in different areas.

- The Disabled Persons Act requires every firm with more than 20 employees to take on a quota of people who are disabled.
- Racial and sex discrimination is *not* unlawful if there is what is known as a "genuine occupational qualification" (a reason why one race or sex is genuinely better suited for the job). However, GOQs are, rightly, very rare indeed.
- If you want to be an Equal Opportunities Employer, you will need to draw up a policy for your company which ensures that you do not discriminate between employees because of race or gender. Once your policy has been drawn up, you will also have to stick to it and make sure it is enforced.

Handling grievances

Draw up a simple, fast-acting company procedure to handle grievances and include it in all contracts. Usually only large companies have one, but smaller organisations have just as much to gain by having this kind of procedure documented and in place from the beginning. It won't take long to put together, as there are plenty of standard forms of words that can be copied and adapted, and it can save time, trouble and a lot of money.

Absence and sickness

Every nine-to-five employee, however long-standing, should have absence and lateness formally logged as a matter of course. This may sound rigid, but as long as it's a taken-for-granted part of the company culture, it won't be an irritant. You must also keep track of people who are working late without formal overtime and putting in extra weekend hours. It works both ways.

With most of your employees, these records will never actually be needed. But for the one in 20 where you have to resort to disciplinary action, or even move towards dismissal, the written records can make the difference between acrimonious and protracted arguments, or even tribunal hearings, and an employee who backs down gracefully when presented with the weight of evidence. A little extra time taken on the record-keeping can save hours or days of time, as well as a good deal of stress, if things don't work out.

On the positive side, this kind of log actually works as a way of controlling absence, simply by making people more aware of their timekeeping and their days off. Some people are genuinely shocked if you can prove to them that they had three attacks of food poisoning and four bouts of flu in the course of one winter. We tend to be almost as dishonest with ourselves as we are with our employers.

Statutory Sick Pay

Sick employees may be entitled to claim Statutory Sick Pay (SSP) under the Social Security and Housing Benefits Act 1982, which covers all employees and employers. The Act states that an employee must experience a Period of Incapacity to Work (PIW) of more than four consecutive days before claiming SSP. This means that if one of your employees regularly takes three days off, with no doctor's certificate, you will be left picking up the tab.

The limit of the statutory Period of Entitlement (POE) is set at 28 days and people are not eligible for SSP if they are:

- on strike
- in prison
- ill outside the boundaries of the European Union
- over 65
- receiving certain other benefits
- temporary employees
- not yet working

And, yes, you do have to pay income tax on your Statutory Sick Pay.

Redundancy

Employees are entitled to redundancy payments if they have:

- a minimum of two years' continuous employment of 16 hours per week or more
- five years' continuous employment of 8 hours per week or more.

People over 65, the self-employed and apprentices do not qualify and people on fixed-term contracts may be asked to waive their redundancy rights.

Calculating the actual entitlements and payments can be complicated, but there are plenty of Employment Department booklets on the subject.

Dismissal

The same guidelines apply to dismissal as to absence. Right from the beginning, be meticulous about noting down problems, so that if the worst comes to the worst at least you can prove how bad it was. After the first oral warning following a breach of contract, all subsequent warnings should be in writing.

Generally employees need to have been in continuous employment for two years or more and to work at least 16 hours per week to claim unfair dismissal. Employees working fewer than 16 hours need to have five years' continuous service. All women are protected against dismissal on maternity-related grounds and should either be offered alternative work or suspended on full pay.

Notice periods can vary according to contract, but the statutory minimum, according to the Employment Protection Consolidation Act 1978 is:

- one week for less than two years' employment
- an additional week for every extra year up to 12
- no less than 12 weeks for more than 12 years' employment.

ACAS, the Advisory, Conciliation and Arbitration Service, recommends that every employer should establish fair and clearly stated rules of discipline which all employees should know.

This makes perfect sense in the smart office, because the object of the game is not to fire people and face the disruption and costs of having to replace them but to get the most out of the people you have already invested in.

DOING IT RIGHT: TRAVEL WITH CONFIDENCE

ARRANGING TRAVEL AT HOME AND ABROAD
Where value flies out of the window
   A question of class and money
Adding value over the Atlantic
What about fares in the UK?
Long haul is more like a real market
To Europe, don a hole in the ground

CREATING ITINERARIES THAT WORK

WHEN IN THE ROME . . . TUNE IN TO THE CULTURE

UNIVERSAL COMMUNICATION
Handle with care
Don't stand so close to me
Enlisting help
Working with interpreters
Going it alone
Entertaining
Women on their own

Smart Office | 11 Steps to a User-Friendly Office

ARRANGING TRAVEL AT HOME AND ABROAD

Sorting out and booking travel arrangements for other people is a thankless task and one that should be sidestepped at every opportunity. The problem is that what seems like a simple matter of logic and logistics gets tangled up with people's undeclared needs, private preferences and attitudes to questions of status.

That's bad enough. But you inevitably find there are company-wide issues to take into account as well. If the firm is in poor shape, most people will agree that the cost of first class air tickets and five star hotels should not be allowed to add another unnecessary straw to the camel's back. But what happens when things pick up again and the prospects are good? If one senior manager gets the five star treatment, does that mean that all of them, plus directors, of course, are entitled to expect the same?

The richest man in America, Bill Gates, 40-year-old head of Microsoft and currently worth around $13 billion, always insists on flying on scheduled airlines, economy class. But then, what does he know?

WHERE VALUE FLIES OUT OF THE WINDOW

If a supplier offered you the opportunity to pay either £5 or over £14 for a certain box of computer disks, you would normally try very hard to make sure you bought at the first price, rather than the second. Next time you are booking flight tickets across the Atlantic, for people from your firm to attend an exhibition or conference, for example, think of the seat on the plane as that £5 box of disks.

If it's a big show, you will know the dates well in advance. If the members of your party are staying in the US at least seven days and you can book 21 days in advance, you will pay something like £288 for APEX tickets from Heathrow to New York. That's the £5 box of disks. If you have to pay full standard economy fare, you will get a lot of extra flexibility over switching, refunds and so on, but you will pay £844 for the same seat – the equivalent of buying your box of disks for roughly £14.65.

Airline marketing staff will yelp that the flexible terms add value to the seat. In a sense, they do. The question for your company is "Do they add that much value?", when it's the same seat, in the same cabin, on the same flight.

Sticking with Heathrow to New York and standard (actually BA-supplied) ticket prices that were valid in early 1996, we can move onward and upward to look at business and first class prices, taking our box of computer disks with us. Most people, including most of those who book tickets on anything other than a very regular basis, have no clear idea of how airline fare structures work. So it's worth a glance.

Appendices

A question of class and money

The disks we're buying are not identical now. They are slightly better quality and the airline is giving bigger, more comfortable seats, better service in the air and on the ground, better food and less cramped conditions. It is also flying this better seat on exactly the same plane, in the same time, between the same airports. On BA's business class – known as Club World – the return fare between Heathrow and New York is £2362. That's £41 for a box of disks. Yes, value has been added. But you may need to ask how much.

In first, everything is bigger, better, brighter and plusher. It needs to be. The equivalent transatlantic fare is £4188 (or £72.71 for a box of disks).

And, compared with that, Concorde, the very acme of transatlantic travel, in terms of speed, if not comfort, is quite a bargain. America and back takes no time at all and costs £4704 (so a supersonic box of computer disks would be £81.67).

ADDING VALUE OVER THE ATLANTIC

Until very recently, there was nothing radically different about first class. In fact, there was little of real substance to distinguish between first class, business class and Y class (the ticket marker for economy – unfairly referred to as Z, for Zoo, class by disillusioned travel experts).

Except on a handful of Far Eastern services operated by Singapore Airlines and Philippine Airlines in the late eighties, there has not been an opportunity for air travellers to stretch out flat and get a proper night's sleep since the end of the flying boat era. Now BA has relaunched its First service with new seats which lower into completely flat beds for every one of the 14 passengers in the First cabin, giving them the chance to sleep their way across the Atlantic and land genuinely rested and ready for business.

That is a substantial difference. If it means your top people effectively save a full day, or arrive comfortable and concentrated instead of red-eyed and stressed, it is worth money. How much, though, is up to you and your company to decide.

WHAT ABOUT FARES IN THE UK?

Pick the right flight, on the right date, through the right travel agent, and you can fly from London or Manchester to New York or Toronto and back for less than the cost of a return to Edinburgh or Glasgow. The standard return price for London-Edinburgh is £234 with BA.

There are a host of different options and prices advertised by both BA and British Midland which may lead you into thinking you can book for, say, £74. But you will usually find that these are far from being no-strings deals.

In practice, the best you are likely to get, without having to persuade your staff to stay over a weekend, is an APEX ticket (£115, but you must book 14 days in advance) from either BA or British Midland. If booking two weeks in advance is not possible, try British Midland's

> Smart Office | 11 Steps to a User-Friendly Office

£182 deal, which allows some flexibility, such as open date returns, though it steers you onto off-peak flights.

The possible jokers in the pack are a handful of smaller airlines that have introduced much cheaper internal flights over certain routes. Ryanair (with cheap flights across the Irish Sea and to Scotland) and EasyJet (which offers Luton to Glasgow or Edinburgh, one way, for £29) may eventually make enough impact to encourage the big carriers to drop their prices. But, for the time being, there seem to be quite enough companies prepared to shell out £200 for a return flight between Heathrow and Edinburgh to keep the load factors reasonable and the fares high.

LONG HAUL IS MORE LIKE A REAL MARKET

If the situation on internal UK flights is a disgrace, and that on many European routes is hardly any better, help is at hand when it comes to long haul flights.

The traditional business travel agents – people like Thomas Cook and AT Mays – will work quite hard to find you a good deal. Trailfinders, once scorned by the trade as a hippy bucket shop, has survived and thrived over 25 years by dedicating itself to the sort of detailed, flexible, personalised customer service that is the envy of all its rivals, combined with the ability to winkle out very cheap routeings and tickets for its customers. Even Lunn Poly, as mainstream as they come, is now aggressively marketing its ability to track down low cost flights.

TO EUROPE, DOWN A HOLE IN THE GROUND

If your executives are not going to fly, they are probably not going very far. But the opening of Channel Tunnel rail services has finally brought the near side of the Continent within reasonable one-day striking distance for people who refuse to fly. London to Paris or Brussels in three hours or so – city centre to city centre and with a lot more legroom than any plane can offer – is an option that compares well with flying on the busiest business routes in Europe.

Ticket prices are not very different from those offered by the airlines. It costs £220 for a full first class return, including a decent meal, £155 for second class returns and £87 (Paris) or £79 (Brussels) for advance purchase, bought 14 days ahead and requiring you to stay over a Saturday night.

But the Eurostar train service has a number of subtle, and quite persuasive, attractions for business travellers, apart from novelty value and the appeal to those who dislike flying. These advantages include:

1. **Late booking** You can buy a ticket up to 30 minutes before departure time
2. **Late check-in** You can cut it fine and arrive as late as 20 minutes before departure
3. **Uninterrupted work time** Once you're on board at Waterloo International, you can concentrate on what you're doing right through to Gare du Nord

4. **Usable work time** There are no bans on the use of mobile phones or laptop computers, which are often restricted in and around planes and airports for safety reasons
5. **No taxi, tube or RER to catch or fares to add on** If your journey really is from one city centre to the other, any realistic comparison needs to cost out the whole trip and allow for the hassles of switching to and from local transport at both ends

There are always going to be some claustrophobics who will hate the idea of taking a tube train to France, just as there are people who find flying a horrifying experience. But at least there is now the opportunity to get round either of these problems by taking the alternative option.

CREATING ITINERARIES THAT WORK

If you're doing something that's harder than it looks, it's often helpful to be reminded of the fact that it wouldn't be a pushover for anyone else either. Mapping out an itinerary for the MD's autumn round of visits to key suppliers or planning the most efficient route for a sales rep whose customers may be scattered across hundreds of square miles are just that sort of job – a piece of cake, till it's you that has to do it.

If you have been left holding the baby (though why it should so often be the office manager who is expected to sort these things out is an interesting question in itself), it may be some consolation to know that even mathematicians and computer experts cannot come up with foolproof answers to this kind of routeing puzzle. In fact, this particular conundrum is the subject of much study in our universities, under the recognised title of The Travelling Salesman Problem.

The TSP is actually recognised as being a mathematical classic – easy to describe but impossible to solve. And no one, still, has managed to come up with any way of finding the optimum route, other than calculating or measuring the length of every possible route and picking the one that gives the lowest total. It's easy enough with just a few customers. But the built-in technical snag is that the complexity of the problem grows exponentially and races away out of sight as the number of visits increases.

You can try to cope with these things by hurling computer power at them – the biggest Travelling Salesman Problem for which a precise optimum route has been calculated involved 7,397 destinations and took a massive array of workstations at an American university to crack. Or you can try to think your way through to a solution – BT's giant research laboratory at Martlesham, near Ipswich, claimed as one of its top achievements for 1994 "World's fastest algorithm for devising routes for travelling salespeople".

Our tip is to politely ask the MD or the salespeople to let you know in what order they'd like to drop in on people, so that you can make the arrangements for them.

Smart Office | 11 Steps to a User-Friendly Office

WHEN YOU'RE IN ROME... TUNE IN TO THE CULTURE

Being polite is important. It's our cultural way of making people feel comfortable so that we can get on with selling them something, making them perform better or persuading them to give us information we need. Politeness is less meticulously practised than it used to be, which gives truly polite people a hugely unfair advantage over everyone else.

In our own environment, politeness and polished communication skills overlap and there are plenty of courses and good books on the subject. But it's much more difficult to fine tune your communication to give you the same kind of advantages when you start to take your business overseas.

A touch, a gesture or a mistimed glance can make the difference between a deal and a wasted air fare, or even between an evening's productive networking and a fist fight in a bar. It's worth doing your homework and even putting in a little practice beforehand – depending, of course, on which way you prefer to spend your evenings.

Better late or never?

It is always a mistake to assume that people from other cultures know what you mean, just because they know what you're saying. Punctuality, for example, is a matter of politeness. But whose idea of punctuality are we going to set our clocks by when we are doing business abroad?

If you ask a German to your party at 7.30, he'll be there on the dot. *Natürlich*.

Your American friends – the ones from the Midwest, at least – will think it only polite to arrive a few minutes early. And the Japanese can be expected any time after 6.30.

The Brits will probably turn up about 15 minutes after the appointed hour, with the Italian contingent appearing at 8.15 or 8.30. The Greeks will be there some time during the evening.

During the working day, Portuguese meetings will not start on time, Danish and Dutch ones will and Italian business people may surprise you by their determination to stick to a timetable, unless there is a genuine reason for delay. Don't guess at these things, though. When in doubt, get it out into the open and ask what the people around you are expecting.

Appendices

UNIVERSAL COMMUNICATION

The words OK and Coca-Cola are just about as close as we've got to global communication these days, though it may turn out that the Internet will be the real icebreaker – in 15 years the new international computerspeak may have achieved what 100 years of Esperanto failed to do.

There's a popular theory in applied psychology at the moment which holds that people's eye movements (up and right, from the observer's point of view, for something they are remembering, up and left for something they imagine) can tell you a lot about their thought processes. Although these patterns differ a little between individuals (and especially when left-handedness comes into the equation) they are held to be broadly universal, across all the nations of the world, with the single exception of the Basques.

If it's really true and we can tell whether someone is sincere or not just by watching their eyes, why should we get so anxious about our business communications when we're away from home? The answer is simply that person-to-person communication is so pivotal. Get it wrong and the deal's lost, the trip's wasted and you could even be in personal danger. That means the stakes can be very high.

The technical arguments still rage and the jury is still out on eye movements, though the theory is obviously worth bearing in mind. Meanwhile, being culturally well informed is the first step towards successful selling abroad.

Handle with care

Eye movements are generally too subtle to get you into trouble. Hand movements are much more problematical. They change as you cross borders and they change with time, too. Just as the English never used to cross their 7s in the Continental manner, our routine digital obscenity was the Great British V-sign, which is even described and defined in the Oxford English Dictionary. Watch young people and fashionable TV now, though, and you'll see a great deal more use of the European middle finger salute, which used to be quite incomprehensible to home-grown insulters.

While it is true that no respectable reader of this book is likely to use either of these ugly signs in casual discourse while travelling abroad, we are all quite likely to use the positive, cheery thumbs-up gesture. Don't. There is a fair sprinkling of countries around the world where it will be seriously misinterpreted. There's nothing more mortifying than trying to be relaxed and friendly with foreign partners only to see a look of outrage and horror as the wrong gesture blights the conversation.

Americans, and some people in Northern France, often use the "OK, that's fine" sign in which the thumb and forefinger form a circle. But the same gesture in Japan signifies a coin, or money. In the South of France, it means "nought, nothing, zero – a thing of no value". And throughout much of Southern and Eastern Europe it is regarded as a peculiarly pungent and offensive obscenity, to be avoided at all costs.

Smart Office | 11 Steps to a User-Friendly Office

Don't stand so close to me

Desmond "Manwatching" Morris is the expert on these cultural quirks and minefields. In his recent book, *Bodytalk: A World Guide to Gestures*, he details the hand signals and other body language he has discovered in 60 different countries. But there's usually someone around who will tip the business traveller off about the most unexpected local conventions. You don't have to be in Thailand very long before people mention to you that it is disrespectful to allow your feet to point directly at another person.

What is harder to pin down is the area of cultural values involving subtle factors like eye contact and personal space. For Westerners brought up on the assumption that honest people look you straight in the eye, the many Eastern cultures that disapprove of meeting your gaze may be confusing.

The person you are talking to may be struggling dutifully to avoid embarrassing you with direct eye-to-eye contact, while steadily building up your impression that he is shifty, potentially devious and possibly dishonest. This is not a recipe for rapport. One or other of you needs the knowledge that will allow the culture gap to be bridged. And since you are the visitor, the onus is on you to do your homework before this kind of situation arises.

Personal comfort zones are a particular problem in the Middle East. Brits and other Northern Europeans like to talk to people at a range of approximately an arm's length. In Arab cultures, half that distance feels about right. So we tend to seem stand-offish, as we back away. And our Arab business partners give us the awkward feeling of being crowded and pursued and backed up into corners, when there may be no such intention.

In grotesquely obvious cases, this kind of mismatch will be spotted and you can do something about it. It is when the cultural pressures are lurking in people's peripheral vision, unidentified and niggling at the edge of consciousness, that they are most disruptive. At times like this, it is often worth investing in some local knowledge.

Enlisting help

The Victorians, whether they were paddling up the Amazon or sampling the fleshpots of Paris, often enlisted the help of native guides. Quaint and outdated as this may sound, it's a custom that many modern businesses are resurrecting – because it works. Quite simply, it means having someone on your side who knows the local rules.

A foreign company, particularly in places like China, Eastern Europe and the remnants of the Soviet Union, will usually be only too keen to provide you with one of its own employees or associates who slightly speaks your language or once passed through London for a few days. But even if these helpful people speak Standard English (RP – received pronunciation – as it is now called) better than you, the fact remains that they are being paid by the people you are negotiating with. It's much better to have your own team going in to bat for you.

Organisations that are expanding to new parts of the globe will sometimes open satellite offices locally. Alternatively, a company may retain a reputable independent consultant in the same field to be there to help with visits, give cover when visiting staff have gone home and generally provide a safe base to operate from.

Depending on the country you're looking at, buying in some local back-up is not always as expensive as you might think.

This can help you save on hotel bills, interpreters and protection money and, most priceless of all, it can cut down on stress. Hiring local mercenaries used to be standard practice when the British (and the Dutch, Spanish, French, Germans, Portuguese and others) set out to expand their empires. Just because most business deals no longer involve stealing someone else's natural resources doesn't mean that you're not going into battle. Being a one-man army takes its toll, so allow for the mercenaries when you calculate your budget.

Working with interpreters

If you can't afford to buy your own back-up troops in Mongolia or Jordan, then consider opting for the services of an interpreter. It's a hundred times better than a phrase book backed up by two months listening to tapes in your car and it's 50 times better than having to rely on the services of a non-professional provided by the company you're visiting.

In spite of the fact that 97 per cent of rock and roll culture is in English (as is everything to do with computing, airlines and air traffic control, high-tech medicine, finance and politics) the translation business is going through a boom period. There are plenty of professional and highly skilled interpreters available everywhere. There are also plenty of expensive amateurs.

Your best bet, if you think you will need an interpreter, is to make the arrangements yourself. This may seem crazy in a situation where you don't even speak enough of the language to phone the translation agency. But bear in mind that you need more than words. You need a cultural guide and for that you will require someone with high professional integrity who will be working only in the interests of the person who pays them (i.e. you). Try to organise it before you leave home via one of the big UK translation agencies.

And when you do find yourself working through interpreters, don't take them for granted. They are human beings, not computers, and however good they are at two or more languages, they may also be:

Ill-informed about your business	If you are in chemical engineering and engaged in technical talks about equipment with a Chinese factory manager, it's no good just asking the agency for someone who speaks the appropriate Chinese language. You really have to specify someone with a technical background, preferably in your particular field. (Interestingly, VW's successful Shanghai factory, staffed by Chinese with a sprinkling of German managers, uses English as its working tongue.)

Smart Office | **11 Steps to a User-Friendly Office**

If it's not possible to get someone with the right background, be prepared to pay them for two or three extra hours and brief them thoroughly in advance about the detailed areas and vocabulary that will come up in the discussions.

Time spent on this also pays dividends in terms of building rapport. You are going to be working as a team with this person, if only for half a day — make sure that you have a little more than a common language working for you. Besides which, if the interpreter is a native of this strange place you are going to be in for the next few days, he or she may be able to help you with a wide range of local information — both for business and pleasure.

Biased

You have no way of knowing this in advance, but you can soon find out. This is another area where you may be glad you paid for some of the interpreter's time before translation duties start. And if you do find out that you have hired a raging anglophobe who wants his own country to come out on top, pay him for the hour you spent to find that out and hire someone else. This is yet another advantage of paying the piper rather than relying on goodwill.

Sickness

If you get someone who's just discovered she's pregnant, who has developed flu overnight or whose wife left him this morning, you are not going to get top performance. Apply your right of veto if you've really got a no-hoper or use your charm and warmth to get the person back on par if there isn't time to call for a replacement.

Deaf to what's being said

Even if the interpreter is not wearing a hearing aid, make sure he or she can really tune in to what you're saying. There was one difficult situation where an Irish businessman who sounded rather like Ian Paisley was negotiating via a Japanese interpreter who had trained in America. It wasn't so much that the nuances were lost — more a case of whole sentences going down the plughole. Accents matter. In places like India, check that you've got the right religion, too, as well as the right language. Some Brahmins do speak Urdu, but your Muslim hosts may not relish negotiating with you through them.

The wrong sort Isn't one interpreter much like any other? No. Some do personal simultaneous translations – the really clever stuff, where they stand alongside you as you listen to the chairman of the foreign board and translate into your ear as he is talking. The French call these people "*chuchoteurs*" or whisperers. It's fiendishly difficult to do well and you have to pay extra for them, so check whether you need this kind of specialised skill. Most interpreters will do concurrent translation, where they wait for you to speak, translate it and then feed back the reply. The best will do both of these and written work as well. If you are on a high pressure trip, where you may want to amend contracts and write formal letters too, someone like this can be invaluable.

If all else fails, you can try to get help in locating a decent English-speaking interpreter through the British Embassy or Consulate or the British Council. Or you could contact the Goethe Institute, where you can be sure of finding another pool of people with a good knowledge of English (though German businessmen should not assume the same tip will work in reverse if they need to find German speakers).

Going it alone

Begin by buying a good book that focuses on the cultural aspects of doing business in the country you're visiting. Then visit the country's embassy in the UK and ask for information about cultural differences, business etiquette and hotels. After that, glean all the advice you can from seasoned travellers. Here is your five-point starter:

- Ideally, maintain perfect health. If you've got no back-up, you can't afford to be ill.
  - Check with your doctor's surgery, well before you are due to go, about vaccinations and malaria. It's a good idea to stay up to date all the time with your jabs (tetanus and typhoid, particularly) and your polio immunisation.
  - Follow the royal family's code of practice while you're away and avoid seafood and anything that hasn't been deep fried or well boiled. Concluding your deal is more important than taking gastronomic risks.
  - Heed Edwina Curry's sage advice and spend the evening at your hotel with a good book (or, preferably, your file notes on the day's events and your plans for tomorrow). If you look hard enough for excitement, you'll undoubtedly find it. But it may not be the sort of excitement you want and the consequences, in many parts of the world, could be grave, long-lasting or both.
- Take your own medical kit. Put it together with two aims: staying alive and maintaining your ability to do business. Small packs from travel shops, department stores and AA offices now realistically include two sterile needles for injections and a few stitches, as well as aspirin, disinfectant cream, plasters and water purifying tablets.

You can now buy most of the items you need to keep functioning in the teeth of minor ailments over the counter in the UK. Experience suggests that whichever member of the party is carrying Contac or something similar (for suppressing cold symptoms), Eurax cream (for bites, rashes and itching), Imodium (for tummy troubles), Piriton (for hay fever and allergy to Eastern European bedding) and Dequadin (for sore throats) is likely to have some grateful colleagues at some point.

- Take all the information packs and brochures you need if you are really going somewhere obscure. If space runs out, cut back on the underwear – it's easier in low-tech parts of the world to get your washing done than your photocopying.
- If you are taking gifts, find out in advance what would be appropriate. Don't guess.
- Go a day early and spend some time talking to people. Watch and find out what they do, how they interact with each other and what basic gestures and hand signals mean.

Entertaining

Coping with the out-of-hours stuff can be far more stressful than the business meetings. Often there are completely different sets of rules for how you behave in the office and how you behave when invited out to eat or back to someone's home. It may also be more difficult to take your interpreter with you. This is where having some kind of office base of your own can be wonderfully comforting – you can even organise the entertaining yourself and invite your hosts to take dinner with you. That way you can introduce some of your own cultural habits and get away with them more easily.

Women on their own

Women supposedly have more problems than men when travelling alone on business. Books have been written on the subject and some major cities have special women's hotels. But women travelling on business are far more likely to be harassed, molested or subjected to ordeal by boredom when they are accompanied by male colleagues.

Civilised women in the civilised cities of the world can be perfectly comfortable when travelling, dining or sleeping alone. Women who are intelligent enough to be representing their organisations abroad are usually quite capable of identifying which bars to avoid, dealing with impertinent waiters and selecting their own liaisons if they need company. Most, however, welcome the rare interludes of peace and quiet when they can catch up on sleep, reports and letter writing, without having to put the demands of others first.

When it comes to doing business, though, there are parts of the world where women do have to be more cautious than their male counterparts. In Japan, for example, although women work, they are still expected to maintain a veneer of submissiveness. A Western woman with an aggressive, masculine approach may find it hard to put her point across.

Appendices

In Muslim countries there are particular problems, though they are not usually insuperable. After all, Benazir Bhutto and Hanan Ashrawi (though she is actually a Christian) are respected and influential in the Muslim world, so nothing is impossible. The best advice is to be as well informed as possible about what the codes of conduct are and then to adopt a very conservative approach, particularly with regard to matters of dress and appearance.

REFERENCES

STEP 5 REFERENCES
Names & Addresses

Teleworking – Telecottage Association Tel 0800 616008 / Fax 01453 836174
For advice on all aspects of teleworking for large and small businesses

Publications

Teleworker Magazine – For members of the Telecottage Association. Provides invaluable information on developments, products, network support and also regular conferences and seminars for the teleworker.
　Contact Telecottage Association above
Home Run Magazine – For people working at home or from a small office
Active Information, Cribau Mill, Llanvair Discoed, Chepstow NP6 6RD
Tel 01291 641 222 / Fax 01291 641 777

STEP 6 REFERENCES

The Health and Safety Executive publishes comprehensive and easy-to-read information on every aspect of health and safety in the workplace from the control of hazardous substances to avoiding musculoskeletal disorders.
　Five Steps to Risk Assessment is particularly recommended but information on all health and safety matters is available on request from the addresses below.

Names & Addresses

Health & Safety Executive Information Centre – Broad Lane, Sheffield, S3 7HQ
Tel 0114 289 2345 / Fax 0114 289 2333
St John Ambulance – Edwina Mountbatten House, 63 York Street
London W1H 1PS
Tel 0171 258 3456
For statutory first aid training and advice

Smart Office | 11 Steps to a User-Friendly Office

Publications

Health & Safety Executive Books – PO Box 1999, Sudbury CO10 6FS
Tel 01787 881165 / Fax 01787 313995

STEP 7 REFERENCES
Names & Addresses

Friends of the Earth – 0171 490 1555
Community Recycling Network – 0117 942 0142
UK Ecolabelling Board – 7th Floor, Eastbury House, Albert Embankment, London SE1 7TL
Tel 0171 820 1199 / Fax 0171 820 1104
Wastewatch – Gresham House, 24 Holborn Viaduct, London EC1A 2BN
Tel 0171 248 0242 / Helpline: 0171 245 9718
Conservers at Work – The Environment Council, 21 Elizabeth Street, London SW1 9RP
Tel 0171 824 8411
Community Recycling Network – 10–12 Picton Street, Montpelier, Bristol, BS6 5QA
Tel 0117 942 0142 / Fax 0117 942 0164

Publications

Paper Chase – A Guide to Office Waste Paper Schemes (£2.50) Friends of the Earth
How to be a FOE – Tips on how to go green (£3.45) Friends of the Earth
A Waste Watch Practical Guide (£9.95) Waste Watch

Notes

A comprehensive list of consultants who will carry out an environmental audit is available from:
   Environmental Data Services (ENDS)
   Unit 24, Finsbury Business Centre
   40 Bowling Green Lane, London EC1E 0NE
Information Leaflets on energy efficiency and management in offices:
   Enquiry Bureau
   Building Research Energy Conservation Support Unit, Watford WD2 7JR
   Tel 01923 664258

For energy audits of offices, a list of energy management consultants should be available from your regional Energy Efficiency Office (EEO) which can also provide information on all aspects of energy efficiency:
  The Energy Efficiency Office
  Department of the Environment, 2 Palace Street, London SW1E 1EG
  Tel 0171 238 3000

STEP 8 REFERENCES

For information on the financial aspects of employing other people, a number of helpful leaflets are published by the Inland Revenue and available from HMSO, local Enterprise agencies, Chambers of Commerce and business associations.

GENERAL INFORMATION

  HMSO Publications Centre, PO Box 276, London DE8 5DT 0171
  HMSO Bookshop, 40 High Holborn, London WC1V 6HB Tel 0171 873 0081
  Federation of Small Businesses, 32 Orchard Rd, Lytham St Annes, FY8 1NY
     Tel 01253 720911/Fax 01253 714651

  and also:
  Chambers of Commerce
  Training & Enterprise Councils
  Enterprise Agencies
  Libraries

BOOKLIST

  Thriving on Chaos, by Tom Peters, Pan Books (February 1989)
  The Pursuit of WOW, by Tom Peters
  Tom Peters Seminar, by Tom Peters, Macmillan (pbk November 1994)
  The Frontiers of Excellence, by Robert Waterman, Brealey (pbk April 1995)
  Inside Organisations, by Charles Handy, BBC (pbk May 1990)
  The Empty Raincoat, by Charles Handy, Arrow (pbk August 1995)
  The Reinvention of Work, by Fr Matthew Fox, Aquarian (pbk September 1994)
  Total Quality Management, by John S Oakland, Butterworth Heinemann (pbk March 1993)
  The 7 Habits of Highly Effective People, by Stephen Covey, Simon & Schuster (pbk March 1992)
  The One Minute Manager, by Kenneth Blanchard, Fontana (April 1993)
  The One Minute Manager Builds High Performing Teams, by Kenneth Blanchard, Fontana
     (April 1993)

Smart Office | 11 Steps to a User-Friendly Office

Now Offices, No Offices, New Offices, by Michael Brill
The One to One Future, by Don Peppers & Martha Rogers, Piatkus Books (pbk May 1996)
Power Shift, by Alvin Toffler, Transworld
20-20 Vision, by Stan Davis & Bill Davidson
Reinventing the Corporation, by Jon Naisbitt & Patricia Aberdene, Oxford University Press (hbk 1992)
Competition for the Future, by Gary Hamel & C.K.Prahalad, McGrawHill (hbk August 1994)
Megatrends 2000, by John Naisbitt & Patricia Aberdene, Smithmark
Global Paradox, by John Naisbitt Brealey (pbk March 1995)
A Vision of the New Workplace, by Francis Duffy & John Davis

Information

Visualisation – Inside Out Publications and Information 0171 491 1468

INDEX

1996 Regulations, 111
80/20 rule, 34

Absenteeism, 151
Access to the system, 68
Accidents, 105
Acetone, 130
Administration Manager – banks, 26
Adventure weekends, 160
Agincourt, Battle of, 157
Air conditioning, 131
Aluminium, 126
Amateur Gardening, 196
Ammonia, 130
Angels, 30
Anorak, 66
APC, 70
Apple, 79
ASLEF, 81
Atriums, 131
AUTOEXEC.BAT., 67

Back up systems, 69
Barbour Index, 107
Barings Bank, 163
Battleships, 64
Beatles, the, 195
Benchmarking, 87–8
Benzene, 130
Bicycle fleets, 127
Bio-effluents, 130
Body Shop, 129,193
Bookkeeper – responsibility, 31
Branch manager – Banks, 26
Brands Hatch, 196
Branson Richard, 56
Brochures – information from, 46
BT, 89

Business centres, 91

Californian studies, 111–12
Canofile, 250, 35
Canon, 34
Capital Radio, 207
Carbon dioxide, 131
Carcinogens, 130
Carpets, 45
Carrot & stick, 81, 145
Cashflow, 31
Catering strategies, 198
CD-recordables, 116
Celebrations, company, 148
Central filing system, 32
CFCs, 125
Chain of excellence, 85–6
Channel Tunnel, 196
Chaos – avoiding, 30
Childcare, 140
Chinese whispers, 102
Chloroform, 130
Chrysanthemums, 130
Churchill, Winston, 159
Civil servants, 105
Clerks, 79
Coaching, 145
Cockpits, 94
Coffee machine, 103
Color Schemes menu, 80
Communication, 28, 80, 152
Company's mission, 25
Competitive quotes, 53
Computer accounts, 31
Computer manager, 26
Computer tick list for ordering supplies, 46
Computer virus, 30

Computers, 79
CONFIG.SYS, 67
Consultants, on environmentally friendly offices, 123
Consumables, eco friendly, 125
Contracts and Agreements, 55–6
Control – computers as a means of, 63
Control (in the office environment), 23
Control of Substances Hazardous to Health, 106
Control software, 66–7
Copier maintenance contracts, 58
Cost savings, 41
Couriers, 198
Cryptography, 67
Customers, 86–7
Customising software to insert file tags, 67–8
CVs, 139, 141, 142

Daily Telegraph, 33
Dartmoor, 160
Data cartridges, 116
Data Protection Act 1984, 74–5
Data protection, 69
Data retrieval, 65
Databases, 33
De Mille, Cecile, 195
Dean, James, 121
Decorative items around the office, 44
Delegation, 29
Delivery notes, 30
Desks for computers, 73
Display Screen Equipment Regulations 1992, 106

Disposable cups, 128
DMI (Desktop Management Interface), 66
DMTF (the Desktop Management Task Force), 66
Document storage, 32
Downsizing, 150
Draft budget, 50
Dragon trees, 130
Duplicate telephone message pad, 169

E-mail, 64, 74, 92, 128
Earls Court, 196
Edifact electronic data interchange standard, 35
Electrical supply problems, 70
Electronic filing systems, 35
Electronic mail, 32, 169
Electronic village hall, 89
Emerson, 70
EMI (electromagnetic interference), 70
English ivy, 130
Entrepreneurs, 34
Equal opportunities, 140
Equipment, 124
Equipment – service and price, 57
Equipment buying – golden rules, 56–7
European Union regulation, 107, 110
European Union, 123
Executive managers, 160
Exhibitions, 194
Exhibitions – as a source of information, 72

facilities manager, 24
File – tagging, retrieving, 65
File identification system, 67–8
Filing system, 29, 30
Financial year, 50
Fire Precautions (Places of Work) regulations, 106
Fire regulations, 101
First Aid at Work, 106
Fitness, 127

Fleet Street, 197
Flipcharts, 206
Floor plan for computer system, 65
Floppy disks, 116
Forests, 128
Formaldehyde, 130
Full Inside Leg Measurement, 33
Full-time staff, 151

Gantt charts, 166
Glass recycling, 126
Green label, 123
Green offices, 122

Harvard, goal setting study, 146
Health, 141–2
Health and Safety at Work Act 1974, 106
Health and Safety Co-ordinator, 108
Health and Safety Executive, 109
Health and safety regulations, 101
Heart attack risk, 105
Helplines, 72
Henry V, 157
Herzberg, Fred, 81
Historical factors in office management, 23
HMS Victory, 196
HMSO, 109
Hoover building, 96
Hotelling, 94
Human resources, 135
Hypochondriacs, 129

Ideas – the currency of computers, 64
Idiot Guides, 72
Illegal access, 65
Illicit applications, 66
Incentives, 148
Information technology, 63–4
Instant offices, 92
Institute of Contemporary Arts, 196
Insulation, 127
Insurance – computer, 65
Intel, 66
Internal presentations, 194

Internet, 68
Interviewing, 138, 140
Inventory – hardware and software, 67
Invoices, 30
Iomega Zip Drives, 69
Ionisers, 129
IPC, 196
IT departments, 66

Japanese multinationals, 193
Jelly babies, 206
Joan of Arc, 159
Job descriptions, 157
Job satisfaction, 135
Journalists, 195

Kardex, 35
Key man insurance, 116–17
Kodak, 34

Lake District, 160
Lanier, 35
Leadership, 157
Lease, 52
Lease purchase, 52
Ledgers, 31
Leeson, Nick, 163
Legal departments, 55
Lighting, 112–13
Lighting efficiency, 124–5, 126–7
Lightning, 69
Living organism – the office as, 27
Lloyds building, 196
Log book for the computer system, 67
London Underground, 146
Loss leaders, 45

Magazines, computer, 71
Magic lantern show, 202
Magneto-opticals, 116
Major budget items, 44
Management consultants, 103
Management of Health and Safety at Work Regulations 1992, 106
Management theory, 85

Index

Managing people, 135, 159–60
Managing projects not people, 47
Manual Handling (Operations) Regulations 1992, 106
Manuals, 72
Marks & Spencer, 193
Maslow, Abraham, 81
Maxwell, Robert, 48
MBA, 81
McGregor, Douglas, 81
Melody Maker, 196
Mentoring, 145
Mercury, 127
Message taking, 169
Methyl alcohol, 130
Microsoft, 66, 79
Milton Keynes, 122
Mini-cartridges, 116
Mission statements, 86
Montgomery, Field Marshall, 145
Mother-in-law's tongue, 130, 131
Moths, 45
Mr Sheen, 84
Multimedia, 201
Mutiny on the Bounty, 42
MVCs (most valuable customers), 34

NASA, National Aeronautics & Space Administration, 130
National Lottery, 195
National Service, 23
National Union of Journalists, 116
Negotiating practice, 50–1, 52–3
Negotiating skills, 47–8
Networked diaries, 32
Networked diary systems, 163
Networking, 34
New Scientist, 196
Newspapers – as a source of information, 72
Nobel Prizes, 195
Noise at Work, 106
Non-numerical information – stored on computer, 63

Office Bible, 46
Office Diary, 165
Office manager, 24
Office Manager, role of, 157
Office managers' meetings, 200
Office protocol, 65
Office waste, 125
Offices Shops and Railway Premises Act 1963, 106
OHPs, 201
Olympia, 196
OMBWA (Office Management by Walking About), 165
One-off opportunities – don't exist, 54
Open days, 207
Optical disks, 116
Optical discs – for filing, 35
Organisation and Methods Manager, 26

Panasonic, 35
Paper, recycling, 124, 125–6, 129
Paper-based systems, 32
Paperless office, 32
Part-time staff, 151
Password, 68
Payroll and other people costs, 42
PC - theft of chips, 115–6
PC – for filing, 35
PC screens, keyboards, 111
PC-driven interactive multimedia presentations, 205
PCs and their peripherals, 110
PDAs (personal digital assistants), 84
Peace lilies, 130
Performance management, 80
Personal Protective Equipment at Work Regulations 1992, 106
Personality – affecting role of OM, 29
Personnel, 136
Personnel and bookkeeping responsibilities, 27
Petty cash, 27
Philodendrons, 130
Philosopher's Stone, 80

Physical factors in creating a UFO, 43
Plastic recycling, 126
PODs, 94
Polaview 105 LCD projector, 205
Pollution, 122, 130
Post-it notes, 169
Postcards for presentations, 201
Poste restante, 92
Power cuts, 69–70
PowerPoint, 205
Pregnancy, 140
Prejudice, in recruitment, 140
Presentations, 194, 199
Press conferences, 194–9
Press kits, 198
Product cycle, 85
Production Office Manager, 26
Productivity, 42
Products, environment friendly, 123
Provision and Use of Work Equipment Regulations 1992, 106
Psychometric testing, 142
Public transport, 128
Purchase evaluation – as a project, 47

Questions, in recruitment interviews, 140–1
Quotations, 52

Rapesco True Image Projector, 205
Receptionist – responsibility, 31
Receptionist, role of, 158, 167, 169
Recognition v competition, 147
Recruitment, 136
Recruitment agencies, 136
Recruitment software programs, 138
Recycled products, 123
Recycling, 122, 125–6
Reducing waste, 126–8
Removable hard disks, 116
Reporting of Injuries, Diseases and Dangerous Occurrences, 106
Representatives – dealing with constructively, 43–4

273

Requisitions, 30
Reuters, 64
RFI (radio frequency interference), 70
Ritz Hotel, 196
ROI, 43
Roles and areas of responsibility, 29
Roles and teamwork, 160
RSI (Repetitive Strain Injury), 73, 111
Rubber plants, 131
Rules for running a computer system, 69

Salaries, 42
Sales conferences, 194
Sales Office Manager, 26
Sales technique, 49, 52
Savoy Hotel, 196
SBS (Sick Building Syndrome), 114–5, 128
Seating for computers, 73
Security control software systems, 67
Self-employed people, health, 142
Self-managing teams, 135
Sensor-operated controls, 127
Shared facilities, 110
Small firm – office management of, 26–7
Smart managers, 42
Smart office – what it's about, 39
SMART target setting, 146, 166
Smoking, 129
Snopake, 41
Social Chapter, 107
Social instability, 142
Sod's Law, 48, 164
Software management, 66
Solar panels, 127
Solitaire, 65
Sony, 193
Spikes, 70
Spreadsheets, 79

St John Ambulance Association, 108
Staff turnover, 135, 145, 148
Staffing levels, 149–50
Standard software, 34
Stationery & consumables, 44
Stress at work, 101
Stress, in the workplace, 145
Subcontracting, 23
Supermarkets, 64
Suppliers, 41
 – as a source of information, 53
 – positive relationships with, 53
Surges, 70
Switchboard operators, 168
Symantec, 66
SyQuests, 116
System – setting up an effective, 30

Tape streamers, 69, 116
Team building, 122, 135–8
Teamwork, 24
Teflon, 130
Telecottages, 89
Teleworking, 23, 82, 88–9
Telford, 122
The Health and Safety Commissions *Approved Code of Practice*, 108
Theory X & Y, 81
Threatening phone calls, 168–9
Time management, 160–1
To-do lists, 164
Toner, 124
Tower of London, 196
Toxins, 130
TQM (Total Quality Management), 84–5, 159
Trackballs and trackpads, 112
Trade shows, 96
Trichloroethylene, 130
Tripp Lite, 70

Tropical hardwood, 125
Typists, 79

UFO, 42–3, 96
UK Ecolabelling Board, 123
Unemployment, 142
Uninterruptible Power Supply (UPS), 69
Unsolicited sales calls, 51
USA – office practice compared to UK, 42
USP – Unique Selling Point, 51

VDU filters, 129
Victorian principles, 81
Video, 206
Videoconferencing, 205
Virtual office, 83
Voice messaging, 169

Wall Street – the film, 47
Waste, 122
Weeping fig, 130
Win/win, 53
Windows, 79, 80
Windows 95, 195
Wolverton, Dr Bill, 130
Word processing, 79
Work smarter instead of working harder, 34
Workplace (Health, Safety and Welfare) Regulations 1992, 106
World environment, 122
World Health Organisation, 114, 128
WRULD (Work-Related Upper Limb Disorder), 111

Xerox, 34, 79
Xylene, 130

Yachting World, 196
Yellow Pages, 194

Zip drives, 116